‘WAY DOWN BESIDE THE REEDY RIVER

The Saga of the Salvation Army in Greenville, SC
1888 & 1904-2004

Raymond W. Kitchen

Published by United Writers Press, Inc.
3505 Koger Blvd., Suite 210
Duluth, Georgia 30096 USA
770-925-4678
www.unitedwriterspress.com

Printed in the United States of America by
King Printing, Lowell, Massachusetts

For information, contact:
United Writers Press, Inc.
3505 Koger Blvd., Suite 210
Duluth, Georgia 30096
1-866-857-4678

ISBN: 0-9760824-2-X
Library of Congress Control Number: 2004114627

This book is lovingly dedicated to the memory of
our precious daughter,
Major Margery Ann Kitchen Duracher *(deceased),*
wife of Major Frank L. Duracher.
She was suddenly promoted to Glory
on March 21, 2003 at 51 years of age.
Margery was the first to read the initial draft
of the original sketch of the book.
She pronounced it "Wonderful, Dad."

'WAY DOWN BESIDE THE REEDY RIVER

"We are down here in this southern corner by ourselves, and yet not alone, for the Lord is with us. Hallelujah! It is true the fight is hard and we have a great deal to contend with: but with it all, the Lord is leading us on, and we are able to report some souls since our last report. Glory to God!"

—Lt. C. W. Kaiser, *The War Cry.* January 1888: Greenville, SC.

The Saga of The Salvation Army in Greenville, South Carolina January-May 1888 and 1904-2004
A Centennial History Book
By: Raymond Kitchen

East Washington Street, c1880s. Details concerning the "Invasion" of 1888 are unknown.

> "On New Years Eve the Soldiers all promised God with us to live closer and do more for Him this year than we did in the same one that had just passed away. May God help them all to be true to their vows. We seek the prayers of the comrades all over the field."
>
> —Lt. C. W. Kaiser, for Capt. Bob Fielding, Greenville, SC 1888

Disclaimer

This book is an individual's effort to portray the history of The Salvation Army in Greenville, SC from inception in 1888 to the "centennial of service" year 2004.

It was compiled to celebrate the "centennial of service" of the Greenville, SC Salvation Army Corps during the years 1904-2004. The parenthesis of time between 1888 and 1904 is largely unaccounted for.

It is based on historical facts commonly obtainable from public, private, and official records of The Salvation Army, and information obtained from written and oral interviews with various members of the units that make up the membership of The Salvation Army's past and present.

The author is the sole compiler and takes full responsibility for the accuracy of interpretation of the records and of the material contained herein. It is a true account, allowing for minor discrepancies of overlapped and under-filled historical records of events.

The annotating "cradling" information in the pre and post entries of the book is strictly the view of the author and does not reflect The Salvation Army's official thoughts or operational methods either past, present, or future. It is, however, an accurate rendering of the Army's methods of operation both past and present.

This "cradling" information is provided to emphasize the fact that no person or organization exists in a vacuum, but must have roots, growth, structure, and depth of experience in order to survive, produce, and prosper.

It contains some descriptions and terminology which have become obsolete in some cases, but which combine to create a historical line of progress in Greenville, South Carolina from the beginning to the present time.

Credits and Sources

The following publications and other sources were used to compile and construct this history of The Salvation Army in Greenville, SC. Some are used merely for reference or cross-reference, and others are quoted voluminously. If, by chance, I have overlooked or omitted a credit, I take full responsibility, apologize, and give thanks for the information.

I am deeply grateful for the works of the publications and institutions listed below:

The Greenville Daily News; The National Salvation Army War Cry; The Salvationist; The Southern Spirit; Greenville History of the City and County in the South Carolina Piedmont by Choice McCoin; The Salvation Army records and files in Greenville, SC; Greenville Public Library System; The Salvation Army Southern Historical Center; The National Salvation Army Archives; excerpts from The Salvation Army Southern Territory Yearbook (Fellowship of Faith Celebration) 1927-2002: Springboard to the Future; Born to Battle by Sallie Chesham; Sweeping Through the Land by Allen Satterlee; The Authoritative Life of William Booth, Founder of The Salvation Army by George Scott Railton; War on Two Fronts by Roger J. Green; Somebody's Brother by E. H. McKinley; Greenville, The History of the City and County in the South Carolina Piedmont by Archie Vernon Huff, Jr.

Photo Credits

Photographs of Carl Sandburg courtesy of Mr. Michael Farrell, Carl Sandburg Home NHS; Salvation Army historical photos from Salvation Army Southern Historical Center courtesy of Mr. Michael Nagy; Photo of CSM Roland Smith and Mrs. Smith courtesy of Linda Vick Griffin; local updated photos and Reedy River Falls, the author; CSM Street's family swearing-in ceremony courtesy of Brigadier Otis Street.

Photos of Salvation Army activities and personnel are from Salvation Army sources and The Salvationist. The photo of William Booth is taken from the booklet, Army Without Guns by Lt. Colonel Cyril Barnes.

Acknowledgements

My wife, Major Hope Casarez Kitchen, is a paragon of patience. That patience was taxed to the full measure while I sat hour upon hour compiling and writing. She waited patiently for me and provided valuable help by proof reading and correcting my basic errors of spelling and grammar as well as providing research of the raw material. Without her I could do nothing. Thank you.

To Ben and Phyllis Kitchen Anderson: Thank you for spot research and key information for the crafting of the book's content.

To Major and Mrs. Stanley and Carlene Cox Melton, Corps Officers of Greenville, SC Salvation Army (2000-2003) for making records and facilities available in abundance.

Special thanks to Captain and Mrs. Greg and Tammy Robinson Davis [June 2003-onward] for continuing access to the records.

To the staff of the Greenville Corps, Boys and Girls Club, and Social Service Department of The Salvation Army: Thank you for gathering and delivering the records to me in a timely manner and in great quantity. Thanks, especially to Mike Foss and Sam Piper of the Boys and Girls Club Council.

Thanks to the "keepers of the archives" who allowed and assisted me to peruse the archived Salvation Army records.

The Soldiers of the Greenville Corps and the former and present Officers contributed abundant material.

Members of the Greenville, SC Advisory Board and the Boys and Girls Club Council and staff were very helpful in providing valuable background material for the book.

I am especially indebted to Mr. Michael Nagy and Major Jacqueline Campbell of The Salvation Army Southern Historical Center for printed material and copies of photographs that are distributed throughout this Greenville Historical Book. Both have given valuable information from the Southern Archives, which has helped in compiling this document. They have done "spot research" on questions raised by the author.

Equally, I am grateful to Ms. Susan Mitchem of the National Salvation Army Archives in Alexandria, Virginia for providing lists of past officers who have served in the various programs in Greenville, South Carolina. She has also helped with "spot research" of the National Archives and provided significant information to substantiate the report.

A valuable source of information was found in the Greenville Public Library consisting of newspaper clippings, books, and microfiche records of publications covering the entire period of history of The Salvation Army in Greenville.

The Greenville Historical Society provided photos and narrative to help illustrate and authenticate some of the entries in the book.

Many of the former Commanding Officers and Assisting Officers have contributed anecdotes and historical information, which serve to bring the book to life. This is valuable material, and I am thankful to receive it.

Additionally, I have received valuable information from several of their family members.

Children and grandchildren of some of the Officers and Soldiers of yesteryear have made valuable contributions of information. This adds authenticity to the narrative.

Likewise, I am grateful to the Greenville News and the Greenville Piedmont and The Salvation Army National War Cry and companion publications, which provided much of the research material centered on the historical past as news items.

So many bits and pieces of information were garnered from so many sources that it is impossible to give proper acknowledgement to all suppliers individually. In the credits section I have listed as many sources as possible.

Thanks to everyone who has made a contribution either knowingly or unknowingly.

If you have touched the Army or have been touched at any point by the Army, this book is for you and about you and your association with The Salvation Army in the City and County of Greenville, South Carolina.

I am grateful for your support and assistance.

TABLE OF CONTENTS

(Sub titles are quoted from religious songs and hymns used in Salvation Army worship services)

PROLOGUE

"One Step at a Time"

William Booth, 1829-1912: Founder and first General of the world-wide movement known as The Salvation Army.

General William Booth, the Founder and first General of The Salvation Army, said, *"The world is still in a poor way. She is sick with a desperate sickness of body, mind and soul and circumstances. For her sickness she has multitudes of would-be physicians and innumerable professed remedies.Some are old fashioned enough; some are modern inventions; some are utterly useless; some only help her move rapidly forward on her onward journey towards corruption and destruction; while others, in the most deadly fashion, poison her outright. There is one and only one remedy, and that is the salvation of God. The salvation bought by Jesus Christ upon the cross. Salvation from sin, salvation into the favor of God, salvation unto holiness and usefulness, salvation free to every man, woman and child on the face of the earth."*

This was written in the nineteenth century. The sad fact is that in spite of all the amazing advances and improvements made by mankind, the statements still stand as a fair description of the state of the world today. In some cases, the situation has improved. In some cases, it has grown worse, much worse.

The Salvation Army Officers are indeed the leading edge of the cutting forces of the message of the gospel and the administration of services brought to the table of need by the organization. They are rightly placed as the leaders and prime motivators of the movement.

There are, in addition, literally millions of citizens, lay members, soldiers, advisors, benefactors, and well wishers, who have formed the basc of the Army's success in thousands of communities around the globe.

Without this "army within an army," The Salvation Army would be unable to function as a fighting force for the dignity of mankind.

A notable example of people participation can be found in Lt. Colonel Sallie Chesham's book, Born to Battle. [Condensed quote]

The world renowned poet, author and humanitarian, Carl Sandburg, is pictured as a lad and later with his guitar.

"In 1888, tow-headed, ten-year-old Carl Sandburg of Galesburg, Illinois, slipped into Army meetings in the 'low-ceilinged battered hall at South Broad Street on the public

> square.' Later, he went there again when Pastor Nyblad formed the Elm Church.
>
> Carl 'got pleasure' from The Salvation Army and sometimes played his *guitar in meetings and stood on the street corner with Salvationists."

*Note: Sandburg historians indicate that he did not learn to play a guitar until he was in his twenties so this episode with the guitar would have been the later date.

A footnote declares that Young Carl Sandburg became the world-renown poet and historian.

Young Carl Sandburg did not join The Salvation Army, but he did touch the soul of it in his early years. His actions, as described by Sallie Chesham's account, served to defend the validity of the new organization from the unusual tirades of the Pastor Nyblad.

Carl Sandburg later moved to the North Carolina mountains. His home place is located in Flat Rock North Carolina, just a few miles north of Greenville, South Carolina. It is where he spent the last years of his life and is today a monument to his life and works. His participation with The Salvation Army open-air meetings and indoor meetings apparently came at a later time in his life. His autobiography, Always the Young Strangers, pages 310-11, recounts his watching a Salvation Army band on a street corner.

Coincidental Juxtaposition

It is interesting to note that in the year of the youthful Carl Sandburg's visits to The Salvation Army [1888] in Galesburg, Illinois, the Army first came to Greenville, South Carolina.

The Greenville Salvation Army at that time lasted only three or four months, but it marked the official beginning of the work, and it is the date of record for the founding of the Greenville operation.

Will You Not Enlist with Me, and a Valiant Soldier Be...

In every community where The Salvation Army sets foot, the “troops” rally in unbelievable numbers from every sector to form the “Army” in Salvation Army. This book pays tribute to these multitudes of men, women, and children who have contributed so much to the success of The Salvation Army.

This is one story: the story of Greenville, South Carolina after one hundred continuous years of saving the lost and serving the needy people in our community. There are many other stories yet to be told in country upon country, city upon city, community upon community, and yes, in life upon individual life.

First and foremost, Jesus came so that the individual soul might have life and that more abundantly. That concept is central to The Salvation Army mandate.

So . . . If you have been touched at any point by The Salvation Army. . . Or, if you have touched The Salvation Army in any capacity...You are the Army...This is your story, too.

CHAPTER I
ARCHITECTURE AND NOMENCLATURE OF THE EVOLVING ARMY
"We're Building Up the Temple of the Lord"

Setting the Greenville, SC Salvation Army Citadel cornerstone: 417 Rutherford Street, c1951.

"People will say, 'What is The Salvation Army?
Who is William Booth?'"

General William Booth himself presented this statement prophetically as a question in an address he gave in defining the combining of the religious and social work as a means of serving the whole person: soul and body (George Scott

Railton. *The Authoritative Life of General William Booth*: p. 190).

That question has yet to be answered in full by anyone, including The Salvation Army, because the Army is always in a state of metamorphosis, growing into that creature of loving service envisioned for the Army by God alone.

The Army is sculptured upon the hearts of all previous, present, and future willing souls who have stood, or will stand, in the human-induced breech of the ramparts of God's love and defend the helpless from the onslaught of hopelessness and helplessness.

Perhaps the Army's true worth and identity will not be revealed until the arrival at the end of the struggle between right and wrong.

As The Salvation Army song of yesteryear states, "And when the battle is over, we shall wear a Crown."

Crown?

Ah!

But first must come the cross.

Jesus said. "And anyone who does not take his cross and follow me is not worthy of me" (Matthew: 10:38 NIV).

Every man must come to the cross of Jesus Christ for salvation and assume a cross of service as a sign of truly following the footsteps of the Master, Jesus, before he can obtain the crown. Love God supremely and love your neighbor as yourself.

The Army, a coalition of mortals, has chosen the servants' cross of compassionate, sacred service to humanity.

To His followers, He said, "My yoke is easy, and my burden is light" (Matthew 11:30 KJV).

God is not through with His Salvation Army yet. He has not added the final parapet to the "Citadel."

E Pluribus Unum

Consider the allegory of the elephant and the blind men. Each blind man was led to a different part of the elephant and allowed to touch it. Each man "saw" the elephant differently: as a "huge tree trunk," a "large fan," a "little snake," a "large serpent," a "sharp spear," etc. Each described his impression of the elephant, but none, in fact, had adequately described the elephant.

It is so with The Salvation Army in the eyes of the general public even in this day. The part of the Army each segment of the public encounters is the part that is imaged in their eyes as The Salvation Army.

The following quote from a letter of appreciation to The Salvation Army for assistance at the September 11, 2001 World Trade center disaster by Amy L. Brenton of Massachusetts who was working with a veterinarian Unit CVT-VMAT illustrates this fact:

> "I must be honest and say I never knew what The Salvation Army did. I always saw people ringing their bells and asking for donations. I often thought it had to only do with those in financial need. I now know it has to do with everyone who is in need. People often asked me how I ate while I was down there. I always reply, 'Great... thanks to the Salvation Army.' The members in my team got raincoats, socks, flashlights, Tylenol, gloves, sweatshirts, food, Band-Aids, and more from The Salvation Army."

The author's own experience during an interview with a technician for a medical procedure at a local hospital in June of 2003 further reinforces the depth of the public's confusion of the dual identity of the Army's vast array of programming:

TECHNICIAN: What is your religion/denomination?
AUTHOR: Salvationist
TECHNICIAN: Where do you go to Church?
AUTHOR: The Salvation Army
TECHNICIAN: (puzzled inflection) I did not know The Salvation Army is a Church.

It actually took several minutes to explain the dual nature of the Army to her satisfaction. It is still doubtful that she fully grasped the explanation.

No one is absolutely certain what to name or how to address the monolith that is The Salvation Army, such is its ever-changing nature and always constant calling.

Could it be that the Army's primary purpose and mandated destiny is no more and no less than the Founder's succinct description of his concept: that of a "saved, sanctified, and servant-slave Army of the living Christ"? And is its form the vessel that God designs to effect that noble purpose in each present age?

The Mission Statement of The Salvation Army describes its mandate as:

> "The Salvation Army, an International movement, is an evangelical part of the Universal Christian Church. Its message is based on the Bible. Its ministry is motivated by the love of God. Its mission is to preach the gospel of Jesus Christ and to meet human needs in his name without discrimination."

(Note: the author has encountered several versions of this statement, but all are essentially the same in meaning and content.)

How did The Salvation Army rapidly grow into the worldwide force of a religiously-oriented conglomerate of social services that now reaches into almost every nook and cranny of the known world? How did it attain that very milestone in the lifetime of General William Booth, the founder?

In 2004, ninety-two years after his death, the Army still heeds that initial calling to be a "saved, sanctified, and servant-slave Army of the living Christ," whose array of services still attempt to fill the depth of human need in the entire world.

The most compelling affirmation is that God is the creator, innovator, and author of The Salvation Army and its service-emphasizing method of reaching the masses with the Gospel of Christ by exemplifying His compassion and Love to the "whosoever" (John 3:16 NIV).

As He leads from generation to generation of development, the Army follows His mandates by nothing less than divine radar. Dare I say figuratively, "A pillar of fire by night and a pillar of cloud by day" (Exodus 13: 20-22 NIV).

Each successive generation takes on the aura and atmosphere of the current shifts and changes of the prevailing times. Yet, the mandate for service and salvation never changes.

Over the years a formal, yet casual grouping of services has emerged all around the world to, as The Salvation Army states, "Meet the need at the point of need."

Thus, if you were to travel around the globe, you would find The Salvation Army at work in almost every culture and climate, administering the work of serving humanity and communicating the gospel in the language and activities of the country's population and cultural make-up.

If one could travel back in time or into the future, he would no doubt see the Army in a different model and position of servitude to the masses of the unsaved and downtrodden. Still, it would be the same Salvation Army carrying out the mission delivered by Divine decree to the founder and to the Army of today that follows on.

Again, the Army expresses in song the sentiment of constant servitude, "...In summer, in winter, no matter, the Army's the same after all." "I'm glad I'm a Salvation Soldier. I promise to stand brave and true to the flag with the star in the center. The yellow, the red, and the blue."

From region to region in every country there are differences enough to cause the Army to adjust and fine-tune its methods and operational forms to accommodate even the most minute of cultures to the location to be served. Yet, it is in essence the same Salvation Army doing the same service: saving and serving the lost of all of God's children.

These adjustments and changes are made in order to fit into the local scenes without imposing a different culture and/or religious regimen for the local citizens to follow in order to obtain the Army's services.

The singular non-negotiable element of The Salvation Army's vast array of services is Salvation, by and through the Lord Jesus Christ and Him alone, and service in His name. Still, no one is required to accept the teaching of The Salvation Army to obtain services; they are given without strings attached.

The Need at the Point of Need

Generally speaking, the standard programs of The Salvation Army are needed and wanted in bulk in almost every corner of the universe of need. After all, a "cup of cold water" is welcomed in any place and in every situation, and essentially, a "cup of cold water" in His Name is The Salvation Army's stock-in-trade. It is the essence of all it has to offer.

The Structure (nomenclature)

Still, the Army is a centrally directed and operated entity with its core policy-making and operational forms in one place.

The International Headquarters is based in London, England. The international head of The Salvation Army movement is the General, described as both an office of responsibility/authority and a singular-person rank of an elected individual of The Salvation Army.

Each country of operation is under the jurisdiction of a National and/or Territorial Commander(s) usually with the rank of Commissioner.

Territorial Commands are divided into Divisional Commands, and Divisional Commands are directors of Corps operational cities and other units within their jurisdictional area. Corps Officers/Directors are responsible for the on-site operations in the local community. Each ascending Commander has an ever-widening scope of responsibility and authority to innovate and implement The Salvation Army's mandate within his/her area of command. In this system there is a direct chain of command from the Corps Officer to the General through a set protocol.

To help them in their tasks, The Salvation Army Officers engage advisory boards, advisory councils, funding bodies, Soldiers, the general public, volunteers, and other donors of time, talent, and treasure. All are volunteers with the exception of the Commissioned Officers and the employees.

This cadre of local members and volunteers generally provides the "Army" in The Salvation Army. Often, they exude a great deal of the Salvation as well.

THE GRID OF SERVICES FROM AN EVOLVING PERSPECTIVE

Over the years, in order to meet this demand for an all-inclusive and well-operated religious/humanitarian program, the Army has developed a loosely knit, centrally directed system of social programs and religious services. These construction blocks to a better society within the community are designated roughly as departments, programs, or other such individual, yet cohesive identifying names.

Listed below are a few of the divisions of programs and services offered through The Salvation Army. In some communities more services are offered and in some communities, fewer. The programs are dependent upon the needs of the community served, and the local Army's ability to provide services.

With the employment of numerous executive councils, advisory councils, professional employees/advisors, legal representatives, local leaders of the community, and at-large experts and specialists, the Army provides services in the following manner:

- The General establishes international policy and maintains continuity.
- The Territorial/National Leaders establish regional policies.
- The Divisional Leaders provide oversight to the Corps Operations within a jurisdictional area.
- The Corps Officers administer the local operations at the local level of service.

Corps Community Centers

Corps Community Center buildings are as varied as the programs offered. On the next page is one such building in Greenville, South Carolina, c2003. A Corps Community Center may be a free standing building or a complex of buildings and recreational areas. It is ideally located in a central community where it is accessible to surrounding families and organizations that make up the bulk of the membership and volunteering personnel of the local Salvation Army unit.

In the past this edifice has been called many names, including: "the Hall," "the Citadel," "the Corps," "the Corps Community Center," "the Center," and "the Church." The list is actually almost endless and sometimes gets comical as one tries to outdo the other with names such as: "the Work," "the Building," and "the Office."

In recent years, descriptive monikers have been attached, such as "the Service and Worship Center," "the Community Church," and other such designations. Lately, ethnic designations have been applied to specific Corps such as "the Hispanic Corps," "the Asian Corps," "the International Corps," and others whose membership is made up of one dominant ethnic group.

None of these names have fully captured the essence of the spirit of service that is carried out within and outside the walls of the building. In fact, those activities are as varied as the names applied to the different edifices. The list is unending. The most succinct description would be simply, "The Salvation Army."

Structures and Standards

The standard make-up of a typical Corps Program schedule, which is the usual designation of a Salvation Army service/worship-center operation, is as follows:

Religious Services

Religious services are open to all the community. Services are administered by members of The Salvation Army under the direction of a Salvation Army Officer, with the assistance of a staff, which is made up of professional and other paid and volunteer personnel. These services follow the traditional array of church related worship and witness services. The local Corps Officer serves as the pastor of the group. These are the basic religious services: Sunday school; Holiness meeting (AM]; Salvation meeting (PM]; Mid-Week Prayer and Praise meeting (PM); Outdoor and Street ministry where allowed and practical.

Other related locally designed religious/character-building and social welfare programs are added as suggested by the local community and approved by the Territorial Leaders. These are presented in another section of this chapter below.

Community Center Membership Rosters

Salvation Army Corps Officers: the administrators/ leaders of the local units. These Officers also perform the duties of pastor of The Salvation Army's local religious communities.

Senior Soldiers: members fourteen years and older who have professed Salvation through Jesus Christ and signed a declaration of faith called the "Articles of War," also referred to as "A Soldier's Covenant," and have been sworn in under the flag of The Salvation Army.

Junior Soldiers: Members from seven to fourteen years of age who have signed a young people's pledge and enrolled in the junior units; they attend weekly worship and training activities and services in children's meetings. The pledge includes a simple declaration of faith.

Adherents: Generally, all adults who want the Army to be their place of worship/fellowship but do not want to become Soldiers. Adherents sign a statement of desire to become an Adherent. The “Adherent” designation can be applied in all Salvation Army units.

Regular enrolled attendees of public meetings: These are those who attend Sunday School, group meetings, and other character-building/religious programs who simply want to attend fellowship/religious services but not join The Salvation Army as members of the organization.

Training Classes: Salvation Army soldier preparation classes are required for prospective Salvation Army Soldiers. Generally no further training is required for Soldiers, but many ongoing classes and courses are offered through the Educational Department of The Salvation Army.

Corps Cadet Training: It is essential training for the future leadership of the Corps programming and The Salvation Army Officer preparation. This requirement has been relaxed in recent times to allow for non-member youth to participate in concentrated Bible study.

Traditionally, these groups are the prospect-pool for recruiting Salvation Army Officer candidates. Although, by no means are they exclusive. Any person who presently exhibits an experience of Salvation through the blood of Jesus Christ and desires to join as a Soldier or Officer-candidate will be considered.

Musical forces: Musical forces include both instrumental and vocal sections. Musical training is offered to all who desire to enroll.

Religious Musical Memberships: These memberships require Salvation Army Church membership. This requirement also has recently been relaxed to include any persons who desire to perform in a Salvation Army-sponsored or sanctioned musical group if they will agree to join The Salvation Army within one year.

—“Sing and Make Music” O&R for Salvation Army Musicians.

Also included are alternative worship musical forces which can be described as almost any type of religiously oriented instrumental or vocal grouping.

The main components of the musical forces used in worship services are: Corps pianist/organist, Corps Band, Corps Singers, Worship and Praise ensembles.

Thespian and other arts expressions have also been added to the array of worship forms in recent years. These are utilized and presented by both in-house groups and by outside troupes.

Community Service Programs: These programs do not require Salvation Army membership, but each is a roll-oriented program and is administered by professional, volunteer, or other staff personnel under the direction of a local Corps officer. These programs are described as "character builders" because they are aimed at teaching awareness of the responsibility of community and include a call to salvation.

These, listed below, are generally United States of America designations. Other terms apply according to the country of operation.

Junior Legion: Fellowship for young children.

Young People's Legion: Fellowship for older youth.

Girl Guards: Fellowship/instruction for older girls.

Sunbeams: Fellowship/instruction for younger girls.

Boys' Adventure Corps: Fellowship/instructions for boys of both age groups.

Youth Brass Band: Youth musical training.

Youth Singing Groups: Youth vocal instruction.

Men's Fellowship Club: Fellowship for adult men.

Women's Ministries, formerly Ladies Home League Fellowship for adult women.

The Senior Citizens Club: Fellowship for older adults.

Camping and recreational trips are offered to all ages and sexes within their own groupings.

Various other programs designed to help individuals and to fulfill specific needs of the community are offered depending upon need and funding available. Those specialized programs are designed and offered by the local Corps lay leadership and the Corps officers and approved by the Territorial Leadership.

Outreach: Generally open to all who desire to volunteer services to the community in The Salvation Army. The term most used for this group is the "League of Mercy." These include volunteers such as:

- Hospital and shut-in visitors.
- Prison Ministries/Visitation.
- Assisted living and nursing home visitors.
- Veterans and related groupings visitors.
- Related Social Services Activities: The disaster and emergency services volunteer program responds to disasters and emergencies within the community as needed.

In addition to the list of activities above, every Salvation Army Corps Community Center operates and maintains a basic stock of family assistance items for delivery to anyone in need.

Counseling, upon request, is provided for all who may be experiencing difficulties. Spiritual, social, and character enhancing matters and needs receive prominence in this setting.

Summer camping programs are offered to all ages as a part of the community outreach program.

Emanating from each Corps Community Center are other community-mandated programs that are designed to meet specific needs of the local area. Some have been requested by the community leaders/agencies, and some have been initiated by the local group of Salvation Army officers and lay-leaders.

Greenville Annual Advisory Organizations' Meeting, c1950s.

Greenville Boys and Girls Club Baseball Team, c1950s.

Greenville Fresh Air Camps Program, c1950s.

Girl Guard Judy Farmer Campbell. Guard Territorial Leader Captain Lillian Blackburn. Greenville Girl Guard Awards Presentation, c1950s.

Greenville Corps Community Center
Activities/Social Service facilities.

The Greenville Social Services Administration Building at 419 Rutherford Street, c 2003.

The Salvation Army provides a conglomerate of services designed to assist citizens of every gender, race, and circumstance. The social services operations cover a large and diverse group of programs designed to assist the community in meeting the needs of individuals and families. Not all services are provided in all units of operation. Availability is dependent on location, size of community, and budgetary resources. In some locations, depending on the size of the community and budgetary constraints, the Corps Community Center and the Social Service program are located in the same building or on the same campus.

Anyone may apply to The Salvation Army for assistance and will be considered for help according to need and/or The Salvation Army's ability to render aid.

Family Welfare Services: Family welfare services include all matters of need for families that find themselves unable to provide minimal support and subsistence for its members. The objective is to hold families together over protracted periods of loss of income or other threatening events.

The tools are generally food vouchers and grocery distribution, utilities and rent subsidies, and clothing and other material items to help the family stay together. Personal counseling regarding family, community life, and spiritual values is also provided as requested or needed.

Homeless Shelter Services: Provided in a dormitory-like facility, homeless shelter assistance requires an array of social-related services to help homeless people in times of loss with the barest minimum of life-sustaining resources. This can also include individual housing for homeless families and transitional housing opportunities for those in distress. Homeless shelter services are provided for both individuals and families, both transient and community citizens.

Adult Rehabilitation Centers: In large metropolitan areas the centers are stand-alone units which care for and treat men and women who have found themselves in dire circumstances because of one or a combination of missteps. These may include alcohol abuse, drug addiction, low self-esteem, or other unusual situations that render them unable to cope with daily life.

This service is provided as an as-available program. It requires a staff of trained counselors and a facility large enough to house the required number of people in a residential and treatment situation.

Corps Salvage and Rehabilitation Centers - Thrift Store and Salvage Operations: As the name implies, this service is provided by a local corps unit on a smaller scale than the Adult Rehabilitation Centers. This program requires adequate living and working facilities and often takes up a large portion of the location in which it is situated.

Men and women who are addicted to alcohol and drugs, and/or who have any number of social and spiritual problems, and desire to break the habits are treated. They agree to attend for a minimum number of days, and to be monitored and treated for their addictions or problems in a setting of occupational training, education, and in-residence living under controlled conditions.

Often, a short stay can alleviate the problem, and they are able to return to their families and jobs. Sometimes treatment takes longer. The length of stay depends upon the rate of progress.

The men and women live in separate living groups, and work as a unit in the Thrift Stores and Salvage program, monitored by professional guidance counselors.

Disaster Relief and Related Services: When disaster strikes in any part of the world, this program goes into action to provide both material and spiritual assistance as required in conjunction with the local and national disaster coordinators who are responsible for the health and welfare of our local communities.

Usually the local unit is first responder and has the option of calling in other units as needed to adequately service the disaster. In this case, a regional disaster coordinator is engaged to consolidate and direct the overall program of service. The volunteer workers are enlisted from a combination of all units of service provided by The Salvation Army and local citizens who desire to serve the disaster-stricken area.

Often the disaster is of multi-regional scope or of national and international proportion and requires extensive and complicated coordination. In these cases, a multi-regional team is assigned for the duration of the need. This team draws experts, other workers, and massive supplies from the entire range of The Salvation Army community to administer aid and comfort to the victims and the other relief agencies in the area. They generally stay as long as needed. Often they do follow-up to help rebuild and revitalize the area.

Christian counseling is offered to both victims of the disaster and the rescue workers.

Disaster relief services are offered by The Salvation Army.
Photo from the War Cry Magazine, June 8, 2002.

RED SHIELD CLUB *for* BOYS AND GIRLS

Sponsored and Operated by The Salvation Army

Captain ROBERT BURCHETT, *Club Director*

26 East Broad Street - - Greenville S. Carolina

TO GIVE the underpriviledged boys and girls of this city a chance to DEVELOP THEMSELVES in the AMERICAN WAY. The Salvation Army Advisory Board, in 1938, started the Red Shield Club, utilizing for this purpose the new extension built on to the Salvation Army Citadel on East Broad Street.

The funds for building this new addition were given by the citizens of Greenville. The building has a gymnasium, two game rocms, a craft shop, library, clinic and assembly room.

The Red Shield Club serves all boys and girls—specializing upon those who are underprivileged—often neglected.

The Red Shield Club permits no age limitations - no restrictive fees—no prcselytizing efforts. It serves all nationalities and creeds—cooperating with home, school and church.

During danger hours after school and before bedtime, the Red Shield Club provides wholesome play, stimulating work, physical training and vocational training.

"Builders of Good Citizenship"

The Greenville Salvation Army Boys and Girls Club of America's present location is on Owens Street in Northwest Greenville.

The Red Shield* Boys and Girls Club: The Boys and Girls Club is usually a freestanding recreational and instructional facility employing the use of Christian, community-oriented leaders and activities. Its goal is to teach and mold young people to become better citizens within the community. Honesty, integrity, and good citizenship are the values instilled within the young people. Christian/religious training is not necessarily the goal of the club, but this trait is implicit in the body of the Boys and Girls Club organization.

Adults are encouraged to interact with the children, but the program is not necessarily geared for senior participation or membership.

In many locations, including in Greenville, the clubs are aligned with the Boys and Girls Clubs of America and are so named to include the affiliation with that organization. In other locations the designation is simply The Salvation Army Boys and Girls Club.

The Boys and Girls Club works primarily with young people of low and moderate means; however, membership is open to all children in the community.

Family participation and involvement is encouraged in order to get the whole universe of the child on the same page and help him have a feeling of self worth in the family as well as in the community.

Membership does not require Salvation Army affiliation. The young people are encouraged to attend and worship at their own Church or Mosque or Synagogue or other chosen religious organization, and become leaders in the community and in their church of choice. A few members do become Salvation Army Soldiers, Officers, and program leaders.

*Red Shield Club is the original informal designation for The Salvation Army's Boys and Girls Club in Greenville mainly because The Salvation Army Red Shield was the identifying logo for the club.

The Boys and Girls Club staff is made up of an Executive Director, Assistant Director, program staff, volunteers, and others who are parents and friends of the children of the community oriented operation. None are required to be members of The Salvation Army.

The operation of the club is shepherded by an advisory council made up of local business and professional individuals in the community, some of whom are members by designation of the local Salvation Army Advisory Boards.

Programming of the Boys and Girls Club must meet rigid standards in order to remain affiliated with the Boys and Girls Clubs of America. It must meet moral and ethical standards to remain with The Salvation Army, and it must meet requirements of success and excellence in order to merit the support of the local community. Of course, the high standard of a successful club includes all of the above.

As mentioned, for The Salvation Army Boys and Girls Clubs, the parent body is The Salvation Army, and the body of national affiliation is the Boys and Girls Clubs of America organization.

The range of programming involves mostly academic tutoring, athletics, and group activities which include citizenship training and leadership instruction.

Mentoring, counseling, and fostering programs are offered and encouraged in order to rescue potentially troublesome children and give guidance over rough spots in the young people's lives.

While not active in every command of The Salvation Army in every community, where there is a Boys and Girls Club, it is one of the backbone programs in the Army's arsenal of weapons to combat poverty and sin. The Salvation Army is a pioneer of the concept of Boys and Girls Clubs as a deterrent to a life of crime and wasted potential in the youth of our nation.

THE CHRISTIAN ARSENAL OF LOVING WEAPONS

I have attempted to paint with a broad brush the components which make up many of The Salvation Army's array of services.

This report only scratches the surface of services and programs that exist as methods of achieving the Army's goal of salvation and relief from the effects of sin and poverty for the entire world. It is neither exhaustive nor complete.

This series of programs can be implemented in whole or in part in almost any setting and in every community. In fact, it has been so from the founding days of The Salvation Army. Different components and combinations of components of The Salvation Army's program structures are in use in every place the Army operates. The program utilized is dependent upon the need and resources at hand.

One of the unique and unifying features of The Salvation Army's presentation of services in every community is the concept of "One Salvation Army, and one operational standard" for the total array of services provided. There can be no separation of programs so that one is deemed more important than another or that one receives more emphasis than the other.

It is The Salvation Army, no matter what the need or the service/program employed to meet the need.

However, this book is not about The Salvation Army's programs in general. It is about the establishment of The Salvation Army in Greenville, South Carolina using a combination of the above methods and means, and some that were not listed above.

Other programs, units of service, and unusual methods of operation will be introduced and explained as the book unfolds. Some are no longer in use, having met the need of the then-current situation and passed on to address other community problems. The core mandates of The Salvation Army are always in effect no matter what the need. These mandates are "to save and to serve."

A photo of a painting of the Reedy River
which hangs in the City Hall

CHAPTER II
1904-1909
PERMANENT AND ENDURING BEGINNINGS IN GREENVILLE AND THE PARENTHESIS OF SERVICE
"The Wise Man Builds his House upon the Rock"

Four views of the Reedy River Falls at South Main Street... Notice the photo of a painting hanging in the City Hall (facing page) depicting the early mill days of the Falls and the same scene in the photo taken in 2003 (above left).

When you walk into the lobby of the Greenville, SC City Hall on South Main Street, you will see the following inscription. It is posted on the wall as a concise statement of the beginning of Greenville, SC.

> "The City of Greenville had its origin in the Indian Trading Station and Mill established about 1768 by Richard Pearis at Reedy River Falls."

In 1784 these lands became the property of Colonel Thomas Brandon who sold to Lemual James Alston in 1788. Alston laid out the town “Pleasantburg” in 1797. In 1815 he sold his 11,028 acres including the town which was then known as “Greenville Court House” to Vardry McBee, under whose imaginative development Greenville emerged as an antebellum trading Center and summer resort.

In the 1850’s, the Greenville and Columbia Railroad, Furman University and the Greenville Female College were built. Following the reconstruction era the building of cotton textile mills converted the town into an industrial center which by 1917 became the “Textile Center of the South.”

After World War II there continued diversified industrial growth, with the expansion of textile and allied industries, earning the city the title of “Textile Center of the World.”

An industrious and progressive people have made this growth possible.

In 1905, The Salvation Army set up a tent as a center of operations directly behind the First National Bank building which was on the corner of McBee and Main Street.

On the sidewalk in front of the Carolina First Bank (formerly the First National Bank building) in downtown Greenville, a plaque states:

> "What makes greatness is starting something that lives after you."
> —Ralph W. Sockman

Beginnings and Parenthesis: Salvo Appleseed

According to the earliest record of Salvation Army Officer Assignment, the disposition of forces, shortened to “the Dispo,” the Army first had an officer, Captain Fielding, and an assistant officer, Lieutenant Kayser (M), on the scene in Greenville in January of 1888. (This is the spelling and name style on the Dispo page. Lt. Kayser also has a listing of Keyser and Kaiser in various reports. Both officers moved to Durham, NC and on to several other appointments together and separately before Lt. Keyser became unlisted at Richmond # 2 Corps on June 1889 with rank of Captain, and Captain Fielding became unlisted in the Dispo at Lonaconing, MD as A.D.C. on July 7, 1889.

The designation, A.D.C. is unknown to this writer except as in Aide de Camp. In that case, he would be a traveling companion/assistant to a higher-ranking officer. This is not verified.)

Taking the Plunge

From the 1870s to the 1880s, the population of Greenville quadrupled, and more. This was the result of an exploding economy in the region (*Greenville Mountain and Daily Newspaper*, 1887).

The building of several new textile and gristmills resulted in the expanded market for cotton and additional jobs for the farmers and others who were dwelling in the city. It also was a time for inbound migration of rural people who were looking for a better life in the city.

However, beginning in the 1880s, the tide reversed, and prosperity gradually sank into unusual hardship inflicted by several converging factors of bad fortune.

In the waning era of this prosperity cycle (1887-1888), The Salvation Army first came to town to set up shop.

By 1885, the textile mills had gone bankrupt and were in reorganization because of their exploitation by the northern owners. This loss of industry and the source of employment quickly added to the growing pool of poverty stricken citizens of Greenville. These and other converging circumstances caused the tide of fortune to change on the local economic front as well, and may have been one of the factors that contributed to the short-lived Greenville Salvation Army operation of 1887-1888.*

*Though not confirmed, The War Cry report of 1888 infers that the Army was at work at the "Watch Night Service" in 1887 which would indicate the Army began in Greenville in that year.

The International Salvation Army was only 23 years old, having been founded in London in 1865 as the East London Christian Society by William and Catherine Mumford Booth. William Booth was known as the "General Superintendent" of the Mission.

The name-change from the "East London Christian Revival Society" to the "East London Christian Mission" to the "Christian Mission" to "The Salvation Army" happened between the years 1865-1878 (The Authoritative Life of William Booth, p. 67). The name change to The Salvation Army in 1878 was only ten scant years ahead of the "invasion" of Greenville.

The apparent shift from the pure preaching form to the dual operational form of social welfare and soul saving caused some defection in the ranks even at that early age (1878). The gist of the problem was that some of the other leaders of the movement wanted to establish a permanent "church" structure and the Booths were pushing for a more widely-scoped organization as an evangelical tool for saving the masses.

It turned out that a headquarters building/organization was established for the fledgling Army in that area. The Salvation Army organization, however, quickly expanded to encompass the entire world under the leadership of the Booth family.

The military terminology and ranking system soon permeated the entire operation from the "General'" right on down the line to "soldier." The nomenclature began, as well, to take on the connotation of military structure and form.

Booth declared that the Army's emphasis had not changed and that preaching Jesus Christ would be the only aim of the newly named Salvation Army. In reality, due to the prolific differences of the far-flung operations and the assignment of largely theologically untrained and circumstantially-bred officers, this promise was already on its way to being impossible to keep.

The wave of circumstances surrounding the Army's drive to succeed and expand in order to spread the gospel of Jesus Christ to the masses mandated social service as a necessary tool for expansion.

The Army had already begun to take on the connotation of a living, growing organism which seemed to be heading toward a destiny known only to the originator and founder of Divine origin—the Spirit of God.

Of necessity in many locations, the preaching mode of operation for the Mission Stations, which had by then become "Corps," was strongly infused with the social welfare work as a practical means of acceptance by the local citizenry and the constituents.

Thus, in the spirit of the fabled Johnny Appleseed, The Salvation Army was planted all around the globe to grow and nurture the twin fruits of salvation from sin and salvation from human misery.

The Parameters of Organization

Lurking always in the background of the Army's first beginnings were two powerful deterrents to both the success of the church function and the success of the social welfare function:

- The Army's leaders had no desire to found another Church, and the public did not want to accept another denomination of the Church. Establishing a Church was not in the vision of the founder.
- The Army's social service endeavor was predicated upon the acceptance of its spiritual mission, which was a Revival Society. At the outset, a Social Service Organization was not acceptable to the founders and leaders as a part of the overall strategy of the "Mission." The reality turned out to be that they could not have one without the other. Thus, the struggle for dominance between the two mandates was begun.

The general public did, however, want and need the social welfare innovations of this new and unique organization with its leaders and laity driven to improve the physical as well as the spiritual lot of all of mankind. They could tolerate the religious peculiarities in order to obtain the needed material offerings of successful social welfare work. However, the opposition from both the established churches and the "dens of vice" was fierce and, at times, dangerous for the new Salvation Army.

A Marriage Made in Heaven

The Army has been successful in "marrying"' the two mandates of Jesus, thus overcoming the obstacles, without being exclusively identified as either, or excluding either from prominence of visibility. Those mandates, taken directly from the lips of Jesus Christ are, "Love God supremely and love your neighbor as yourself." (An appropriate Scriptural reference would be Matthew 22:35-40.)

"My Best Men are Women"

—A saying attributed to William Booth

Although Catherine Mumford Booth (Mrs. William Booth) was mainly at work behind the scenes gathering financial and moral support from the West End of London for the Army, she was, in fact, a powerful player in the founding and the success of the movement in its infancy and beyond. She also did her turns at preaching to the masses of the East-Enders of London along with her husband. She was one of the champions of women's rights to the pulpit all through her life.

So arduous were her work and other efforts in the early days that she rightfully earned the title of co-founder of The Salvation Army along with William Booth. The endearing term, "Army Mother" is a tribute to her power and influence on the formation of the organization.

Much of the furious growth and expansion of the early day Army was directly attributed to the labor and effective leadership of its female members and of the Booth family.

Catherine Mumford Booth: January 17, 1829-October 4, 1890.
Mrs. William Booth, General.
Notice the American Crest with the Eagle. It was used for a time in the USA but was eventually replaced with the English Crest of the International Salvation Army.

Most of the "slum" work was effectively done by brigades made up of the girls and women who dedicated themselves to the task of reclaiming the lost ladies of the streets with love and compassion.

Although retiring and quiet by nature, Catherine Booth later became a crusader for women's rights to preach. Her famous pamphlet on "Female Ministry" is still highly regarded. She was of compassionate temperament, tender-hearted and gentle, yet in every sense a warrior. She contributed a great deal to the ultimate establishment of The Salvation Army.

—*Excerpted from a short biography of Catherine Mumford Booth*

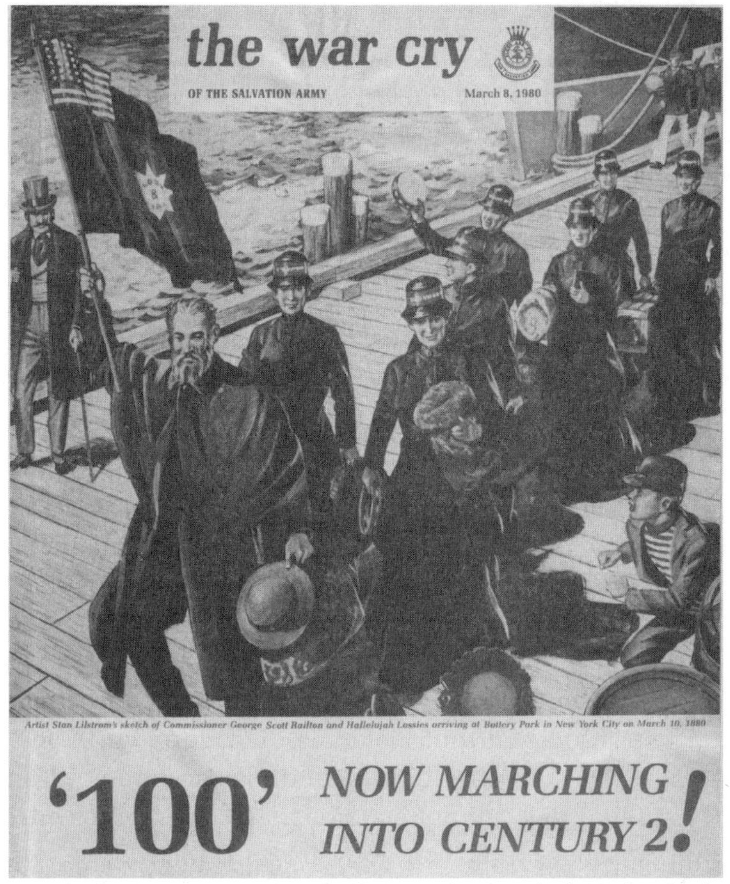

the war cry
OF THE SALVATION ARMY
March 8, 1980

Artist Stan Lilstrom's sketch of Commissioner George Scott Railton and Hallelujah Lassies arriving at Battery Park in New York City on March 10, 1880

'100' NOW MARCHING INTO CENTURY 2!

Commissioner George Scott Railton and seven lady Salvationists land in New York, 1880. National War Cry: March 8, 1980.

FALTERING STARTS and SCHISMS

The first Greenville, SC opening in 1888 was effected only eight years after Commissioner George Scott Railton and the seven "Hallelujah Lassies," a title not conferred by The Salvation Army but by the public, landed in New York City in 1880 to officially commence the Army's work in America.

Commissioner Railton was a trusted emissary of the General, and his forte was, among other things, traveling all over the world establishing the work of the Army in new countries. In fact, he is accredited with owning third place in importance behind General William Booth and his son Commissioner Bramwell Booth in the structure of the now burgeoning upstart of a quasi-religious misfit called The Salvation Army. (Note: This is the author's view of the attitudes of factions of the opposition.]

Note: Commissioner George Scott Railton also authored the book *The Authoritative Life of General William Booth, Founder of The Salvation Army*. New York: George H. Doran Company, Hodder and Stoughton, 1912.

Upon the death of the Founder in 1912, his son Bramwell Booth was appointed by confidential letter to succeed his father as the second General of The Salvation Army. This was the method of transference of leadership chosen by the General at the outset of the organized mission.

Later on, the method of transference was altered to include catastrophic circumstances as a trigger to choose a general by the convergence of the Commissioners Conference. This body was named "The High Council." It was comprised of the leadership of the world wide Salvation Army and was first convened in 1929.

General Bramwell Booth wrote in the preface to Railton's William Booth book the following:

> "I hope also that to some, at least, the great message of this life will stand revealed in these pages. I believe it to be that, while God can do little or nothing by us until we are completely submitted and given up to Him, He can work wonders of infinite moment by the world when we are. Asked, a few months before his death, if he would put into a sentence the secret as he saw it, of all the blessings which had attended him during his seventy years of service, the General replied: 'Well, if I am to put it into one sentence, would say that I made up my mind

> that God Almighty should have all that there was of William Booth.' It was in the beginning, that entire devotion to God and its continued maintenance which could, alone, account for the story told in these brief records."

An Earlier Start in America

In 1878-79, almost two years earlier than Railton's arrival, a young lady named Lieutenant Eliza Shirley, who immigrated to America with her family, established a creditable Salvation Army-like operation in Philadelphia with the assistance of her family. (See pictures on facing page.) She had served in Booth's Army in England before moving to America. At that time she would have been sixteen or seventeen years of age.

So vision-oriented was she, it is said, that she called on the General to leave England and come to America to command the operation. She reasoned that the prospects of success were so much greater in the New World than in England. That first Corps in Philadelphia is today known as the "Pioneer Corps." It is a thriving and successful Corps operation to this date.

Go Forward, Go Forward, Go Forward

From Railton's 1880 beginning, there were many attempts to get the work started in all corners of America, and many of them ended in failure because of ill timing, lack of financial support, overabundant enthusiasm, or some other misstep on the part of the American contingent.

In fact, Commissioner Railton, himself, ran afoul of the city administration of New York shortly after he landed in that city because of too much success in establishing indoor meetings. He wanted to take to the streets with his mission because he felt that the Army should be in the streets where the people congregated and not primarily in a building.

The mayor would not have it.

Railton moved the operation to Philadelphia in protest of the restriction.

Shirley's Valentine corps

TO celebrate the 125th anniversary of Coventry City Corps an exhibition is currently being held in the city's Herbert Art Gallery and Museum. The event began on 6 September and continues until the 26th of the month.

The poster advertising the display depicts Eliza Shirley, one of the earliest soldiers at the corps, who was converted in March 1878 and at the age of 16 became a lieutenant. Together with her parents she opened the Army's first overseas corps in Philadelphia, USA, in 1879.

The exhibition includes photographs and artefacts, among them uniforms, dating back to the 1870s, and not only tells the story of the corps – which was originally the 35th Christian Mission station – but also gives an indication of the Army's worldwide work.

The roll call of former corps officers at Coventry City includes many well-known names. Among them are Caroline Reynolds – who founded the corps on Valentine's Day in 1878, and went on to become the first woman divisional commander in the Army; Elijah Cadman, the Hallelujah chimney sweep; George 'Sailor' Fielding, of Salvation Navy fame; and the 'angel adjutant' Kate Lee.

Eliza Shirley in The Salvationist July 18, 2003.

Lt. Eliza Shirley's parents at Philadelphia, Pa. c1878-79, as published in the Salvationist.

An Earlier Start on the Reedy River

The Salvation Army in Greenville, South Carolina was born during a period of upheaval both in the Army ranks and the country in general. This was especially true in the South because of the aftermath of the Civil War (1861-1865), the reconstruction era (1865-1878), and the destruction and looting of the Southland by the over-running mobs and other looters and robbers and, yes, the "carpetbaggers" who came to exploit the poor, impoverished, defeated Southerners.

For reasons unknown to this writer, and not discovered in the records, the work in Greenville did not flourish but folded almost immediately and was not listed in the Disposition of Forces after May of 1888, barely three months after the "invasion" date.

There is no readily apparent record of buildings, activities, Soldiers, formal opening or public reaction to the Army at that time. The only evidence of the original opening is the entry in the Disposition of Forces in 1888.

There is also a notation in The Salvation Army *War Cry* of January 1888, which began publication in America in 1881, that indicates the scope of the struggle and hardship the Greenville officers in 1888 were encountering.

Lieutenant Kaiser (correct spelling, according to the *War Cry* account) wrote,

> "Greenville, S C:
>
> We are down here in this southern corner by ourselves, and yet not alone, for the Lord is with us. Hallelujah! It is true the fight is hard and we have a great deal to contend with: but with it all, the Lord is leading us on, and we are able to report some souls since our last report. Glory to God!
>
> On New Years Eve the Soldiers all promised God with us to live closer and do more for Him this year than we did in the same one that had

> just passed away. May God help them all to be true to their vows. We seek the prayers of the comrades all over the field."
>
> —*Lt. C. W. Kaiser, for Capt. Bob Fielding.*

However, if there were Soldiers and Officers at a "Watch Night" service in 1887, there may have been an even earlier start in Greenville. No records exist to substantiate this hypothesis. Nor could this writer find any other entry in the *War Cry* reports.

The local newspaper copies perused by the author contained no references at all to the Army's presence in 1888. The local Salvation Army records are silent as well.

The Corps opening in Greenville, SC in 1888 is reported to be the first in the state of South Carolina. It is assuredly among the first in the entire Southern Territory.

An Early Setback

In 1881, less than two years after Railton established the work in America, Major Thomas E. Moore was sent to replace Commissioner Railton as the leader of The Salvation Army in the New Army World. Commissioner Railton was urgently needed in London to assist the General with other pressing duties. This was the beginning of a serious and devastating period in the history of The Salvation Army in America. A scant four years before the Greenville opening in 1888, the first real schism in America reared its ugly head in the form of the formation of "Moore's Army."

As it turned out, other equally or more devastating activities were on tap for the near future as well. This was a period of internal upheaval of The Salvation Army in the United States.

First, there was the seceding of Major Thomas E. Moore, whom General William Booth had appointed as the National Commander, and his contingent of Soldiers and Officers, followed by the formation of what came to be known as "Moore's Army" on October 21, 1884.

Due to Moore's burning desire to incorporate as the "American Salvation Army" and separate the organization from the Hierarchy of Booth's "International Salvation Army," he took a bold step away from the English Leadership.

Major Moore copyrighted and seized by legal claim and incorporation most of the Army's publications, symbols, and property in the United States and claimed them for his own operation. As well, a large number of Soldiers and Officers joined with him in the defection. That schism was partially resolved a few years later. The Salvation Army resumed its onward march under new and more dynamic leadership.

The operation in South Carolina was probably located more to the South of Greenville around Columbia, if it existed at all. Apparently Greenville, and for that matter, the entire Southern part of the United States, was not a high priority on either his, or the International Army's agenda.

The Tie that Binds

A newly minted Captain named Richard E. Holz who had defected with Moore saw the error of his ways and immediately petitioned for reconciliation with the main Salvation Army organization.

It took a few years for him to regain the favor of the Army's leadership, but he was instrumental in helping to heal the breech and bring the defectors back into the fold of the International Army. He became one of the giants of the cause of The Salvation Army in the ensuing years.

Change under Fire

Commissioner Frank Smith, a British Salvationist, was sent to command the Army in America in 1884 upon Moore's rebellion. He refused to talk to the rebel officers and soldiers who had seen the error of their ways and requested readmission to the International Army.

So it was not until Ballington Booth, a son of the General, took command of the USA because of the failing health of Commissioner Smith that the reconciliation process was started.

The young Captain Richard Holz was eventually restored to a place of high service and ultimately produced among his offspring several top leaders of The Salvation Army, including Divisional, Territorial, and National leadership of the movement. He, himself, occupied the high offices of command during his tenure.

Below is a biographical sketch of Captain and Mrs. Richard E. and Mary Powell Holz and their family. Mrs. Holz also was an officer and worked alongside him in every aspect of The Salvation Army's march through the Southland. He served primarily in the East but headed up the Province that included the Southland, with Headquarters in Philadelphia, PA.

Commissioner and Mrs. Richard E. and Mary Powell Holz retired as Territorial Commander and Director of Women's Services, respectively, of the Eastern Territory, USA.

Holz emigrated from Germany to the USA in 1881. He was converted in a Salvation Army meeting about 1881 or 1882 in Buffalo, NY.

Lt. Colonel David Holz, a grandson of the original Captain Richard E. Holz, supplied this information for publication.

> "Re: my grandfather, Commissioner R. E. Holz.
>
> Somewhere I have seen a copy of a picture of him at the dedication of a building in Greenville—possibly the early 20's when he was Provincial Commander of the Southern Province headquarters in Philadelphia and took in most of the South all the way to Key West."

(NOTE: This would be the dedication of the Emma Moss Booth Memorial Hospital in Vardry Heights, Greenville, SC in 1921. National Commander Eva Booth was in the party but was too ill to participate in the dedication of the hospital, and Captain R. E. Holz had a prominent role in the dedication. The Commander was the principal speaker at the 1st Presbyterian Church on Sunday. See the chapter devoted to the Women's Social Service Program—Chapter XIV. rwk)

"He had four daughters and one son. All became officers. They are: Brigadier Ernest R. Holz (my father); Mrs. Commissioner Claude (Elizabeth) Bates, Territorial Commanders in Central & West; Mrs. Colonel G. Blair (Ethel) Abrams (Trust & Annuity Dept-Eastern); Mrs. Major Maude Goellner (DHQ Officer-East); & Mrs. Major Kathleen Gifford (DHQ-West - husband killed in accident). Mrs. Commissioner Bates had one daughter, Mrs. Lt. Colonel Marie Seiler, THQ East.

My father and mother had eight children, five sons and three daughters:

- Commissioner Richard E. Holz: Territorial Commander in West & Central
- Commissioner Ernest W. Holz: Territorial Commander in Southern Territory and National Commander in the USA
- Lt. Colonel David Holz- DC in 3 Divisions - Southern territory
- CSM Edwy Holz - Miami Sunset Corps
- One son and three daughters are not soldiers.

Commissioner and Mrs. (Ruby Walker) Richard E. Holz have one daughter and three sons:

- Commissioner Keitha Holz Needham-South; [Director of Women's ministries]
- Dr. Richard Holz-Territorial Music Director-South;

Dr. Robert Holz: attorney with Bank of America. He is an active Salvationist and just moved to Charlotte. He was Songster Leader & Bandsman at the Norridge Corps [near Chicago] and also at Dallas Temple. He is the Songster Leader at Charlotte Temple Corps.

Dr. Ron Holz: Music Professor at Asbury College and Bandmaster of the Asbury SASF Band.

Commissioner and Mrs. (Wilimina Krunsberg) Ernest Holz have two sons and two daughters:

One daughter, Colonel Mary Holz Jones, serves at National Headquarters. Ernest Holz works for DHQ in Washington.

William Holz is not an active Salvationist.

Christine Holz Goodier attended Corps when she and her husband Bob lived in Washington. No Corps in the area they live in now. Emeline and I, Lt. Colonel and Mrs. David and Holz, have three children. One daughter, Karen Holz Kinlaw and her husband Keith Kinlaw, are soldiers of the Corps in Charlotte, with their four children. The two other children are Sharon Kathleen Holz and Dr. D. Keith Holz.

CSM & Mrs. Edwy Holz have two children. Their daughter, Mrs. Captain Carl Avery and husband are stationed in a Corps near Syracuse, NY. Commissioner and Mrs. Philip Needham, Keitha Holz, have two daughters. One daughter, Holly Needham, was just commissioned Captain. She is the assistant Officer at Charleston Citadel, WVA. Note: The other daughter is Heather Needham."

The following note is found in the SA bulletin service of current events April 29, 2004:

> "Mrs. Commissioner Florence Needham is a proud great grandmother - again. We received word that her granddaughter Heather (Needham) Hawkins gave birth to a baby boy. Ryan Philip was born on Friday evening, April 23, 2004. Ryan weighed 8 lbs. 10 oz., 21 inches long. Heather and Jack Hawkins are the proud parents. The proud grandparents are Commissioners Phil and Keitha Needham. Big brother Will is also excited."

HEALING: AND A NEW CHAMPION OF THE AMERICAN SALVATION ARMY LEADERSHIP

In 1887, Ballington Booth, a son of the Founder, was appointed along with his wife, Maude, to lead the International Salvation Army (as opposed to the Army splinters which had grown out of the schisms) in the United States. They were highly successful in restoring the Army's wholeness and became very popular in America. Both Ballington and Maude Booth applied for and won citizenship in America. Both were dynamic and charismatic leaders who soon won the hearts and loyalty of the American public.

But a greater problem was looming ominously upon the horizon.

When the time came for the General to transfer the Ballington Booths to another appointment in 1896, they decided to split from the International Salvation Army and form another "Army" more suited to the American way of life and culture.

Ballington Booth persuaded a large contingent of Soldiers, Officers, and local supporters, to defect with him. Many others followed him into the new venture. The new organization is known today as the Volunteers of America, and is the only unit of the schisms still in successful existence in the United States. Although the Volunteers of America was initially patterned along the lines of The Salvation Army, it soon took on a new and vastly different set of by-laws and operational procedure. It is now mostly a social service operation. In this and other respects it failed to supplant The Salvation Army in America.

According to a statement by Chairman and CEO of Volunteers of America, Mr. Charles Gould, in presenting a book written about the organization, the Volunteers of America is "a National non-profit, Spiritually-based organization providing local human service programs, and opportunities for individual and community involvement" (Quoted from the Internet 1/8/2003).

The Volunteers of America organization provides many services that truly benefit the needy of our land. Affordable housing is one of the most outstanding examples, according to their literature.

There were other splits and splinter groups forming due partly to the sense of rebellion that pervaded the newly formed Salvation Army in America. Even today, look-alike 'Armies' surface and claim to be valid operations, but they are largely personal operations. Some succeed, but most fold within a few years.

A Local Tempest in a Tea Pot

The Stella Fuller Settlement in Huntington, W.Va. is another such operation that has lasted beyond a few years. It has been in existence since 1933 as "The Salvation Army Outpost," and since 1943 as the "Stella Fuller Settlement." It operates today as a local "Army-like" charity of the 1940s era in the West End of Huntington. (Stella Fuller was a Salvation Army Officer before she decided to strike out on her own.)

Although this operational split came years after the two major schisms in America, it follows the same line of progress as the others. The Booth family, and later their successors, were adamant about not recognizing a separate leadership model apart from the International Salvation Army's chart of operational procedures.

Stella Fuller joined The Salvation Army in Huntington, WV after hearing a young Salvationist testify in an open air meeting in that city about 1916. She was quickly hired as an employee and sworn-in as a Soldier and later was promoted to the rank of Envoy [non-commissioned officer] in charge of The Salvation Army outpost at the corner of Fourth Avenue and Third Street in West Huntington, a dreary place called "Johnson's Lane," now Virginia Avenue, and just the kind of place the Army has always sought out for service.

Friction built up between the main Huntington Headquarters and the West End outpost because of some of the successful and unorthodox methods of the outpost and because of the popularity of the outpost, mainly due to the dynamic leadership of Stella Fuller. In 1943, Fuller left the Army and formed the highly successful Stella Fuller Settlement, an Army-like program complete with religious services, brass band, softball teams and a playground for the youths of the area. A salvage program was added and social welfare work was a mainstay. The Settlement was truly a "haven of rest" for the weary, downtrodden residents of Johnson's Lane in the West End of Huntington.

After she left The Salvation Army, Stella Fuller attempted to align with the Volunteers of America organization, but the leaders of the City of Huntington would not endorse the Volunteers of America as a recognized institution. She formed a Board of Directors who immediately coined the name "Stella Fuller Settlement," and the operation succeeded and thrived. Today the Stella Fuller Settlement is still rendering Salvation Army-like service, in reduced quantity, in the same location.

The Fuller family is no longer the principal operator since the death of Stella Fuller in 1981 and her son, Robert V. Fuller in 1991. The board runs the operation with part time help and volunteers. However, a grandson of the founder, Mr. Phillip Fuller, is a member of the Board of Directors (Excerpted from: *Missing Chapters: West Virginia Women in History by The West Virginia Women's Commission*: Courtesy of Bette M. Whaley, Executive Director, Stella Fuller Settlement, 10/2/2002).

Community Support Necessary

The overriding requirement for the Army's service in any given community is the financial and moral support of the community leaders. Lacking this support base, The Salvation Army cannot operate and pay its bills. The only alternative is to abandon the work and move on to more fertile fields.

In some communities a larger command or the divisional command may provide a small subsidy to help the Corps over rough spots. This is a temporary arrangement, and the small Corps must eventually survive locally or fold. The social and financial upheavals of the formative days caused financial and logistical trouble, and many of the Corps' operations simply went broke.

The Salvation Army did not have a Southern Territorial Command at that time. The southern section of the United States was in a state of confusion due to the after effects of the Civil War and the period of destruction and rebuilding going on all over the Southland. The reconstruction era was still an open fresh-wound, chaffing at the Southland. Dixie was not a prime prospect for Salvation Army operations.

Unsettled and Unwanted

In fact, for a number of years the Southern part of the United States was like the early Social Service program in esteem and desirability among officers. It was a mark of demotion to be assigned to either, and officers resisted the command to go to either field. It is a testimonial to the tenacity of the pioneer Army leadership that the USA Southern Territory is today one of the most esteemed Territories in the world and the International Social Service program is the backbone of The Salvation Army's salvage and reclamation arm today.

Finally, Respect and Creditability

The Southern Territory became a reality in 1927. Atlanta became a Territorial Command with its own Territorial Commander, instead of a Divisional Command under a Chief Divisional Headquarters.

Commissioner William McIntyre was the first Commissioner - Territorial Commander of the South. Colonel Alfred Augustus Chandler was the first Chief Secretary (see the details under the dateline for 1920-1929, Chapter IV).

It is speculated that Colonel Chandler was the driving force behind the Southern Officers' Training School in Atlanta. He studied the National Training system in London and was assigned to The Salvation Army Training Homes in New York in 1907. Among his burning passions was the training of Salvation Army Cadet Officers (*The Salvation Army War Cry*: July 6, 1907).

Greenville: early 1900s. The Mansion House is the second building on the left. The Salvation Army tent was located behind the Carpenter Brothers Drug store on the right beside the Records Building. East Court Street runs between Carpenter Brothers and the Records Building.

An Enduring Start in Greenville, South Carolina

In 1904, Evangeline Booth, daughter of the Founder, was appointed to the office of Counsel and National Commander for The Salvation Army in the United States.

Oral history places Salvation Army Officers in Greenville in January 1904, or sometime in the latter part of 1903. June 1904 is the actual public re-commencement date of The Salvation Army work in Greenville, South Carolina. The official date of re-organization according to the Dispo is October 1904.

By 1904, the economic tide had changed once again, and the Upstate of South Carolina had become the undisputed king of the cotton mill; Greenville was the textile center of the world and at the center of the hub of prosperity.

Into this situation The Salvation Army stepped to bring the love of God in word and deed to the fallen masses of the population who did not share in the prosperity of the region for a number of reasons. It preached the Gospel and administered aid to the slum dwellers of the city.

The regional headquarters for The Southern Salvation Army was in Cleveland, Ohio, and Divisional Headquarters was based in Atlanta, Georgia. All of which was a part of the Eastern Territory with headquarters in New York where Commissioner George Scott Railton and seven "Hallelujah Lassies" had established the work in 1880. New York was also the National Salvation Army Headquarters.

There were Provincial Headquarters (called Chief Divisional Headquarters-CDH) in some major cities, with a Provincial Officer (called the Chief Divisional Officer-CDO) giving supervision to two or three Divisional Offices. The Southern Division was commanded out of Philadelphia-via Cleveland, Ohio-via Atlanta.

Establishing a Command Structure

Upon approval of General William Booth in London, England, the United States Department of the West was formed in 1905, with Headquarters in Chicago. This would later become the Central Territory. Commissioner Eva Booth retained command of the Department of the East headquartered in New York; also, she retained the National Command responsibility. All were subject to the authority of the General in London. Part of California was under the direct command of England and the General.

This divided the command structure into three Territorial Commands:

The Eastern Territory with headquarters in New York. Generally the Eastern Time Zone boundary, including the Southland.

The Western Sub-Territory with headquarters in Chicago. Generally: the Central Time Zone boundary.

The Western territory with headquarters in California. Generally: the Western Time Zone boundary.

The upheaval and turmoil generated by the Salvation Army revolutions of the 1880s and 1890s cost dearly in drastically reduced funding, loyalty of some of the officers and soldiers, and public leadership and support. Birthing and growing pains were very much in evidence in the entire Army world.

A MAJOR CHANGE IN THE VISION: AND A STUCTURE CHANGE FOR THE ORGANIZATION

In Darkest England and the Way Out

Between the two major devastating splits of Army loyalty in America, 1884 and 1896, General William Booth was formulating his Cab Horse Charter and in 1889-90 was ready to publish his book *In Darkest England and the Way Out.* Both publications revealed a giant change in emphasis of the Founder's thoughts and the Army's thrust into the realm of sin and poverty.

From strictly preaching salvation for the soul to the lost and unloved masses of humanity, Booth went to a parallel theme with the preaching and enactment of salvation of the body as well as the soul.

These documents did not initiate the Social Service mandate; it was already well entrenched in the fabric of operations in almost every unit virtually from the outset of the Army initiative. Rather, these publications crystallized and articulated the Founder's deeply rooted feeling of ministry to the soul and the body as a dual mandate for the Army, with each playing a complimentary role to the other.

In other words, the emphasis of The Salvation Army's "vision" was now truly a marriage between the social work as a partner in importance with salvation for the lost soul of man. In a word, "Soap, Soup and Salvation," as expressed in one of the many Salvation Army slogans.

There were, no doubt, several major influences in Booth's deliberations, not the least of which were his "inner circle" of advisors and the converging socio-economic problems of the world, particularly in England, and of the current relief organizations' inability to properly address the problems.

The Greenville Invasion by The Salvation Army

As previously noted, into this period, on January 1, 1888, The Salvation Army came to Greenville in the persons of Captain Fielding and Lieutenant Kayser [Kaiser]. It promptly folded after about three months of operation.

In January 1904, The Salvation Army was re-established permanently in Greenville by Ensign and Mrs. J. W. McSheehan and Cadet Pearl Hewitt.

Ensign and Mrs. J. W. McSheehan and Cadet Pearl Hewitt, 1904.

Enlisting an Army of Soldiers

Generally, advisory boards were not officially utilized up to 1920 or thereabout; however, Salvation Army officers from the Booths up to the present time sought out and won the favor of influential, wealthy, and interested individuals to mentor, support, and foster the fledgling operations in every successful community operation. Sometimes the successful service and industriousness of the officers impacted the community so forcefully that the local leadership sought to volunteer its support and goodwill.

It was after WWI that Commander Evangeline [Eva] Booth (USA), who preferred the title of "The Commander," began to see the value of having outside consultation on community matters. She later became the General of The

Salvation Army. Knoxville, Tennessee became the first city in the South to form a formal Salvation Army Advisory Board (Captain Allen Satterlee, *Sweeping Through the Land*).

Up to that time, officers were instructed by the appropriate headquarters to go to this or that place and commence the work. Off they went with little more than their belongings in a satchel and their hearts firmly rooted in their belief in the power of God to prosper them and sustain the effort.

According to a witticism related by Major Stanley Melton, "Newly commissioned officers were given $50.00 and the commission to go and open the work in a designated location. Sometimes they came back and reported that the work would not open." Then, they were sent to another location, and another, until one did open. Then someone else was sent to the original location until it opened. Such is the stuff Salvation Army people are made of.

At other times people who have had contact with Army programs and were transplanted to another location commenced the work and petitioned the headquarters to send an officer to command and expand the work they had established. The officer made himself available to the community in whatever capacity was needed or wanted. Generally, he associated himself with a local, current problem or issue and worked with the citizens and community leaders to address the solution. His implicit mission was always to preach the Gospel of Jesus Christ and assist the downtrodden of the community in the name of Jesus Christ.

The resulting conglomerate of services, both social and religious, was as varied as the locations invaded and the people who invaded them for the Army.

Booth and his Motley Crew

There was neither intention nor design on the part of the Founders, nor their successors, to establish another church, or for that matter, a social service organization. But in the days of the Founder, the people congregated around him until he was forced to form an organized system of progress and proficiency, which encompassed both the church and the social service operations.

The Founder said on one occasion of the newly congregated followers:

> "My first thought was to constitute an evangelistic agency, the converts going to the churches. But to this there were three main obstacles:
>
> 1. They would not go where they were sent.
> 2. They were not wanted when they did go.
> 3. I soon found that I wanted them myself."

And the more time he spent amongst them, the more the sense of responsibility with regard to them grew upon him. He had discovered what mines of unimagined power for good were to be found amidst the very classes who seemed entirely severed from religious life: There they were, and if only proper machinery could be provided and kept going they could be raised from their present useless, if not pernicious, life to that career of usefulness to others like themselves for which they were so well qualified. They could thus become a treasure of priceless value to their country and to the world. (George Scott Railton, *The Authoritative Life of William Booth*, p. 64)

This is the prevailing and overriding directive of The Salvation Army today: To preach the gospel to every creature and render service in the name of Jesus Christ.

Although the Church vs. Social Service question is hotly debated within and outside the rank and file of the Army to this day, The Salvation Army declares itself to be a Religious/Charitable organization, a branch of the Christian Church, lately, an international movement. To fulfill this self-proclaimed mandate, the Army adamantly declares autonomy of operation and independence to the point of doctrinal discipline and operational style in its conduct of the "warfare" on sin.

Its leaders are Officers and its members are Soldiers, or Adherents. These designations make up the entire membership of the Christian Organization. Volunteers, donors, program members, and clients make up the bulk of the remainder of The Salvation Army's vast numbers of people from all faiths and walks of life.

The Local Structure of Command Volunteers

Usually, a Corps Sergeant Major (local officer) was appointed on the field from among the first converts in the community. Other converts were commissioned as needed to form a chain of command and a plan of action for the local Salvation Army under the command of the appointed Corps Officer. This method of selecting leaders was developed and refined until it produced the modern-day model of command in the Corps' centers. That is, a tightly defined and indoctrinated compliment of local officers who assist in leadership of the Corps' programs under the supervision of the Corps Officer.

Leaders on the Local Front

The main and most essential local officers in every community are Corps Secretary, Corps Treasurer, Corps Sergeant Major, Recruiting Sergeant, Young People's Sergeant Major, Corps Cadet Counselor, Bandmaster, Songster Leader, Home League Secretary, Torchbearer Leader (lately, Youth Local Officer).

Other local officers and sergeants, too numerous to mention, are added as the need arises. Often the list is as long as the imagination of the local Corps Officer and his Soldiers.

This group works mainly with the church operation called the Corps.

A second group of local business and political leaders make up the advisory organizations to assist The Salvation Army Officer in the conduct of community business and relationships. These are listed in another section of the book.

"GO FOR SOULS AND GO FOR THE WORST"

—Attributed to William Booth

The more colorful and gripping the story of the converts, the more public acceptance the Army could secure from the local citizens. Many "Trophies of Grace" are recorded in every part of the realm of The Salvation Army universe. One definition of a "Trophy of Grace" is a notorious local person who has been radically changed from a depraved life and empowered by the Holy Spirit; he gives abundant witness of the fact by living a changed life.

Hence, the General's admonishment to "Go for souls and go for the worst" was one of the manifestations of material success for the early Army. This concept of success extends into the modern day. These dramatic conversions and successes often brought with them more and greater financial support and public acceptance of the Army's programs within the communities.

No doubt, it was not General William Booth's intention for the emphasis of his charge to the officers, Go for souls and go for the worst, to be placed on the public relations aspect of the work. He sincerely coveted the worst sinners for the saving Grace of God. God works in mysterious ways!

Building and Shaping the Army in Greenville

Following Ensign and Mrs. McSheehan's 1904 re-establishment of the Army in Greenville by the novel means of street and tent preaching, there developed rapidly a network of social/religious services to the community that deeply ingrained the Army into the fabric of the city's leadership and all levels of society.

Even in this early day, the social service successes were instrumental, along with but slightly ahead of the religious work, in enhancing the Army's esteem in the eyes of the general public. And it sparked an undying love affair between the Army and the upper and middle class of citizens as well as the lower classes that reaped the benefit of the Army's work in the community of Greenville and all around the world. However, to the Army Officers and Soldiers, the emphasis was always upon the religious preeminence in all things.

The Army's Arsenal of Loving Weapons

One of the old battle songs popular in The Salvation Army long ago contained the lines, "The Salvation Army has a right to beat the drum, the tambourine and the banjo to make the devil run. Come join our Army and get the gospel gun. 'Shoot' it at the devil if you want to see him run."

Over the years the arsenal has been augmented and expanded to include almost anything in sight. A partial listing of the early day Salvation Army activities, or weapons, in Greenville have included:

- The home and hospital program for unwed mothers.
- Bruner Home for orphans and abandoned children.
- Red Shield Boys Club, which later became The Salvation Army Boys and Girls Club of America.
- Transient and homeless shelter for men, women and children.
- Fresh air camps for underprivileged youngsters.
- A standard menu of religious, character building, and homemaking activities.
- Family welfare centers.

- Specialized services such as parole officer duties, medical clinics, burial services for indigents.
- Rehabilitating programs for men and women.
- Thrift stores.
- Alcohol and drug treatment programs.
- Prison and hospital visitation programs.
- Disaster response teams.
- Special holiday relief programs such as during Christmas, Thanksgiving, and Easter.
- Specialized operations to meet specific needs of citizens all round the globe: the World Services Programs.

And of course, the Army has the ever-present drum and tambourine, and the banjo, though the cornet in most cases has replaced the banjo. In this modern day, the substitution has increasingly turned to the guitar, trap drums and keyboard. The Salvation Army brass band is still in vogue in a number of places. And, occasionally one will hear the banjo ring out its pickity sound in a meeting.

The list of services is as varied and unending as the needs of the community. Every program is of vital importance to the welfare and well being of the local neighborhood at the times of inception.

UNIQUE AND FOCUSED SALVATION ARMY PROGRAMS IN GREENVILLE

The Women's Rescue Home program, Maternity Home and Hospital, and the Bruner Home for Children, were operated under the command of the Women's Social Service Department and not directly attached to the Corps operation except that officers assigned to these Social Service programs were listed as Soldiers of the Corps.

These officers often spent their free time attending and worshipping and serving the needs of the Corps as well as carrying out the duties of their specialized assignments. These units were co-operational and always presented a unified Salvation Army to the community. Additionally, many of the clients, volunteers, and employees became Soldiers by joining the early movement.

The membership pool is as wide as the community is diversified. Members are attracted from every walk of life and every persuasion. The only requirement of Soldiership in The Salvation Army is salvation from sin and upright living.

IN THE BEGINNING AN UNCERTAIN START IN TURBULENT TIMES

Following is a chronological history of The Salvation Army in Greenville, South Carolina including the quasi-start in 1888, and a parenthesis of about sixteen years.

1888:

- CO: Captain Fielding (Given name, Robert; nickname, Bob)
- ACO: Lieutenant Kayser (M) (Correct name Lieutenant C. W. Kaiser)
- ABC: No record
- CSM: No record

According to the Appointment Disposition of Forces, The Salvation Army first "opened fire," or became established, in Greenville, SC, in January 1888. It closed within three months.

This period of establishment and parenthesis was concurrent with the time The Salvation Army in the United States was going through a series of schisms and splits and many Corps were realigning or closing because of lack of support or mixed feelings of loyalty. The South, itself, was in a deep state of poverty and despair.

The names of Captain Fielding and Lt. Kaiser in association with the Greenville Salvation Army were not found in the Disposition of Forces after April 1888. Nothing else is known of the first effort in Greenville.

Interestingly, 1888 was the same year the Washington Monument in Washington, DC first opened. As a point of reference, the Greenville Post Office/City Hall was completed on West Broad and South Main Street in 1892. It later became the City Hall and, subsequently, the City's Government Center in 1936. The structure was demolished, but the courtyard area is still intact, and the wide steps from the sidewalk to the courtyard are there. The photo shown below of the local Corps' brass band on the steps of this edifice depicting such renowned Salvation Army leaders, then soldiers, as Colonel Frank Longino with his trombone, a youngster named Wesley Bouterse, and another named Rigsby Satterfield, also Doris Baker, along with the Corps Officer, Adjutant and Mrs. Archibald Baker. There are other officers and soldiers, and a group of Bruner Home band kids in the photograph.

Eyewitness to History, Also a Maker of History

One report by Mrs. Marie Smith Summey, daughter of CSM and Mrs. Roland Smith, one of the pioneer Soldiers and the mother of Brigadier Dorothy Summey, retired, states that Ensign and Mrs. J. W. McSheehan were in Greenville in 1903. The work did not officially commence in Greenville until October 1904 according to the Disposition of Forces for that period (Courtesy National Headquarters Archives).

However, *The Greenville News* reports in its June 6, 1904 edition, the earliest reliable record, that June 5-6, 1904 was the opening date, with a full complement of prospective Soldiers, Officers, and Divisional Officers participating. Included in the article is a printed program of the services that weekend. The Official "building" was a tent erected on East Court Street beside the cigar factory, behind The Carpenter Brothers' Drug Store.

The most reliable eyewitness report places the officers in Greenville in January of 1904, or earlier. This information would indicate that The Salvation Army work actually started earlier than October 1904. However, the author believes the unofficial opening date was the June 5-6, 1904 date. The first contingent of Soldiers was enrolled on August 14, 1904. The official opening is listed as October 1904.

The photograph shown on the facing page does not include the Divisional and visiting Officers, so it is doubtful that it depicts the actual "opening ceremony date." It is either an earlier or a later photo of the nascent Salvation Army in the city of Greenville. The date on the photograph is 1903. Ensign and Mrs. McSheehan were officially listed as the Corps Officers from 1904 to 1905, according to the Dispo.

The first known contingent of soldiers, officers and others in front of the cigar factory on East Court Street, c1903-04. Some of names are misspelled.

Greenville Album Of Yesteryear

Photo contributed by Joseph L. Arnold, Route 3, Danville, Va.

GREENVILLE SALVATION ARMY—Greenville's Salvation Army workers in 1903-04 gathered beside the old cigar factory on East Court street for this photograph. Members of the band hold their instruments in their hands. Standing, left to right, are Bub Braziel, a Mr. Turner, Norean Willbanks, two unidentified ladies, a Mr. Norris, a Mr. Thompson, another Mr. Norris, a Mr. Honeycutt, Dell, Wilson, Miss Know, Major Morgan and Tommie Turner. Middle row, sitting, left to right, are Stella Wilson, Bula Davis, Mrs. Macshin, Capt. Macshin, Cadet Hueu, Mrs. Turner, Mrs. Honeycutt, and little Miss Gooding standing. Bottom row, left to right, are Miss Bessie Braziel, Miss Ada Davis, Joseph L. Arnold, Mont Braziel, Joe Davis and three Turner children.

1904-1905

- CO: Ensign and Mrs. McSheehan from 1/1/1904 [estimated date]
- Captain and Mrs. Orr Hanna, appointed 1905
- ACO: None assigned

  Note: Although not listed in the official roster, a Cadet from the School for Officers Training was assigned with the McSheehans and played a significant part in the opening of the work in Greenville in 1904. Her name is Cadet Pearl Hewitt. It is assumed that she transferred out along with the McSheehans in 1905.
- ACO: Lt. Coleman (M), appointed 1905
- ABC: Unknown: A key benefactor could possibly be Mr. C. E. Graham of the Camperdown Mill and Huguenot Mills.
- CSM: Roland Smith, enrolled Soldier sheet #2, 8/14/1904. Smith is thought to be the first Corps Sergeant Major in Greenville.

Corps Sergeant Major and Mrs. Roland Smith, c 1904.

Note: In regard to the CSM: In the photograph of the first contingent of soldiers and officers around 1903-04 beside the cigar factory, the caption lists a local citizen, Mr. J. C. Morgan as "major." He is in full Salvation Army uniform, thus indicating that he is actually the acting CSM of that date. Mr. Roland Smith is not listed in the caption as being in the photograph. Mr. Morgan was enrolled as a Soldier on 8/14/1904, the same date of the enrollment of Mr. Smith, according to the record sheet from that period.

The Salvation Army regulations state that a person must be enrolled as a soldier before being enrolled as a local officer. The date of the photo is not revealed except as 1903-04. No recorded evidence of local officer enrollment exists in the records. No other records can be found of earlier enrollments.

The Pioneer Senior Soldiers' Roll Book entries: 1904-1910 (arbitrarily set by the author to begin the division of chapters into even ten-year periods or to coincide with Officer appointments as closely as possible to the date)

8/14/1904: J. C. Morgan, A. B. Norris, Roland C. Smith, Lee Turner, Tom Turner.

1/1/1905: C. H. Norris

3/14/1905: J. Rivers Lebby-SFOT. Entered training in August, 1905 and upon commissioning became ACO in Greenville in June 1906. After many years of service, he was appointed as Divisional Commander of Georgia with the rank of S/Captain. (See his bio below.)

J. Rivers Lebby, the first Officer Candidate from Greenville, South Carolina.

According to the Lebby biographical book entry, the Georgia Divisional Headquarters was located in Augusta, GA in 1927-28 at the creation of the Southern Territory. The Salvation Army yearbook, which is the official record, locates the Georgia Divisional Headquarters at 54 Ellis Street, Atlanta, GA at the inauguration of the Southern Territory, and not in Augusta, GA.

The South Carolina Divisional Headquarters was later moved to Columbia, SC for a short period of time. Soldiers listed were:

1/15/1906: Fannie Smith
11/15/1906: James V. Breazeale-SFOT
11/15/1906: Emma Breazeale-SFOT
12/8/1907: Nora Boggs-SFOT, Pearl Thompson
1/26/1908: Susie Turner Foster
6/25/1909: Gertrude Elbert, Mrs. Norean Willbanks McCarter: Jr. Soldier 8/10/1904, transferred to Sr. Soldier 1909. This would place Mrs. Norean Willbanks McCarter as the first known Junior Soldier enrollee of the Greenville Corps. (See note of interest in 1966-1975 decade section)
3/6/1910: Lala Smith, SFOT
3/8/1910: Mrs. Lundy Morgan
3/12/1910: Ernst V. Brazie-SFOT
3/12/1910: Mrs. E. V. Brazie-SFOT
5/31/1910: George Loren Webb

The Pioneer Junior Soldiers' Roll Book 1904-1910

These roll sheets bear no dates and are listed by the tenure of the Enrolling Officer.

Enrolled by Ensign McSheehan 1904-1905:
Leonard Arnold, Bessie Breazeale, Mamie Breazeale, Monte Breazeale, Cecil Howelton
Enrolled by Captain Orr Hanna: 1905-1907:
Marie Smith-SFOT: Ollie smith-SFOT: Tweedie Smith-SFOT.

A report by Mrs. Linda Vick Griffin, who went to the SFOT at a much later date, states that the three Smith girls eventually went to the Training School for Officers and were commissioned as lieutenants. No other records are apparent.The names listed were Ollie Smith, Ruth Smith, and Bessie Smith Williams. 3/6/1910: Doris Riddle, Ella Smith.

There were other attendees who were not enrolled as Soldiers and some of the names are listed in the caption with the photo of the first group in front of the old cigar factory, 1903-1904.

These are Bub Breazeale, Noreen Willbanks [later married to A. B. McCarter], Mr. Thompson, Mr. Honeycutt, Dell Wilson, Miss Know, Stella Wilson, Bula Davis, Mrs. Turner, Mrs. Honeycutt, Miss Gooding, Miss Ada Davis, Joseph L. Arnold, Joe Davis, "three Turner children."

Nomads in a Distant Land – "Way Down South"

The Army publicly re-commenced works in Greenville in June 1904 and has continued uninterrupted to present.

The earliest record mentions a tent as the "building" located on East Court Street behind the Carpenter Brothers Drug Store and beside the old cigar factory on East Court Street.

The Carpenter Brothers Drug Store at South Main and East Court Streets and the cigar factory on East Court streets; the area behind the drug store where the tent would have been located in 1904. Photos c2003.

There are two other tent locations mentioned in other reports on different dates prior to, and shortly after, the Court Street location. One is at East Washington and Brown Streets, prior to the Court Street location. The other is on West McBee Street behind the First National Bank Building, in 1905 after the Court Street location. One report mentions the vacant lot beside the 1st Baptist Church on McBee Street as the location of the tent. This would be the same location as the rear of the First National Bank Building. Both the Brown Street and the McBee Street locations are apparently valid, but the detail and verification is patchy.

Two other locations are reported between the time of the Manley Street residence and the Broad Street building. These include a meeting hall over a livery stable on Laurens Street just south of the (1960s) bus station, and a two-story frame building at Falls Street and McBee. This building later burned and forced a move back to the tent on West McBee Street until the completion of the new structure on Broad Street in 1907.

The Charleston & Western Carolina Railway built a new train depot on the site at Falls and McBee Street in 1905. The exact address is 310-320 East Court Street, which would be the vicinity of McBee and Falls Street. This also indicates that East Court Street extended more than one block from Main Street in the early days of Greenville.

In 1905, The Salvation Army was located on the corner of McBee and Falls Street for a short time, intersection shown here. John Wesley UMC in background at E. Court Street. Photo, 2002.

In the 1980s the depot was razed, and the American Federal Building was erected. The site was later used for the Central Carolina Bank, which is the present structure. It covers a large portion of the area around McBee and Falls Streets, including a portion of the now closed 200 block of East Court Street, which is a part of the complex of parking lots for the bank.

The John Wesley United Methodist Church stands on the corner of Falls and East Court Streets: Number 101 East Court Street. The Church was built in 1900 and is still in operation.

The Early Army in Greenville

Apparently, the Officers Quarters were at the Manley Street location during this mini-migratory experience in and around the city. There is also mention of open air meetings being held on Manley Street where the first officers had an apartment; some reports indicate it was a five-room house. If these reports are correct then the original first meeting in late 1903 or early 1904 would have been on 317 Manley Street. Unfortunately, the street number given is not now, nor was it then, in existence, and no other details are currently available. (Manley Street numbers only go from 00s through the 100s in the year 2004.) The 1903-04 city directory does not list numbers for Manley from Washington Street to East North Street except 202-218, which are residences.

It also lists the family of S. L. McCarter as residents of 206 Manley Street. Since there is a connection between the McSheehans and the McCarters through Noreen Willbanks in 1904, there is the possibility that 206 was the house number of the original quarters of the first officers in 1904. A Mr. McCarter married Norean Willbanks, one of the pioneer Solders, in 1914. She lived in the same vicinity.

This location is the present day location of the Baptist Courier, which covers present day numbers 100-108 (then numbers 200-208). It is the possible location of the original open air meetings held by the McSheehans and Cadet Hewitt outside of their quarters. No confirmation is offered.

So We'll Roll the Old Chariot Along...

In Walsh's Directory of the City and County of Greenville, SC, 1903-04 Edition, The Salvation Army Citadel is listed under "Churches" as being at 540 Rutherford Street. This cannot be confirmed by other sources, and there is no other corroborating information in the existing official records.

It is interesting to note that the Bruner Home for Orphans was founded in 1906 in the 500 block of Rutherford Street. (The Salvation Army did not operate the original Bruner Home for Orphans at that time.) The earliest official location of The Salvation Army on Rutherford Street was the Women's and Children's Rescue Home in 1908. This was in the 600 block.

The Bruner Home for Orphaned Children was operating under the leadership of a Miss Sarah Davis in the 500 block of Rutherford Street in 1906. The record mentions a three-room house where the Television Station, WYFF Channel 4 is now located.

The Baptist Missionary Children's Home, under the leadership of the Southern Baptist Convention, was founded and operating in 1904 in the 400 block of Rutherford Street. In 1914 the Bruner Industrial Home, Inc. purchased the Baptist Missionary Children's Home. Bruner was sorely in need of additional space due to the expanding enrollment of orphaned children. The Baptists had established a new English schooling system for all Missionary Children, and its Rutherford Street operation was no longer needed.

Eventually, in 1917, The Salvation Army assumed responsibility for operating the Bruner Home. In 1927, The Salvation Army acquired ownership of all three operations. They were consolidated into one location in the 400 block of Rutherford Street.

The Bruner Home, under the directorship of the Women's and Children's Rescue Home program of operation was continued to 1949 when The Salvation Army, at the request of the local Community Chest, closed the service out. It was merged with another home for children under the direction of the Community Chest. This operation was also phased out at a later date and passed into the history books of social service innovations in Greenville.

In 1951, The Salvation Army Citadel program at 26 East Broad Street was closed. The new citadel was opened at 417 Rutherford Street on the site of the demolished Bruner Home.

The building on 26 East Broad Street was turned over to The Salvation Army Boys and Girls Club for its exclusive use. In 1969 the Broad Street Salvation Army Boys and Girls Club was abandoned for a new facility on Owens Street. The Broad Street location was sold in 1971 and subsequently demolished.

The Rutherford Street location is now the principal base for all Salvation Army operations in Greenville with the exception of the Boys and Girls Club of America, which is located on Owens Street and operated as The Salvation Army Boys and Girls Club of America. Salvation Army Thrift Stores are located in various parts of the city.

Official Verification

The following article is quoted from the *Greenville Daily News*, June 6, 1904:

SALVATION ARMY WORK
MANY SPECIAL SERVICES TO BE HELD TODAY

The two day special campaign of The Salvation Army began yesterday and will continue through today. The local force is being assisted by Ensign Widgery and Staff Captain Berriman of Atlanta.

Capt. Berriman will preach in the First Presbyterian Church this morning at 11:30 o'clock. He is one of the most forceful and entertaining speakers in the Army and a man of wide experience. He has charge of The Salvation Army work throughout the entire Division. No doubt his sermon this morning will be interesting and beneficial.

Meetings will be held in the open air this morning at 7 o'clock. There will be a lecture in the tent at 3 o'clock by Capt. Berriman; and meetings again at 10 and 11 o'clock led by Ensign Widgery.

Capt. Berriman will hold a service in the open air at 3 o'clock and a Praise service in the tent at 4 in the afternoon, when recruits will be sworn in (Note: Recruits are entered on the roll at least one month before Soldiership is allowed, rwk.) Again in the evening there will be services at 7 o'clock and 8 o'clock. Everyone is cordially invited to attend.

Looking for a Home

In the ensuing years the location was moved around the city and several important operations were established and abandoned as needs arose. These will be entered in the appropriate years of chronology.

A Centennial Family

Corps Sergeant Major Roland Smith was commissioned shortly after the establishment of the work in 1904. He served in that capacity for many years. Mr. Smith was listed as the second Soldier enrolled in the Greenville Salvation Army. (He was promoted to glory in 1935.)

His descendants include Mary Summey Vick, Mrs. Linda Vick Griffin, Mrs. Sharon Anderson Mason, David Griffin, Captain Kenneth Vick [deceased], Steve Vick, Major Thomas Vick, Major Donald Vick, Mrs. Dottie Vick DiRico, and Mrs. Frances Vick Woods. All of the above are the offspring of Mrs. Mary Summey Vick and her husband, Homer Leyton Vick.

Others of Mary and Homer Vick's children and grandchildren are directly related to Mr. Roland Smith, the early day CSM of The Salvation Army in Greenville. Several members of the "first family" are serving as Salvation Army Officers at the present time. Others are faithful local officers and employees of the Army in several locations around the South.

Steve Vick, Corps Sergeant Major in Pensacola, Florida, is serving as Territorial CSM in 2002. His family is also active in The Salvation Army. The Corps Sergeant Major (CSM) is the leading Local (non-commissioned) Officer of The Salvation Army.

Members of the Roland and Fannie Smith family, c.2003.

Many of the early-day and current lay leaders of the Army are related to Roland Smith. Mrs. Linda Vick Griffin, currently employed by the Army and serving in addition as the Home League Secretary in Greenville, SC submits the following genealogy-trail, tracing the Smith family from the 1904 opening to the present day.

Roland Smith Family Tree (Descending)

Name	*DOB*
John David Griffin	2/22/1983
Mother: Linda Vick Griffin	11/3/1946
Father: Johnny Mitchell Griffin	10/27/1954
Grandmother: Mary Francis Summey Vick	10/18/1929
Grandfather: Homer Leyton Vick	6/10/1923
G/Grandmother: Marie Estelle Smith Summey	6/18/1895
G/Grandfather: Claude Preston Summey	7/7/1891
G/G/Grandmother: Francis Elizabeth Sizemore Smith	Unknown
G/G/Grandfather: Roland C. Smith	11/25/1873

This personal note was added by the Smiths' family:

"There was a time when they (Roland and Frances Smith) planned to go to training and become officers. However, Frances would not leave her children. [At that time it was required that the children of cadets be left at home with relatives while the parents were in training for officership. The sessions lasted for about one year and were held in New York, NY, rwk.]

Roland gave his heart to the Lord in 1889 and attended Asbury College in 1892. He met The Salvation Army in 1903 in Greenville and was enrolled as a Soldier on August 14, 1904. He became a local officer shortly afterwards and was Corps Sergeant Major for twenty-seven years."

The Children of Roland and Frances and the Army:

Marie Smith Summey: A Soldier for many years. She held many local offices and raised her children in the Army.

Ollie Smith: Salvation Army Officer

Ruth Smith: Salvation Army Officer

Bessie Smith Williams: Salvation Army Officer

Miller W. Smith: Only Son

Marie Summey's Children:

Dorothy Summey: Retired Officer, lives in Bradenton, Florida

Tommy Summey: deceased

Ollie Summey: deceased

Mildred Summey Anderson: deceased.

Mother of Sharon Anderson Mason (Current Greenville YPSM), and Cathy Anderson Mooney.

Grandmother of Destiny Anderson, Shane Mason, and Chuckie Mason.

Great Grandmother of Brand, Dorian, Dylan and Chase Mason;

Also Great Grandmother of Kinsleigh Anderson.

Mary Frances Summey Vick

Mother of Major Tom Vick, Major Don Vick, Captain Ken Vick (deceased), Corps Sergeant Major Steve Vick (Florida), Greenville Home League Secretary Linda Vick Griffin; Former Young People's Sergeant Major Frances Vick Woods, and Dottie Vick DiRico.

Mary Vick is also the Grandmother of seventeen children and great-grandmother of five children.

This family tree listing was provided by Linda Vick Griffin to establish the continuity of the same family beginning from the opening of The Salvation Army in 1904 to the present time. (Other branches of the Roland Smith family, not involved with The Salvation Army, also exist.)

Corps Sergeant Major Roland Smith and a wagonload of youngsters in front of the Citadel on East Broad Street, c 1900s.

- CO: Captain William Orr Hanna until 6/9/1907
  (Orr Hanna died in June of 1907)
  Captain Mrs. Katherine Hanna from 6/9/1907
- ACO: Lieutenant Coleman (to 1907)
  Lieutenant John Wells (1906-1907)
  Lieutenant J. Lebby (1906-1907)
  Captain K. Downes (appointed 1907)
- ABC: Unknown (doubtful that an Advisory Board existed)
- CSM: Roland Smith

A Principal Convert of the Greenville Salvation Army

The J.V. Breazeale family dates back to the time of the opening of the Corps in 1904, when he was converted in the tent. Some of his descendents served as Salvation Army officers. Some members are Salvation Army soldiers in other cities around the Territory. The native Breazeales served in commanding positions in Greenville at three separate times in the history of the Corps. Unfortunately, there are no available records of the J. V. Breazeale family tree.

Change is Inevitable (and Frequent)

The Army in Greenville was making great strides both spiritually and on the social service front under Ensign and Mrs. McSheehan's ministry when Captain and Mrs. William Orr Hanna were appointed as Commanding Officers to replace the founding Officers in 1905.

Although the McSheehans were in Greenville only a few months, they succeeded in establishing an impressive cadre of local supporters and prospective members among the citizens of the community. This dynamic team of Salvationists attracted both rich and poor.

In addition, they obtained and occupied several key locations for short periods of time. Each exceeded the other in visibility and prominence of location to enhance the growing work in the city of Greenville.

Captain and Mrs. Orr Hanna continued the migration to several sites before the final completion of the Citadel on Broad Street. Unfortunately, the exact progression cannot be fully documented with the exception of the "tent" on East Court Street. The locations are Manley Street (Officers' quarters), the corner of Brown and East Washington Streets, South Laurens Street, and open air stands in town on main Street.

When Captain and Mrs. William Orr and Katherine Liston Hanna came to town, or shortly before, the Army moved to a hall over a livery stable on Laurens Street just south of the bus station. From there they moved to the Falls and McBee Street Address, then to the McBee site of the tent, and ultimately to the Broad Street location in the newly constructed Salvation Army Citadel in 1907.

All the while, during this time of moving about, the Army continued to impact the problems and difficulties of the citizens. The community accepted and applauded the work being done in the name of the Lord. The list of new soldiers and supporters grew in proportionate measure to the work being conducted.

Captain William Orr Hanna was commissioned out of the New York Training School in 1902 at the age of 23 years. He was a very sick man, and was Promoted to Glory (died) on June 9, 1907, three weeks after the dedication of the new facility.

His widow, Captain Mrs. Katherine Liston Hanna was appointed Commanding Officer and served in that position for a year after his death.

He is buried in the Springwood Cemetery in section C, according to the records compiled by interested citizens. The exact location of the grave is: Section C, (row 2) Lot 137-A. It is listed as a single grave. A very fine headstone is there along with a granite border with the name "Hanna" engraved. There is a grave monument in the plot depicting the status of Captain William Orr Hanna as a Salvation Army Officer.

In the same cemetery in section U, next to what was "potters field," is a burial plot for indigents that was maintained by The Salvation Army for that purpose. The exact location of this plot cannot be determined. (See 1909-10 section of the book.)

National Recognition

As a point of reference, in 1905 George Bernard Shaw produced the play entitled "Major Barbara" as a professional show production. The play was a spoof of The Salvation Army's methods and means of service. It received mixed reviews from the general public. At a later date another play/musical was produced, "Guys and Dolls," which depicted The Salvation Army in action with a tongue-in-cheek theme.

The leaders of The Salvation Army hardly gave these plays a second thought. So accustomed were they to the public's reaction to The Salvation Army's unique operation, the plays were just old hat stuff to them. ("Guys and Dolls" still appears from time to time and has been produced as a television program.)

In an article by Dr. Glen Horridge and Bob Brettle published in The Salvationist: January 24, 2004, there are listed a whopping 57 movies and productions featuring The Salvation Army. One of them features none other than the icon of child movie stars, Shirley Temple, as a bell ringer.

In 1905, Captain Orr Hanna moved The Salvation Army operation in Greenville from the Laurens Street address, thought to be a loft over a livery stable, to a frame building on the corner of McBee and Falls Street. The upper level of the building on Falls Street was later destroyed by fire. The Salvation Army moved to a tent on West McBee Street behind the First National Bank, or in a field beside the Downtown Baptist Church in the same general location. In 1905, the C&WC Railroad Station on Falls Street and McBee Street was completed on the site of the burned out building formerly rented by The Salvation Army.

S/CAPTAIN J. RIVERS LEBBY, A PIONEER SOLDIER AND THE FIRST COMMISSIONED SALVATION ARMY OFFICER FROM GREENVILLE, SOUTH CAROLINA

According to an entry in a book by E. Detreville Ellis published in 1967, *Nathaniel Lebby, Patriot, and Some of His Descendents*, an interesting and informative excerpt emerges (Courtesy of Mr. Michael Nagy of The Salvation Army Southern Historical Heritage Department). One of Mr. Nathaniel Lebby's sons, John Rivers Lebby, was enrolled as a Soldier in The Salvation Army on March 14, 1905 and entered The Salvation Army School for Officers' Training in New York on August 8 of the same year. The Soldier's Record sheet in Greenville, SC only records the enrollment with the notation "Gone to Field," which is the Army's unique notation for "entered the ministry." No other information is given on the roll sheet signed by Ensign McSheehan. Following is a quotation from the Ellis book:

> "J. Rivers Lebby, upon leaving school studied telegraphy and worked for various railroads and commercial companies in the East and Western States. He early felt the call to work for humanity, as did many others of the long family line.
> He joined The Salvation Army on March 14, 1905 as he felt he could do the most good for humanity in that organization. His ability was early recognized and August 1905 he was sent to The Salvation Army Training College in New York City, from which he was commissioned a lieutenant in June 1906. Lieutenant John Rivers Lebby returned to Greenville, SC after Commissioning in June of 1906 and served as Assistant Officer in this appointment until 1907. Then followed many appointments as assistant, and finally commanding officer of a Corps.

In the meantime he was called to fill so many pulpits and make so many addresses to clubs that he decided to study more homiletics, public speaking, and pulpit platform work, and took a furlough from The Salvation Army.

He attended classes by day at the Congregational Seminary, Atlanta, and worked at night as an expert Morse Telegrapher to defray expenses.

Upon completing the course, he was ordained as a regular minister of the Congregational Church and had many attractive offers.

He returned to The Salvation Army, however, helping the poor and sick, the homeless women, the drifting men and in providing some recreation for growing children to keep them off the streets gave him the most joy and satisfaction.

During World War I he was in charge of several hostels for Soldiers, after which came an appointment as Divisional Special Efforts Secretary and Superintendent of Booth Memorial Hospital, Covington, Kentucky. On November 1, 1927 he was appointed to the post of Divisional Commander of Georgia with the rank of Staff Captain.

In 1923 J. Rivers Lebby was married to Lillian B. Doby and they served together until his death in 1929. At the funeral both Commissioner MacIntyre and Colonel Ernest Pickering paid high tribute to his ability, dedication, and leadership qualities. Commissioner MacIntyre said, "I count him our outstanding Southern Officer."

It is interesting to note that the Congregational Seminary on 1032 Stewart Ave, in Atlanta was later to become The Salvation Army Southern States School for Officers Training (SFOT) in 1938, sometime after the formation of the new Territory in 1927.

This would make Staff Captain J. Rivers Lebby the first Officer to attend the Southern CFOT, years before it actually became The Salvation Army School for Officers Training.

I quote from correspondence from Mr. Michael Nagy of The Salvation Army Southern Historical Center:

> "We have two documents that will confirm this. First is a copy of a letter, on the letterhead of the Atlanta Theological Seminary, 1032 Stewart Avenue, Atlanta, GA, in 1928. It is a discussion of options for movement of the school, to be joined with some other Congregational school in another state. (Note: The Congregational Church has since become part of the United Church of Christ.)
>
> On the back of this document is a proposed sketch of campus development, showing the main administration building that still exists today.
>
> The second document is a copy of the December 3, 1937 deed from the Atlanta Theological Seminary Foundation (which had by this time merged with the Vanderbilt Divinity School) for the property at 1032 Stewart Ave., Atlanta, to The Salvation Army.
>
> Also note that the first Southern Territory Training College was located on Luckie Street in 1927, and did not move to the current location until 1938, after the property was secured from the Atlanta Theological Seminary."
>
> —Michael Nagy: Archivist/Curator for The Salvation Army Southern Historical Center

A Home at Last

Construction was begun on a Salvation Army Citadel at 26 E. Broad Street in 1905; the building was completed in 1907 and dedicated that year. The Army finally had a permanent home in Greenville. The building lot on Broad Street and $1,000.00 was donated to The Salvation Army by Mr. C. E. Graham of the Huguenot and Camperdown Mills in gratitude for “saving” one of his “ornery” workers at a meeting in the tent on Court Street. He became, in Army jargon, a "Trophy of Grace." (See page 56.)

This story is reported by Brigadier John. V. Breazeale. He also states that Greenville was the first Corps opened in South Carolina, with Spartanburg the second.

Brigadier Breazeale says in a letter that he assisted Colonel Richard E. Holz in laying the cornerstone for the Citadel on Broad Street in 1905. The total cost of the Citadel on Broad Street was $8,500.00 (*War Cry* 6/29/1907).

Breazeale was a native of Greenville. He was saved in the tent on June 23, 1904. He was enrolled as a Soldier in September 1904, married on November 4, 1906, and entered The Salvation Army School for Officers Training in 1906, along with his wife, Mrs. (Emma Kirby) Breazeale, who was also enrolled as a Soldier on 11/5/1906.

There is a record roll sheet for Mrs. Breazeale, but none was found for J. V. Breazeale. There is also no record roll sheet for Emma Kirby. According to Breazeale’s letter, they were assigned to Macon, GA upon commissioning in 1907.

An Elusive Cornerstone, but an Enduring Army

It was a stellar accomplishment to complete a made to order building from the founding of the Army work in 1904 to completion in 1907, a span of only three years.

The cornerstone was inscribed:

TO THE GLORY OF GOD AND
THE WELFARE OF MANKIND 1906.

The building was dedicated in 1907. It was sold in 1971, and demolished. Unfortunately, the cornerstone has been lost. In a story published in The Greenville Daily News at about the time that the Broad Street Citadel was demolished in 1971, the Corps Officer mentioned that the Cornerstone would be preserved for future observances. It has not been found. A time capsule was placed with the cornerstone of the new Citadel building on Rutherford Street in 1951. Perhaps it will reveal more of the answer to the mystery of the Broad Street cornerstone.

There was also a plan to incorporate the cornerstone into the new Administration Building on Rutherford Street. This building was in progress at the time the Broad Street Building was being demolished in 1971, though there is no visible cornerstone erected in the new building.

First Building on the Block

The Citadel Building apparently stood alone on Broad Street for some time. Then the entire region began to become developed all the way to Main Street, including the Piedmont News building, which faced Main Street, and a drug store and several other businesses. Later, in the 1920s, the Greenville County Jail was erected at 32 East Broad Street, next door to the Citadel Corps building. Both structures were demolished at a later date to make way for the new Greenville Daily News complex, which occupies the site at present. The jail was demolished in the middle or late 1990s.

THE FIRST SALVATION ARMY SPECIFIC BUILDING IN SOUTH CAROLINA

On the next page is a copy of the original dedication service of the Citadel Building at 26 East Broad Street: (Replicated as nearly as possible)

SOUVENIR PROGRAM
Dedication Services
May 18th and 19th, 1907

THE SALVATION ARMY CITADEL
BROAD STREET
Col. R. E. Holz, Officiating
Mr. C .E. Graham, Chairman

PROGRAM
Saturday, May 18, 8:00 p.m.Musical Meeting
Sunday, May 19th, 11:30 a.m.
First Baptist Church..Col. R. E. Holz
Presbyterian Church.................................Major J. M. Berriman
Buncombe Street Methodist Church..................Adjutant Johnson
DEDICATION SERVICE, 3:30 P. M.
OPENING SONG, Onward Christian Soldiers
Prayer:
Solo...Captain Widgery
Visiting Officers
Offering..Adj. Berriman
Duet...Adj. and Mrs. Johnson
Address by Mr. C. E. Graham,
Introducing Col. R. E. Holz, of Cleveland.
*Doxology...

Evening Services, 8:00 O'clock.
Conducted by Col. R. E. Holz - Assisted by Major J. M. Berriman.
All visiting Officers taking part.
Special Songs and Music.
Address by Col. R. E. Holz.
*DOXOLOGY:
*The Salvation Army doxology consists of lyrics and motions as follow:
Congregation standing: Singing
Praise God I'm saved
Praise God I'm saved,
All's well...(Raise the right hand above your head)
All's well...(Raise the left hand above your head)
He sets me free...(Bring the hands down in a waving motion, and clap hands in applause as the song finishes.]

The Salvation Army Citadel at 26 East Broad Street,
Greenville, South Carolina, 1907-1951.
Boys and Girls Club: 1938-1969.

In a *War Cry* report on 6/29/1907 Captain William Widgery gave the following report:

> "Greenville South Carolina---The opening of the Citadel in this city was an event that will long be remembered by the people. From start to finish they tried to show how highly they esteemed the work of the organization.
>
> The Citadel is an up to date two-story brick building costing $8,500.00. On the lower floor is a fine auditorium, with a library and office attached. Upstairs is the officers' quarters also rooms for charity cases. The building is nicely furnished, and speaks well for the hard work of Captain and Mrs. Hanna and their assistants.
>
> A large crowd was present at the raising of the colors and when the doors were opened to admit the public to the auditorium, another great crowd gorged the place and standing room was hard to find.

Colonel Holz took charge of the service and thanked the vast audience for their kindness in making the dedication of the Citadel possible.

Mr. C. E. Graham was chairman of the meeting and spoke very highly of the work the Salvationists had accomplished in this place.

Mr. Graham is a warm friend of the cause and shows his friendship by donating liberally to the work.

The dedication service was a glorious one but was surpassed by the night meeting when a large crowd flocked again to a real old-fashioned salvation meeting.

The Colonel delivered a very masterly address and appealed to those in sin to turn from the errors of their ways; and at the close fifteen men and women came forward, some of whom promise to make good Salvation Soldiers.

Everyone seemed delighted with the week-end meetings, and when the visiting officers returned to their several Corps the next morning they went back with their hearts aglow, realizing that it had been good to be present at this glorious event. The people of Greenville, S. C. gave over $415.00 in the collection for the weekend."

—Captain Wm. Widgery

Captain William Orr Hanna lived only three weeks after the completion of the new Citadel on Broad Street. His wife, Mrs. Captain Katherine Liston Hanna assumed command until Captain and Mrs. W. F. Brown were appointed as Commanding Officers in 1908. (Note the change of rank designation of a widow officer from Mrs. Captain Orr Hanna to Captain Mrs. Katherine Hanna.)

Later, following Captain Orr Hanna's death, in 1910, Captain Katherine Hanna was remarried to Arthur Cook. It is unknown if he was a Salvation Army officer.

An article in the *War Cry* dated July 9, 1907 reported Captain Hanna's obituary:

DIED AT HIS POST

CAPTAIN WILLIAM ORR HANNA

Incurably ill with that dread disease consumption, brave, devoted Captain Hanna stuck to his post to the last, fighting with his latest breath and living to see the completion and dedication of the splendid Army Citadel that he had toiled so hard to erect in Greenville, S.C. Three weeks later his spirit took its flight. Dear Mrs. Hanna was supported in this trying time by her adopted mother, Mrs. Major Gaiety.

She and her sweet babes will sorely miss the bright beautiful spirit of the husband and father who left them for a time. But God has not failed them, nor will He ever.

Captain Hanna came out of New York #3 and was commissioned on November 18, 1902. Three years ago he was married to Ensign Katie Liston, who has been a true helpmeet for him in all his work and in the suffering that has latterly been his lot.

He will be missed by his comrades of the *O.K. Province in which all his officer-days have been spent. The funeral service of the dead warrior, conducted in Greenville on Wednesday, June 12th, by Major Berriman was most impressive.

*Note: (speculation) O. K. (Ohio and Kentucky) province was the commanding unit of The Salvation Army in the Southland at that time. (rwk)

1908

- CO: Captain, Mrs. Katherine Hanna (to 1908)
  Captain and Mrs. W. F. Brown (1908)
  Ensign A. Patterson (1908)
  Captain and Mrs. John Pringle (1908)
- ACO: Captain K. Downes
  Lieutenant E. Campbell (W)
  Lieutenant A. Goodland (W)
- ABC: Mr. C. E. Graham seems to be a prominent and permanent supporter of The Salvation Army.
  The Advisory Board concept is not in effect.
- CSM: Roland Smith

After establishing and maintaining the array of programs in the new Corps building following her husband's death, Captain Mrs. Katherine Hanna was relieved by Captain and Mrs. W. F. Brown as the Commanding Officer.

"REINFORCEMENTS NOW APPEARING"

(From The Salvation Army battle song "Hold the Fort")

Added Unit on Rutherford Street

In 1908, the Army's programs in Greenville became so burdensome that another division of the work was needed to enhance and expand service to the community. The Salvation Army Women's Social Services Department opened the shelter for homeless women/maternity home in May 1908. Captain Mary A. Minton was the opening officer. Other officer appointments followed shortly the same year. The complete listing of officers is found in the Women's Social Chapter of this book. This facility was in operation until it was closed November 1931. (Commandant George Lewis was the closing Officer).

The location of the Women's Rescue Home during the period 1908-1931 is thought to be 621 Rutherford Street according to one report. A *War Cry* report in 1917 places the Women's Rescue Home at the outskirts of Greenville about a block from the Bruner Home for Children. This would indicate that the location at 621 Rutherford Street is correct. A large metal storage building is standing there at this time.

The original Bruner Home was located in the 500 block of Rutherford Street. In later years the 500 block of Rutherford Street became the home of the local Television Station WYFF News Channel 4. This was the original location of the Bruner Home for orphaned children in 1906.

When the present Salvation Army complex was constructed at the site of the Bruner Home on *417 Rutherford Street in 1951, the Army was using a large white frame structure adjacent to the Bruner Home as a shelter for homeless people. This has been demolished, and new structures have been built to house the office and command complex.

*Note: The owners of the Bruner Home for Orphaned Children purchased the Baptist Missionary Children's Home in the next block, and moved from its location at 500 Rutherford Street to 417 Rutherford Street.

1909:

- CO: Captain John Pringle to June 1909
  Captain and Mrs. William J. Purdue from 6/1909
- ACO: None Appointed
- ABC: Not in existence
- CSM: Roland Smith

The Pringles served as Commanding Officers for one year carrying on the many programs of service and activities established by former officers and assistants.

Assistant officers were almost always appointed as trainees and moved in and out quite frequently in order to broaden their experiences in preparation for commanding positions.

Commanding Officers were also transferred frequently due the fast-evolving schedules of services carried on by The Salvation Army, and the need for a particular field of expertise in different parts of the country.

Captain and Mrs. William Purdue were appointed in June of 1909. They hit the ground running. According to a report in the *War Cry* of 12/11/1909 the Corps was given a new paint job. It was "the prettiest building in downtown Greenville."

The Greenville City Council elected Captain Purdue youth offenders parole officer, no doubt, with the hopes that the parolees would attend The Salvation Army and "get religion."

The Citadel on Broad Street contained facilities for parolees and transients as well as the religious/character-building programs and services, and the officers' quarters. It was also used as a distribution point for welfare services and other humanitarian services.

This arrangement was the norm for Salvation Army operations at that time and for many years thereafter. In some small and medium-sized locations it is still the method of providing services to the community.

Multi-Purpose to the Max

The Greenville Salvation Army Citadel building has been used at times for almost every conceivable purpose according to the needs of the community. This arrangement has not been altered very much down through the years.

In an article written on December 11,1909 by the Editor of the *War Cry* there is described a typical Salvation Army adjustable-program format used in almost all cities of the time. The use of the facilities and personnel was, as always, adapted to meet local needs:

> *A Splendid, All-Round Work*
>
> *Greenville, S. C., An Army Town*
>
> The Salvation Army has been at work in Greenville, S. C. for nearly six years.
>
> Ensign and Mrs. McSheehan were the first Officers and they did a most excellent work during their command. Captains Lebby and Breazeale were both converted under them, and a good work was begun, which was afterward carried on to such grand issues by Captain and Mrs. Orr Hanna.
>
> It was during their command that the magnificent edifice now occupied by the Army was built, and which was said to be the first citadel built by The Salvation Army in the South. (This is the Citadel at 26 East Broad Street, rwk)
>
> It is very sad to relate that soon after the completion if this Temple of God, which was dedicated to God and the good of mankind, Captain Hanna passed away to his reward. He literally gave his life's blood for the accomplishing of this purpose-the building and completion of this structure. One of the most sacred places in Greenville is the grave of our warrior of the cross. (Note: Captain William Orr Hanna is buried in Section C of Springwood cemetery. This is the same cemetery where The Salvation Army buried indigents. The Salvation Army indigents' burial plot was in section U according to a cemetery map printed in that era.)

Continuing the article:

> We are told that "he that loses his life shall find it," and that "a good man's work doth follow him" and we add our testimony to the truth of the word and fulfillment of the promises. The influence of Captain Hanna's life will never die.

Mrs. Hanna (now Ensign Hanna of Baltimore #3) and Captain Downes of Hazleton, PA stood faithfully by him and assisted in the glorious work he was enabled to perform while in command of this Corps.

(Note: Captain Mrs. Katherine Hanna was in command of the Corps until 1908 after Captain William Orr Hanna's death. Captain and Mrs. Brown, of Charlotte, N. C. were next in command and carried on the work very successfully during their stay in this beautiful little city. Then followed Adjutant Patterson who was succeeded by Captain and Mrs. John Pringle from Oil City, PA. These Officers were followed by Captain and Mrs. William J. Purdue.

The story continues in a related article by the Editor of the *War Cry*:

Property Improved

The citadel property has been greatly improved with a coat of paint both inside and out and the opinion of all who have seen it is that it is the prettiest building in the city.

During the summer the public was supplied with ice water free of cost. The Salvation Army putting out ice water barrels on nicely painted stands on the most propionate corners of the City's streets.

The ice was donated by John B. Marshall, Mayor of Greenville. The barrels were painted in Army colors [red for the blood of Jesus Christ, yellow for the fire of the Holy Spirit, and blue for purity of heart. rwk], and the most scientific methods were used in filling and emptying the same. Ice was also given to the poor supplied through the kindness of Mr. Marshall.

When the City Council was elected Captain Purdue visited them and congratulated them upon their success and informed them that they could depend upon him for his heartiest co-operation in every effort toward the betterment of the City.

They personally assured him they would deeply appreciate his help in all matters, and the mayor said he wished to be advised by Captain Purdue. Since that time they have often sought his advice, and have co-operated with each other.

Captain Purdue appeared before the newly-elected Aldermen and addressed them on the work of The Salvation Army after which one of them rose and moved that a donation be given to the Army each month. Mayor Marshall then appointed an Alderman to the chair and, taking the floor made a most eloquent appeal for The Salvation Army. They spoke in glowing terms of our work, and needless to say the donation was given, and even better support was promised later.

Soon after, a mass meeting was held. Mayor presided and several prominent citizens were present.

The question was agitated as to the formation of a Juvenile Court and the appointment of officers, chief among them being that important ever-acting position of Chief Probation Officer. The other position was duly filled Mayor Marshall being made president, and other very prominent men being elected to vice-president, secretary and treasurer. The mayor proposed, and in fact, said that no one else should have the position of Chief Probation Officer than Captain Purdue. So he was appointed with acclamation and given power to appoint his own assistants.

He is consulted in the trial of all young offenders and when they are found guilty he appeals for suspension of sentence, which is always given and he secures their release on condition that they behave and visit The Salvation Army when ordered to do so.

In the meantime, Captain Purdue watches over them and secures them work with good surroundings to encourage them in every possible way to be good.

A card index system will some day tell some remarkable stories; but one thing is sure it will prove that the probation system is a complete success and that the old order of sending first, and especially young, offenders to the chain gang was nothing short of a crime.

Friendly Doctors

Since taking charge of this Corps, Captain Purdue has secured the services of every Doctor, whenever needed, to attend to the poor, and many have helped in the way. It is one thing to get a physician to attend and prescribe for a patient, and it is another problem to have the prescription filled, but this is now all attended to here by the Ladies Aid Society paying to have them filled in the...(Unreadable).

Without doubt one of the...(Unreadable) Charities of Greenville are the children's treatment of eye, ear, nose and throat.

It is estimated that since Captain Purdue has been in charge that over $1150.00 has been given to the poor. Print literally fails to describe the relief that has been made possible to those who, were it not for the clinic, would have to suffer in silence.

It might be added that The Salvation Army and the Physicians made no distinction regarding sect or color-all in need of relief are attended to.

Two leading specialists visit the Citadel daily and eyeglasses are provided free of cost to those unable to pay for them.

Captain and Mrs. Purdue are intensely interested in the young people, and have made splendid advances in the junior work. They have won their way into the hearts of the young, and, in that way gathered many around them that will do anything to please them. They are well trained and in drills show to good advantage.

During the summer and early fall three outings were given to the children. The first outings were for juniors who were taken in wagons to Saluda Dam, a miniature Niagara Falls. The second was made possible through the kindness of the Streetcar Company who donated the use of their cars to carry the children. This was at night and was called our "moonlight ride." One of the favorite yells that night was, "We are it, yes we are, The Salvation Army, rah, rah, rah." The last outing was for the poor mothers and children of the city and the mill villages. The Streetcar Company again donated the use of their cars to carry the children to the depot, and the Greenville and Knoxville Railroad donated the use of a special car to carry them to Travelers Rest. The Superintendent of the Road accompanied us to see that no accident happened, and also to see how The Salvation Army treated its guests. The day was ideal and everything went off without a hitch.

Other Unusual Services Provided by The Salvation Army in the Early Days as Reported in the Same Story

> Many other arrangements are being made that will mean the advancement of our work in this City...Such as:
>
> Doing charity work for the County.
>
> Burying the poor in a regular lot in the cemetery to remove the stigma of a pauper's grave.
>
> We also have a nice Young People's Legion (older teens group, rwk), band of love [young children group, rwk], and Company meeting [Sunday school all ages, rwk].
>
> —Editor, *The War Cry*

There were photographs of Mayor John E. Marshall, Police Chief Robert H. Kennedy, and Captain and Mrs. William E. Purdue accompanying the article. They are not clear and could not be reprinted.

Many and Varied Methods

From inception, The Salvation Army has used many and varied methods to serve the local citizenry and especially to help relieve suffering and pain. All this is done in the name of the Savior, Jesus Christ. Each succeeding year and change of command brought other and more varied programs to the Citadel on Broad Street and later, to the other locations as the Army marched through time and the neighborhood.

The Salvation Army is still at work today using modern methods and more sophisticated avenues of service to perform the same acts of loving service to humanity. The Army is the same, after all.

During that time the Citadel had a most vigorous workout, and the city of Greenville saw The Salvation Army in action as it moved from need to need without missing a beat. As the needs changed, so did the solutions provided by the Captain in charge and his able assistants and volunteer supporters.

Officers Come and Go but the Work Goes on Just the Same

The Army is still at its innovative work, seeking and saving the lost, and ever-expanding its scope of operations to that end. Captain and Mrs. Purdue were commanding officers in Greenville from 1909 until 1910.

The normal rotation of officers is in June, when the newly commissioned officers are graduated from the Schools for Officer Training. Of course, all officers are not moved around at the same time or in larger numbers than absolutely necessary to enhance and improve the Army's work. There are exceptions to this rule in order to accommodate circumstances that arise in the disposition of the forces.

In short, there is no generally set routine for transfer of officers. Transfers are effected as need arises. Officers must be ready at short notice to farewell and report to a new command.

CHAPTER III
1910-1919
A WORLD AT WAR AND AN ARMY AT PEACE: WW I
"At Peace with My God"

1910-1917:

- CO: Captain and Mrs. William J. Purdue to June 1910
  Adjutant and Mrs. John Crook from June, 1910
- ACO: No Assisting Officers assigned
- ABC: Advisory Boards have not yet come into vogue. However, there is almost always a person or group that takes the Army under its wing as mentor and significant supporter. Greenville city officials and executives of the mills were involved in the Army's backup during this time. None are specifically identified at this juncture.
- CSM: Roland Smith

"...To End all Wars"

When Captain and Mrs. John Crook took command of The Salvation Army in Greenville, little did they realize that before their term finished, America would be involved in yet another war. This war would be a worldwide conflict that would earn the high sounding title, "The war to end all wars."

Alas, that was not the case because evil will always find a way to challenge the forces of good as long as the world remains in its present form. Or, in some cases man will trip over his own finitely endowed seat of wisdom, and this will result in a catastrophic event for large numbers of people.

Hardship of a Different Kind

In addition to facing and conquering the usual line-up of hardships, the Captains Crook would have to contend with the hardship of being without most of the male help because they would be off to fight World War I. The women would be involved in home front activities largely unrelated to Salvation Army business. But, The Salvation Army would be involved in the thick of the fray on unique errands of mercy.

Most roads were still not paved, and the rain made a quagmire of the clay that permeated Greenville, especially the "muddy bottom" around the South Main and Broad Street area where the Reedy River snaked through Greenville and the Reedy River Falls graced the landscape with cascading liveliness.

View of the Reedy River looking west from the Gowers Bridge at South Main Street.Photo c2003.

The automobile had not yet been mass-produced in the early part of this decade, and most personal travel was by foot. Transportation was by horse and wagon, barge, or rail. Getting around the town, much less outside of town, was nearly impossible, especially on the rain soaked days. The city of Greenville also operated a streetcar line up and down Main Street at the time.

The flooded Reedy River of 1910 sparked the rebuilding of the *Gower Bridge over the River at Main Street.

Originally a wooden structure, it was replaced by a concrete bridge. The trolley tracks, which ran along side the bridge at a lower level, were also washed out and were replaced. The trolley was the main mode of transportation along Main Street.

*Note: The Gower Bridge was named for the founders of the coach factory along the banks of the river, which was a landmark business in Greenville for many years.

REMEMBER THE FOUNDER'S STATEMENT, "SALVATION OF THE SOUL AND BODY?"

In 1910 the Citadel on Broad Street was being used as clinic and hospital ward for indigent citizens. There was no totally organized hospital system in regular operation in the city. The Salvation Army Citadel was apparently one of the first buildings to be used as an Emergency Hospital in the city of Greenville.

The Women's Hospital Board, not directly connected to The Salvation Army but operating as an independent group to help alleviate the suffering of the needy, raised the money and secured donations to operate the facility. They chose The Salvation Army Citadel because it was in a convenient location, and the innovative Salvation Army Officer was willing to embark on yet another mission of mercy in the city of Greenville.

The Salvation Army at that time also maintained a plot in section U of Springwood Cemetery and buried indigent persons there. As mentioned earlier, Captain William Orr Hanna, Commander from 1905-1907, is buried in section C of Springwood Cemetery.

In 1912, a private sanatorium was built by private subscription on Arlington Avenue. An article by Brigadier J. V. Breazeale in the Greenville News at a later date mentioned that The Salvation Army in conjunction with the Women's Hospital Board set a tent up behind the Citadel to house a man afflicted with TB. The article speculates that this was the initial start of the TB Sanatorium.

The TB Sanatorium was primarily for alcoholics and mental patients. The sanatorium was later sold to the city of Greenville and became a part of the city hospital system. Under the city administration, it was expanded and began to accept other patients as well.

Soul and Bodywork Side-by-Side

Not much information is publicly recorded of the church work of The Salvation Army, but it was going on in some form at the same time all the other activities were running. The religious work is the founding mandate of The Salvation Army's existence. Lacking that, they could lay claim to neither the name of "Salvation" nor "Army."

Character building programs, emergency services, disaster services, and other programs and services were added as needed by the community and as deemed appropriate by The Salvation Army Administration.

A Marriage Made in Heaven

In the topsy-turvy onward march through the world, the other programs became the definitive view of The Salvation Army in the mind and eye of the public. However, the mandate "to preach Jesus" was and is paramount in the plan and purpose of The Salvation Army Officers and Soldiers. Thus, the so-called "lost identity"* battle began early on.

The Salvation Army, especially in the United States, was never regarded as a bone-fide Church structure; although, churches sought out Salvation Army speakers for "pulpit duty" because they recognized the true power behind the organization.

*Lost identity refers to the general public's confusion about the Social vs the Church identification of The Salvation Army. Even today the Salvationists are often rebutted with the statement: "I did not know The Salvation Army is a Church." Some have described The Army's religious foundation as "the best kept secret in America."

The Army has been described as a religious/charitable organization, and this descriptive terminology has prevailed, not only in the United States, but also as the standard description in the entire world.

This description is by determination of The Salvation Army policy-making administration derived from the founding mandate of William Booth and his advisors. The Salvation Army was never involved in purely church building activities.

Concentrating on the church work and neglecting the community work may have been a cause of the failure of the original 1888 Salvation Army in Greenville. This is unconfirmed, and perhaps the real reasons for the failure will never be known.

The social service work of The Salvation Army was elevated to partner-status by the revision of William Booth's thinking, which was crystallized and put into operation with the publication of his book *In Darkest England and the Way Out*, published in 1890.

This publication, along with his Cab Horse Theory became the central manual of operation and continues to be so at the present time. However, the interpretations of the documents are almost as varied as there are individuals serving in the Army.

A simple explanation of the Cab Horse Theory would be: If the horses that pull the cabs through the streets of London are guaranteed a place to sleep, eat, and work for as long as they live, then why are not the highest creatures, mankind, also entitled to at least the same guarantee or opportunity, as the case may be. (rwk)

An article in *The Greenville News* dated Saturday May 31, 2003 from the Associated Press with a Charleston, SC byline indicates that the Carriage Horse debate is still ongoing. The title of the article is: "*Carriage Horses Get a Break from the Steamy Summer.*" The gist of the article is that the Society for the prevention of cruelty to animals (SPCA) revised its guidelines to protect the horses when the weather and humidity reached a certain point.

The book, *In Darkest England and the Way Out*, ignited a spark all around the world because it outlined a workable plan to alleviate the suffering that plagued the whole of the human race, that is, rank poverty and excruciating human suffering. There is an interesting theory about the exact authorship of the book, but it is much too involved and complicated for the purpose of this report.

Both documents provided a straightforward rationale for the change of direction from a singular-purposed religious Army to the plural definition of a religious-charitable organization. This set the stage for the future thrust of the Army's rationale for existence. That is, that all mankind should be guaranteed at least a reasonable opportunity to pursue basic needs in order to survive and be spiritually fulfilled, the key being a viable relationship with Jesus Christ in the plan of salvation from sin.

Our Corps Social Service centers became "show me" Christ first and "tell me" Christ second operations with the emphasis on "show me." As the saying goes, "You can't effectively preach to a man who has an empty stomach." The prevailing thinking is "fill his stomach (material needs) first; then, he will be receptive to the gospel message." The plan bordered on a socialist state mentality for the Army and its members and constituents. It reflected the main thinking of one of the co-authors of the book *In Darkest England and the Way Out*, Commissioner Frank Smith of the 1884 era.

In the words of General William Booth in an address to the Social Department Officers about a year before his death, in 1911:

> "I said, 'They shall hear; we will make them hear; and if they won't hear any other way, we will feed them, and accompany the food we give them with the message to which they so determinedly turned a deaf ear.'"

In another section of the address Booth continued,

> "But it was not until the end of 1883 or thereabouts, that anything like a systematic effort in this direction was organized on their behalf"
> —*The Authoritative Life of General William Booth,* p. 188

Evidently the problem was that the people who were the object of The Salvation Army's desire were much too occupied with the worries of obtaining basic necessities to hear the message of the gospel. Thus, the way was opened for the "Gospel preaching" and the "social service dispensing" Salvation Army to be codependent and equally emphasized in word and deed. This became the mandated method of service and progression and ultimately spread around the world as The Salvation Army's scope of endeavor.

This led to the facilities of The Salvation Army being available for use in any capacity and for any purpose deemed beneficial to mankind, especially the downtrodden and destitute citizens of every community. As a matter of fact, most Salvation Army buildings are designed and constructed with a multiple-usage theme as its central strength. This has been the norm from the beginning. One of the Army's statements of fact is, "Everything we do is religious."

From the Founder's Mouth...

When a reporter asked William Booth if The Salvation Army proper had suffered from the competition of the social operations, the Founder replied that to his mind, "It is all The Salvation Army proper." —*Captain David Cavanagh, in The Salvationist, July 2002*

A Successful Marriage

The marriage of the social and the religious work in The Salvation Army became consummated figuratively in 1878 when the name changed from "Christian Mission" to "The Salvation Army," expanding its scope, distance, and thrust. It became functionally official in 1890 when the Cab Horse Charter and the book, *In Darkest England, and the Way Out* became the defining publications. Thus, was The Salvation Army officially set on course to become a religious/charitable organization in word and in deed.

Almost every Salvation Army unit was bent upon enacting the messages sounded in Booth's book, In Darkest England and the Way out. Up to this time the Army dabbled in social service work in order to reach the unsaved with the gospel message. This theme played out in almost every institution of the Army throughout the world.

Not a Church only and not only a Social Service Agency but, a Religious/Charitable Organization, a militant [later changed to 'Evangelical'] arm of the Christian Church with the two-fold resolve to minister to human needs and preach the Gospel of Jesus Christ.

In recent literature this statement is rendered, "The Salvation Army, an international movement, is an evangelical part of the Universal Christian Church."

...And the Savior's Love Will Be the Theme of our Song...

The usual method of religious operation in Greenville was to hold Sunday and weekday services in the Citadel auditorium hall. Other sources of meetings included jail meetings and open air meetings around the city. Before moving into the new building, all meetings were held in a tent or in the open air or in rented buildings. The officers were invited to preach in some of the local churches on special occasions.

Any place would be acceptable to the Army as a venue for the preaching of the Gospel. In Greenville it was in such places as street corners, tents in open fields, private residences, a hall above a livery stable, and finally, a real church/social service building.

Sources of new membership were:

- Reclaimed and converted persons
- Families from the welfare rolls
- Migrants who came through on the trains
- Homeless and transient men and women
- Fallen ladies
- Drunkards
- Productive citizens who would heed the call to service
- And anyone who would show the slightest interest in The Salvation Army's ministries and enlist as a supporter

Both Sides of the Tracks

The enticing, adventure-laced work of The Salvation Army also attracted members from across the tracks, some of whom became innovators and top leaders in the movement of the Army throughout the world. The spirit of the Army captured and captivated supporters and well-wishers from every spectrum of society.

Not "Business as Usual"

Often, dramatic and unusual methods and demonstrations designed to capture the imagination of the congregation and the public marked the meetings outside and inside the buildings.

One officer used an open coffin in the open-air procession. At an appropriate time he would sit up in the coffin and begin to preach, much to the surprise and delight of the onlookers.

It is said that the Commander, Eva Booth, was unusually adept at using the dramatic to captivate the attention of a congregation. In one meeting she wrapped herself in an American Flag and shouted "Hiss this if you dare" to a crowd of detractors.

Music of all stripes and gender, and every type of instrumentation was used to attract attention. Brass instruments became the weapons of choice because of the carrying power and the apparent ease of operation of a brass instrument. This evolved into the brass bands of The Salvation Army, of which it boasts some of the best in the world.

Most secular tunes of the early days were adapted and fitted with religious words and used in and out of meetings to capture the attention of the crowds. The Salvation Army Battle Song, Hold the Fort was adapted from the Rebel Army's battle song of the same name.

Recruiting and Training Leaders

Recruits for membership were made of converts who accepted the Gospel of Jesus Christ, demonstrated for a period of time a change of heart and habit, and desired to enroll in The Salvation Army. Often the converts were pressed into service for the Army and put right to work converting others and volunteering to do other tasks related to the building of the Kingdom of God.

Many were offered a place in the School for Officers' Training, and upon completion of a nine-month course, they were commissioned and returned to the field with the rank of Lieutenant.

It was not unusual for a person who demonstrated leadership ability and intelligence and who had accepted Salvation to be commissioned on the field and given the rank of "Supply Sergeant," "Envoy," "Auxiliary Captain," or some other designation and placed in charge of a unit of operation.

During the week, youth and adult activities and classes were held to enhance the social and religious skills of the recruits and members of the general public who were not interested in joining but interested in learning.Out of these programs came the standard character building activities employed by the Army today in every Army operation around the globe.

This activity was occurring simultaneously with the social and outreach programs. Social work in The Salvation Army is in the tacit mandate of all officers, "You see a need, you meet the need." Or, as General William Booth said to his son on one occasion when a need was apparent, "Bramwell, do something."

Usually the Corps Officer was the prime motivator and innovator of the projects operated by the Army in the community. Often the community leaders suggested local problems that could be addressed by The Salvation Army and offered to help establish a program to facilitate the solution. More often than not the officer set right to work with the leaders of the communities to accomplish the objective if it would help the community and provide an opportunity to preach the gospel.

Where Do You Live?

In the early days, the Corps Officers' living quarters were, mostly, "on the building," or in a boarding house nearby. Thus they were available at all times to all who came to the door for whatever need or reason. It was not until years later that official quarters were provided away from the building for officers and their families.

Who Are Your Neighbors?

In the 1904-07 migration, The Salvation Army was located on South Laurens Street sandwiched among bars, livery stables, a shoe shop, dancing halls, the jail, and the City Hall.

In 1926, Greenville County constructed a county jail next to The Salvation Army Citadel on Broad Street. The Army probably became actively involved in the care and keeping of some of the prisoners and those who were paroled. No doubt it ministered to their families as well. There is no proof of this, but the scope of Army work has always included prisoner-relief. This jailhouse building remained there until 1996. The Army moved out of the Citadel in 1969.

Major Tom Vick and Mrs. Judy Campbell, former members of the Greenville Corps, each mentioned in separate interviews with the author of being in meetings at the Citadel in the 1940-50s and being able to see the prisoners in their jail cells, so closely built-together were The Salvation Army and the jail at that time. Don Campbell added that the prisoners often engaged in conversations with passersby from their cell windows.

The Salvation Army Citadel sandwiched between the County Jail and the newspaper building, c1940s.

The Salvation Army Citadel was demolished in 1971 to make way for the Greenville Daily News complex. The Salvation Army and the County Jail sites became a part of the Greenville News' parking lot. All other structures along Broad Street to Main were purchased by the newspaper and became a part of the media edifice that stands there today.

THE WAR IS ON AND THE ARMY IS INVOLVED IN A STRUGGLE OF A DIFFERENT KIND

1917-1919:

- CO: Commandant and Mrs. John Crook to 6/1917
- Ensign and Mrs. George Storey from June, 1917
- Ensign and Mrs. William Price from June 1919
- ACO: Lieutenant Dallas Holder 1917-1918
- Supply (non-commissioned Officer) Mrs. Gallear 1919
- ABC: Doubtful that an AB existed. Mr. and Mrs. W.G. Sirrine were keenly interested in The Salvation Army operated Bruner Home, along with the Bruner Family. There was a large and active Board of Directors overseeing the operation of the Bruner Home at the time of transition to The Salvation Army.
- CSM: Roland Smith

The War Goes On ...On Both Fronts

These were dark times for the nation as well as the whole world. WWI was in full swing, and the effects were prevalent everywhere. Salvation Army Officers Crook, Storey, and Price were at the helm at different times in Greenville during this period of time.

In 1917, Textile Hall was built. This building was a monument to the huge success of the entire cotton processing industry in the Upstate of South Carolina. The Woodside Building on East Main Street was completed in 1917. This was a modern skyscraper and the tallest building in the city, in fact, in the entire state of South Carolina.

In the month of June 1917, The Salvation Army assumed operation of the Bruner Home under the auspices of its Rescue Home for Women. This was a home for orphaned and abandoned children. The Women's Missionary Union of Baltimore, an auxiliary of the Southern Baptist Convention, previously operated the home. Its purpose was to house children of missionaries while their parents were on the field in foreign countries. Subsequently, it was sold to the Bruner Industrial Home Incorporated to serve children needing shelter.

Officers Assigned

The first Officer in charge of the Bruner Home in 1917 was Brigadier Mary E. Bebout. Adjutant and Mrs. George Graves were appointed later that year and became Superintendents of the Bruner Home shortly thereafter.

The Bruner Home was established and supported by the efforts of Miss Nell Davis, founder; Miss Bruner, benefactor; and Mr. and Mrs. W.G. Sirrine, a prominent Greenville attorney and his wife, mentors. Also, the Duke Foundation supplied operating funds. Food was donated by local businesses, and the local citizens made up a creditable Board of Directors.

In 1917, The Salvation Army became the operator, and in 1927, the proprietor of the Bruner Home for Children and Orphans. The Bruner Home was located at 417 Rutherford Street at the site of the present Salvation Army complex. A small recreational building constructed on the campus in 1932 is all that remains of the original farm and huge Charleston style house that was the actual Home. The Bruner Home was closed in 1949 due to constraints of budget requirements and consolidation with another children's home operated by the United Fund.

Subsequently, The Salvation Army complex was built on this site and occupies the entire compound, including a Corps building, the rehabilitation programs, shelters, all social service programs, and the Salvage Operation.

A historical narrative of the Bruner Home, pictures, and anecdotes by former children of the home can be found in a booklet compiled and edited in 1994 by Captain Gail Fleeman, who along with her husband, Captain R. Curtis

Fleeman were Salvation Army Corps Officers in Greenville in 1993-1998. This was to commemorate the 90th anniversary of continuous service to Greenville by The Salvation Army. Further information, including officer and resident personnel, can be found in the Bruner Home chapter of this book.

You're in the Army Now

World War I became one of the defining moments for The Salvation Army in unique service to the troops. The Salvation Army "Doughnut Girls" of the battlefield gave a lasting, worldwide presence to thousands of service men who were reminded of the Love of God and the importance of home. The Salvation Army lasses, who took refreshments directly to the front, endeared themselves to the men and women who were in the fight for worldwide freedom.

The Doughnut Girls were the Poster Child of Salvation Army service during WWI and for many years afterward, but in actuality The Salvation Army served right alongside the combatants to help alleviate their fear and suffering in every phase of the War.

Several Salvation Army Officers were commissioned in the United States Military Service as Military Officer Chaplains. They served their country and The Salvation Army in that capacity.

While the world was at war, The Salvation Army was at work exemplifying and preaching the peace that Jesus gives. This is true on both sides of the conflict. The Salvation Army knows no enemy except sin and its consequences.

CHAPTER IV
1920-1929
RACING TOWARD THE CRASH WITH A LOT OF FAITH AND LITTLE CASH
"Faith Turns the Night into the Day"

Women's Home and Hospital, Greenville, S. C.

The Emma Moss Booth Memorial Hospital in Vardry Heights Greenville, South Carolina, c1921-31.

1920-1924:

- CO: Ensign and Mrs. William Price to June 1921
- Commandant and Mrs. Archibald Baker from June 1921
- Captain Eva Bivans from June 1924
- ACO: Lieutenant Ida Larmon 1921
- Lieutenant Edna Saunders 1922
- Lieutenant Sarah Painter 1923
- Lieutenant Mattie Dyson 1924
- ABC: Unknown.
- CSM: Roland Smith

There were four main components of The Salvation Army programming in operation in the city of Greenville.

These were:

- The original Corps Program
- The Women's Rescue Home
- Emma Moss Booth Memorial Hospital
- The Bruner Home for Children.

Many local citizens and leaders were involved in these programs, but none are mentioned or identified as an Advisory Board as such.

In the 1920s, the advisory board concept was born, and many cities, at the urging if the *Commander, were rushing to enlist local business and political leaders as mentors and supporters in a formal setting of board affiliation. This proved to be a masterstroke of development throughout The Salvation Army world.

When the advisory board concept came prominently into play in the 1920s, the various individual volunteers and supporters were organized into groups in order to present The Salvation Army's programs as peer to peer in the community. The advisory board also served to give organizational stability and business guidance to the local Salvation Army unit leaders, the Corps Officers.

Up to this time, the local Salvation Army officer was charged with the responsibility of enlisting local individuals who would see the need and contribute time, talent, and treasure on a one-on-one basis. He now had the impetus to formally organize such a group.

Thus, from the 1920s, every Salvation Army operation has been guided and mentored by a local group of advisors who enhance and enlighten the work in the community.

*Commissioner (Counsel) Evangeline Booth, Daughter of the Founder and National commander.

The various advisory boards are not boards of directors. They serve as advisors to the local Corps Officer who is responsible to the Divisional Commander for the ongoing work within the established framework of The Salvation Army. The advisory board members also serve as liaisons to the public in matters of Salvation Army community services. Members are often involved in public relations and fund raising for the local operations.

The legal responsibility for all Salvation Army operations ultimately rests upon the Territorial Commander and the General via the Divisional Commander. These supervising officers work in conjunction with the Divisional Command structure to effect continuity of program and other matters on a regional and worldwide basis. The local units serve as the delivery point of all Salvation Army services and programs to the communities around the world.

GRAVITATIONAL CERTAINTY
"What Goes Up Must Come Down"

The early years of the 1920s saw a great surge in the success of the stock market that resulted in successful building and business growth all over the land. But this, as it turned out, was the big build-up before the inevitable crash that always seems to come when success gets out of hand.

The Stock Market Crash of 1929 destroyed huge accumulations of personal and corporate wealth and set the stage for a worldwide recession that was to last for many years. The era of the crash would actually see once wealthy people literally begging in the streets for food for their families.

The Salvation Army was not unaffected. In fact, it experienced some of its most dramatic and traumatic moments both locally and internationally during this period.

A New Healing Institution

In January 1921, after two years of construction, the maternity hospital was dedicated where the present downtown St. Francis Hospital stands in Vardry Heights. The official name of the hospital was Emma Moss Booth Memorial Hospital. It was named for Captain Emma Moss Booth who gave her life in the service of The Salvation Army. She was killed in a train wreck while traveling to inspect a Salvation Army operation in Colorado. At that time she was on the way to Chicago to meet with her husband for Officers Councils. She was the wife of the USA National Commander appointed by the Founder, following the secession of Ballington and Maude Booth, and Eva Booth's intervention. The correct name-style was Frederick de Lautour Booth-Tucker and Emma Moss Booth-Tucker (Sallie Chesham. *Born to Battle*, p. 97). The hyphenated name was in keeping with the practice of all members of the Booth family being individually recognized and all male in-laws taking on the name of the Booth family for legal and possible historical identification.

MUKTIFAUJ
Commissioner Frederick St. George de Lautour Booth-Tucker

On April 10, 1888, Emma Booth, the Founders' daughter, was married to Frederick St. George de Lautour Tucker. They were appointed to Command the work in the USA in 1896, replacing Ballington, the Founders' son, and Maude Booth who had resigned to establish the Volunteers of America. Note the American Crest with eagle.

An Enormous Capital Expenditure

The cost of construction of the EMBMH was reported to be approximately $250,000.00 including equipment. According to a published report of that time, the public donated about $125,000, and the Army took out a note with the bank for about $125,000. Substantial donations to build the hospital were provided by most of the mills and other manufacturing plants, which were proliferating in the Greenville area at that time.

Below is a copy of a published financial breakdown following the close of the hospital.It is an audited report of the condition of the EMBMH, cost of construction, and operating deficit. It was published at the 50 year celebration of The Greenville Salvation Army in 1954.

Land and construction
Total cost..$272,508.11
Furnishing and equipment... ....$19,728.00
Total construction and furnishing cost.......... $292,236.11

Contributed by the mills and the public.........$187,236.11
Loan from THQ New York............................. $30,000.00
Local Bank notes negotiated...........................$75,000.00
Grand total cost...$292,236.11
Income: 1925-1930.......................................$309,362.34
Expenses: 1925-1930....................................$349,465.07
Operating deficit for period.......................... ($40,102.73)
Total Salvation Army loss from construction of building
and operations:. ....($145,102.75)
Proceeds from sale of hospital building (1931)....$55,000.00

Net Salvation Army loss................................ ($90,102.75)
(from hospital and services)

The Emma Moss Booth Memorial Hospital operated as one of the main city hospitals for the employees of the mills for about ten years. The main thrust of operations was toward a maternity home and hospital for pregnant, unmarried girls and young women, but it admitted others as well on an as needed basis. The hospital program included an accredited School of Nursing, operated by The Salvation Army.

Due to the Depression and other causes, which inflicted operational deficits, the hospital was closed in 1931 and sold to the Catholic Order of the Little Sisters of the Poor who began operations as the Saint Francis Hospital in 1932. The chapter in this book on the Women's Social Service Department provides more detail about the Home and Hospital in Vardry Heights.

THE LADIES HOME LEAGUE MOVEMENT IN GREENVILLE

On November 2, 1924, the Ladies Home League program was initiated in Greenville, South Carolina. Captain Eva Bivans was the Commanding Officer in November 1924.

According to a story in The Salvation Army *Southern Spirit* on December 2, 2002, by Colonel Rodolph Lanier, Eva Bivans was one of several siblings of Captain John Bivans who occupied a large presence in the Southern Salvation Army in the early years of operation. A number of his descendents and converts are presently serving as officers and soldiers.

He was directly and indirectly responsible for introducing many of the leaders and laymen of the movement to The Salvation Army as he traveled about the Southern Territory in Corps assignments.

Ladies Only, Please

The Ladies Home League program was designed to provide a social and interactive experience for women and girls who had no other means of congregating with their peers in a regularly scheduled fellowship and learning experience.

The Salvation Army Ladies Home League sewing circle at the Broad Street Citadel, c1932.

Typical Ladies Home League group service, undated. Annual Advisory Organizations' meeting.

The following article was found in the Greenville Daily News on November 1, 1924:

OFFICER TO FORM LEAGUE IN THE CITY
Col. (Mrs.) Gauntlett has seen service in several foreign cities.

Col. (Mrs.) Sidney Gauntlett from The Salvation Army Headquarters in New York, accompanied by Staff Captain and Mrs. Herbert Smith and Captain E. Pickering of the Divisional Headquarters of Charlotte, is now in the city for the purpose of organizing a local Women's Home League.

Special meetings will be held in the Citadel at 11 o'clock tomorrow morning and at 7:30 o'clock tomorrow evening.

Colonel Gauntlett is an officer with a strong personality and has preached the gospel in many countries. She first became a Salvation Army officer in Denmark early in 1887 and has been a member of the faculties of Salvation Army Training Colleges in Denmark, Germany, and Switzerland. She was Principal of the Switzerland Officers Training College where instruction was given in three different languages.

The object of the Women's Home Service League, which Mrs. Gauntlett will organize here, will be to afford an opportunity for women of moderate means who are deprived of the privilege of ordinary social and club life to gather for a weekly meeting. The meetings will be informal and primarily of a social nature. The women will bring their sewing baskets or knitting needles and spend the afternoon making garments and other articles for poor women and children. Instructions will be given those who do not understand sewing and other forms of needlework.

Mrs. Gauntlett has been home league secretary for the Southern and Eastern States since the death of her husband last Thanksgiving Day. She was married in Switzerland to Colonel Sidney Gauntlett who was Chief Secretary of Switzerland and Italy. After nine years of service in these countries she and her husband went to Chicago. Mr. [sic] Gauntlett was Chief Secretary of the Central Territory until his death.

The Ladies Home League program has attracted hundreds of ladies in Greenville, and many thousands around the world over the years, and has been a source of valuable fellowship and mentoring among the women of the community. It is active today with a larger scope of activities and opportunities for fellowship for women.

The Ladies Home League has been described as the largest women's group in the world. It is also one of the main programs of The Salvation Army in every community. The female officer of every command from the General right on down to the Corps Officer is charged with the oversight and responsibility of the Ladies Home League program.

There is a note in the Greenville Ladies Home League scrapbook of 1954-55 that alludes to Mrs. Major Arne Lekson starting the Home League in 1932. This could have been a re-establishment of the program after a hiatus of some time. The Home League in Greenville was first begun in 1924 when the Territorial HLS came to town and initiated the Home League program.

One of the Home League projects is preparing meals for special events. A Corps members meeting, c1932.

The first commissioned Home League Secretary in 1932 was Mrs. Callie Taylor. Three succeeding HL Secretaries were Mrs. Norean McCarter; Mrs. O. P. Fletcher; and Mrs. Carrie Street. It is unknown how long each served as HLS. It is also unclear who was serving as HLS from 1924 to 1932. The information is taken from a Home League scrapbook dated 1954-1955. At that time Mrs. Carrie Street was HLS and Mrs. Emma Hammond was Assistant Home League Secretary.

The name of the Ladies Home League has recently changed to that of Women's Ministries to reflect the broad changes in make-up and programming for women of all ages and pursuits whether in the home or in the marketplace. Sewing and knitting needles are icons of the past as the main tools of the League. However, homemaking is one of the featured programs in the fourfold Worship, Service, Fellowship, and Education list of activities in today's Home League service.

A Family Affair

In 1924, Ruth Evangeline Baker was converted in Greenville at the age of twelve years. She later married William Southwood, and they advanced to the rank of Brigadier. She was promoted to glory on September 25, 2000. It is assumed that she was the daughter of the Corps Officers in 1924, Commandant and Mrs. Archibald Baker.

1925:

- CO: Captain Eva Bivans to June 1925
- Captain Bertha Sanders from June 1925
- ACO: Lieutenant Letitia Adams 1925
- Lieutenant Leila Lowery 1925-1926
- ABC: Unknown. Advisory Board participation was still apparently being carried out on a one-to-one basis at this time.
- CSM: Roland Smith

The ongoing programs of social and religious work at the Citadel were growing and expanding when Captain Eva Bivans was transferred out and Captain Bertha Sanders replaced her as the Commanding Officer. Captain Bivans married soon afterward, and the marriage produced several officers and leaders who occupied staff leadership positions in various Divisions of the Army.

Following is a quoted e-mail from Lt. Colonel David Mikles, retired, who along with his wife, Lt. Colonel Jean White Mikles served as Divisional Commander and Director of Women's Services, respectively, of the North and South Carolina Division for several years.

> Captain Eva G. Bivans married David Roscoe Mikles in 1926. She was the mother of Lt. Colonel David Mikles, NSC Divisional commander from 1991-1997.
>
> She is also the mother of Lt. Colonel John Mikles who served as DYS for the Carolinas Division (probably 1969-71).
>
> Eva Bivans Mikles also has one daughter, Emma Mikles Townley of Ft. Myers, FL.

(Note: John Mikles also served as the Divisional Commander of the Kentucky-Tennessee Division, Alabama-Louisiana Division, Texas Division, and as the Assistant Chief Secretary of the Southern Territory until his retirement on August 30, 1995. He is married to a young lady who lived in Greenville for a while, Irene Baugh Mikles.) (rwk)

At that time, also, The Salvation Army was operating the Bruner Home for abandoned children. The Emma Moss Booth Memorial Hospital was also operational and thriving at that time.

Although the Corps Officer at the Citadel on Broad Street was not directly involved in the operation of either of these units, the cross-support of one and the other produced a highly infective and effective Army presence in the community.

1926-1927:

- CO: Captain Bertha Sanders to June 1926
- Captain and Mrs. William Burnell from June 1926
- ACO: Captain Evan Coles 1926
- Lieutenant James Parton 1927
- ABC: Unknown
- CSM: Roland Smith

In the 1920s the stage was being set and negotiations were underway to divide The Salvation Army in America into four Territorial Commands. The Southern Territory would become the fourth command and would include the southern states of the Civil War era—Dixie. The Central and Eastern Territories would give up a part of their area to facilitate the new boundary.

The battle cry of the newly minted Territorial Commander, Commissioner William McIntyre, was "Dixie for God." This, of course, echoed the cry of William Booth's "The World for God" and the Commander Eva Booth's "America for God." It was, and is still, a fitting and noble quest for the Army all around the globe, substituting, of course, the appropriate name of the country whose Salvation Army leaders are uttering the challenge.

Captain Evan Coles, who is listed as an assisting officer in Greenville in 1926, is the grandfather of Walter Coles and his brother David Coles. Neither is an active officer at present, but they are partners in a consulting firm of Coles & Associates that specializes in program studies and fund raising for Salvation Army units all around the world. Both are active Soldiers and take part in Army activities as lay leaders of The Army. It is not known how long Captain Evan Coles was stationed in Greenville.

LONG AWAITED DIVISION

In 1927, the Southern Territory was established and added to the three Territories already existing. At that time, Atlanta, GA, which was the Divisional Headquarters, became the Southern Territorial Headquarters under the command of Lt. Commissioner William McIntyre.

The Southern Territory extended generally east to the Atlantic Ocean, West to and including Texas, South to the Gulf of Mexico, and North to and including a portion of Kentucky, which was divided with the Eastern Territory. It encompasses generally, the original boundary of the Confederacy.

There was a reshuffling of divisional boundaries and re-naming of the newly formed Divisional operations throughout the new Southern Territory.

Unknown to anyone, in a few years the financial situation would become so difficult both in terms of funding and needed services, that the new boundary lines would have to be changed radically once again. The Southland command was formed at a most inopportune time.

S/Captain and Mrs. J. Rivers and Lillian Doby Lebby: Divisional Leaders of the Georgia Division, c1927.

It is in this shuffling that S/Captain J. Rivers Lebby* was appointed Divisional Commander of the Georgia Division with Divisional Headquarters in Augusta, GA. (Actually, the yearbook does not list the headquarters as being in Augusta; rather it is listed as being located in Atlanta, rwk)

*Captain J. Rivers Lebby was the first cadet out of Greenville in 1905.

PROPERTY ACQUISITIONS

Bruner Home for Children, Greenville, S. C.

The Salvation Army began operating the Bruner Home in 1917; the Army owned the home beginning in 1927. Photo, c1920's. The home was built in 1904.

The Bruner Industrial Home, Inc. deeded the Rutherford Street property to The Salvation Army on June 6, 1927. This was the same Bruner Home property which was operated by

The Salvation Army since 1917 and owned by the Southern Baptist Convention until 1914; it was owned by the Bruner Industrial Home, Inc. until 1927.

1928-1929:

- CO: Captain and Mrs. William Burnell to 6/1928
  Ensign and Mrs. Harry Turkington from 6/1928
- Captain and Mrs. Albert Mattson from 6/1929
- ACO: Envoy Annetta Bell 1928-1929
  Lieutenant Gunnar 1929-1930
  Captain Ila Davies 1929
- ABC: UNKNOWN.
- CSM:Roland Smith

RURAL SERVICE EXTENSION UNITS FOUNDED

In 1928, a new method of service delivery was invented in Bennington, Vermont. I quote from Sallie Chesham's book, *Born to Battle*, pp.188-89:

> "In the summer of 1928, although unplanned, a most successful Salvation Army program of services, first called Rural Service, then service extension units, was initiated. Envoy William A. Nichol, a non-commissioned officer was seeking funds for general work in Bennington, Vermont, the center of a mountainous rural area and a non-Corps town.
>
> Bennington's bank president reported happily that $500.00 had been raised as an annual contribution to the Army.
>
> The funds would help needy urbanites and also help support institutions which rural citizens might use in times of special distress.
>
> As Nichol left, the banker mentioned an elderly woman he knew of who needed fuel for the winter. 'We can't have that,' said Nichol, 'give her $100.00 of the money you raised.'

> When he returned to Boston and reported the incident, it was decided to repeat this kind of action in other non-corps areas.
>
> In this manner 'service units' were pioneered. Twenty per cent of the amount raised annually by Salvation Army designated community leaders was retained for local needs.
>
> The principle of the service was, and still is, mutual aid for The Salvation Army and for the rural community. Local men and women community leaders volunteered to represent The Salvation Army. They raised funds annually and controlled the use of the allocation kept locally for emergency needs. Primarily, the units existed for unusual and emergency relief, which no local agency could meet.
>
> Although already benefiting from statewide and interstate services of the Army, the non-Corps areas would now have a part in the regular support of such services as homes and hospitals for pregnant and unwed girls, camps, emergency-disaster services, missing persons bureaus, services for the armed forces, aid to prisoners and their families, children's homes, emergency shelters, and centers of rehabilitation for alcoholic and other distressed men."

1928 was the year following the formation of the Southern Territory, and the idea spread to the Southern States and eventually to Greenville, Pickens, and Oconee Counties in particular. Greenville is the center, and the counties are the rural service extension units.

It is not known in what year the service extension unit program was initiated from the Divisional level in the North and South Carolina Division but is assumed that it was early on.

Greenville began to spearhead the Corps operated Service Extension Unit in 1974 in those counties.

Also in the settling formation phase, control of the service units was vested in the divisional headquarters at one time and in the local Corps unit at another. Today both

Easley and Seneca are full Corps Operations. Greenville is no longer responsible for these Corps.

Mill Strikes Vex Service Providers

In addition to the devastating crash of the American Stock Market in 1929, there was also a new set of vexing problems in play in the community that caused a polarized contention between the citizens and most social welfare agencies. The mill strikes by the workers from Tennessee to South Carolina provided a new definition of "need" of a self-inflicted variety.

The strikes were for a good cause: higher wages, better working conditions, etc., but they could not have come at a worse time in the economic sector. Just as trouble or death, there is really no good time for problems to happen.

In the communities already at poverty level because of the general economic conditions of the times, the striking workers' families were forced to seek assistance in order to survive and were being turned away by the local charitable organizations. Whole communities were split down the middle as to what to do when the mill workers came to file for humanitarian assistance from the agencies.

The striking workers who voluntarily left their paying jobs had plunged their families into hunger and want. These mill hands who were voluntarily out of work were taxing the resources of the relief agencies and actually taking away from the community instead of contributing to the welfare of the truly out of work people who, through no fault of their own, were in need.

One side of the community wanted to help all that came regardless of the reason of their need. The other side saw no reason to assist people who had jobs but would not work. The only two valid relief agencies in the Greenville area were the American Red Cross and The Salvation Army. These two organizations were caught up on the horns of a dangerous, raging moral and political dilemma.

Both took the stance of the latter. This was probably due to the constraints of the shortfalls in funding in the community. They did not, however, refuse aid to the people who were truly suffering, that is, starving.

The safety net of public and private assistance was being stretched unusually thin. All relief agencies were forced to walk a fine line between want and need, as was the relief community in the entire population of the world. The need was protracted, and the resources were severely constricted.

Restructured

So severe was the need for capital that the South Carolina Division was dissolved and then merged with the North Carolina Division with Headquarters in Charlotte. According to a note from Lt. Colonel David Mikles, a former Divisional Commander in the Carolinas, the South Carolina Division was actually divided into two parts. One part was added to the South Atlantic Division with Headquarters in Jacksonville, Florida. The other part was added to the North Carolina Division with Headquarters in Charlotte, North Carolina.

From shortly after the formation of the Southern Territory up to the split-up of the South Carolina Division, the Divisional headquarters for the South Carolina Division was located in Columbia, SC. Consolidation and mergers of Divisional Headquarters were the rule rather than the exception in those dark days.

THE FIRST HIGH COUNCIL IS ENACTED TO ELECT THE GENERAL

In 1929, another milestone was reached and surpassed by The Salvation Army. The succession of the office and rank of General was originally determined by the Founder naming his successor in a sealed envelope and upon his death, the legal counselor opening the envelope and announcing the new General. Then he, in turn would do likewise to continue the line of leadership. This method resulted in the appointment of the Founder's son, Bramwell Booth as the second General of The Salvation Army in 1912 upon the death of the Founder.

In 1878, at the formation of and the name change to "The Salvation Army" as the official designation for the movement, and upon advice by his friends and mentors, General Booth also enacted another emergency and contingent means of electing the next in line for the position. This contingent means was to be used in the event of incompetence for health reasons or other causes which would be detrimental to the ongoing cause.

This change was to be made by a group of sitting world leaders formed into a group called the "High Council."

In 1929 it was evident that General Bramwell Booth was not competent because of deteriorating health problems. The High Council was enacted for the first time to select the new General by vote of the members of that body. This resulted in the election of the third General of The Salvation Army, General Edward Higgins, who was then the current Chief of the Staff. The result of this election process was to destroy the envelope filed by General Bramwell Booth, not revealing his selection.

From that time onward the General has been elected from among the sitting commissioners by vote of the body of the High Council members. This important change could be described as yet another "phoenix" experience for the Army, when from the potential ashes of ruin, the resurrected life of the organization took on new form and rose to higher and more effective avenues of strength and stability.
This potential threat could be true both in the leadership succession problem and the devastating world economy catastrophic occurrence in 1929. Somehow, the benevolent hand of the Lord is manifested to the good of the Army at all times and especially in crisis times.

CHAPTER V
1930-1939
SURVIVING, NOT THRIVING
"Though Thunders Roll and Darkened Be the Day, I'll Trust in Thee"

1930-1931:
- CO: Captain and Mrs. Albert Mattson to June 1930
- CO: Commandant and Mrs. James V. Breazeale, from June 1930
- ACO: Ensign S. Patterson from September 2, 1931
- ACO: Lieutenant Clarence Bates 1930-?
- ABC: Mrs. A. Foster McKissick [This is the first mention of an Advisory Board in Greenville that could be found]
- CSM: Roland Smith

Eyewitness to History of Greenville Salvation Army
On November 11, 1930, the Piedmont Newspaper posted the following story by reporter Mildred Edwards:

> *Local Citadel was first Salvation Army Building of its kind in the South. Commandant Breazeale finds old records showing history of the Post on Broad Street.*
>
> The Greenville Salvation Army here was the first building constructed for the organization in the South. It is shown by records unearthed by Commandant J. V. Breazeale who recently came here to take charge of the work and who lived in Greenville County back in 1904 when the work was first started here and is familiar with developments since that time, though he has lately been stationed elsewhere.
>
> From the small beginning made here in the early history of the Army have grown the City Hospital, The Salvation Army Hospital, Tuberculosis Sanatorium, which is now the Greenville County Sanatorium, the Bruner Home and the home for homeless men on Falls Street.

Just how these have grown from it was described today by Mr. [sic] Breazeale as follows:

Open air meetings in '04

Ensign and Mrs. J. W. McSheehan came here from Atlanta about January 1, 1904 and rented a five-room house on Manley Street. They held open-air meetings for about two months, then they put up a tent on East Washington Street in front of the old Pates & Allen Livery Stable. That was before there were any paved streets in the town and the tallest building was the four-story Mansion House.

At that time this was the only Salvation Army Corps in the State, and one of the 19 in North Carolina, Georgia, Florida, Alabama, Mississippi, and parts of Tennessee and Louisiana. Now there are about 250 Corps in the same area and 40 in North and South Carolina.

Use tent in winter

Meetings were held every night. When the tent was too cold in the wintertime a stove was [brought in] and the meetings went on. There were no picture shows or other entertainment and The Salvation Army service was the principal attraction each night, Mr. [sic] Breazeale said today.

A number of the town's worst sinners and drunks were converted, in addition to a large corps of others, among whom was Commandant Breazeale who was a lad at that time.

Later a tent was put up near the present site of the cigar factory and this was kept about two years. Another move was made then to a frame house on the site where the C. & W. C. now stands. This was a two-story house. A family lived upstairs and the hall below was used for the Army meetings. A fire burnt the roof off the house and so meetings had to be held only when it wasn't raining.

At the end of the first two years of work Captain and Mrs. William Orr Hanna came here and it was during their administration that the Citadel was erected.

At that time the Army had bought a frame dwelling for the Officers in Atlanta, and there was a shack owned by the Army in Savannah, but this was the first building ever erected by the organization in the South.

Citadel is built

Jamison and Morris constructed the Citadel and J. E. Sirrine was the Architect. Colonel R. E. Hols [sic], now Commander of the Eastern Territory with headquarters in...(Section obliterated)... laying of the cornerstone.

The contract was signed August 18, 1906 and called for the expenditure of $5910. It is estimated to be worth double that amount now.

It was dedicated May 18, 1907. Dr. T. W. Sloan, pastor of the First Presbyterian Church and the late C. E. Graham were largely responsible for [providing for] the building.

Mr. Graham gave the lot and the first $1000. Toward the building and Dr. Sloan was friendly to the work, allowing meetings to be held in his Church, and Commander (Eva) Booth and other high officials of the Army to speak in behalf of The Salvation Army.

The Salvation Army was the first charity to enter the city and the first to stage Christmas charity after it was prepared. That condition is not true now when many are pleading for help. For about 10 years the army had the field to itself here.

Charity Aid Founded

About 1910, the Charity Aid Society was formed lead by Mrs. W. G. Sirrine and Mrs. W. W. Burgiss.

Captain (W. Orr) Hanna had died and Adjutant J. H. Crook [who] was in charge of The Salvation Army did all the investigation for the Society and much relief was given.

An Emergency hospital was set up in the three rooms at the Citadel, which are now used as an emergency home for women and children.

The day the hospital opened a man fell off a building, which he was constructing and he spent several weeks recovering in the hospital. This was the only free hospital in the city at the time and is thought to have been the only public one.

The City Hospital grew out of this work, Commandant Breazeale said today.

Find Man in Hut

About that time a man was found lying in a hut near the southern Depot. He was ill with tuberculosis. There was no place to put him.

A tent was erected behind The Salvation Army Citadel by the Charity Aid Society and the man placed there. Hopewell Tuberculosis Association and the Sanatorium had their beginning there, Breazeale said.

Taking Away the Straw and Demanding More Bricks

One of the first causalities of the 1929 stock market crash and the resulting loss of financing and critical community support was The Salvation Army. This was ironic because the front lines of defense in the war on poverty in Greenville were The Salvation Army and the

American Red Cross. Other "charities" were in operation and no doubt felt the pinch of immediate loss of support, as well.

A GOOD PROGRAM BUT WOEFULLY UNDERFUNDED

Troubles of a high and aggravated nature were piling up on the Emma Moss Booth Memorial Hospital. Although one of the most caring and efficient hospitals in the region, the Emma Moss Booth Memorial Hospital was in arrears about $39,000.00 and was amassing debt at the rate of $10,000.00 per year.

It was closed in 1931 and sold to the Catholic Church's Little Sisters of the Poor in 1932. That organization began operating the facility as the Saint Francis Hospital. This hospital stands on the same property and was used until 1971 when it was razed to make way for the new hospital system. Through the years the Saint Francis Hospital system has grown to a major hospital system in Greenville.

On the social services front at the Corps, this was a time of extreme and protracted need because of the effects of the crash of the stock market. The workloads of The Salvation Army social service program increased by more than twice.Appeals were made to merchants and citizens, who themselves, were struggling for survival. Donations of any kind to help feed the poor and destitute were aggressively pursued by The Salvation Army.

Failed Appeal

In the latter part of 1931, The Salvation Army Commander, Captain J. V. Breazeale and other relief agency directors were in a meeting with the local Community Fund. They decided to launch an emergency appeal for $10,000.00, but the drive failed and the need for funds could not be met. As a result, gathering and distributing old bakery products and other foodstuff became the way of life for The Salvation

Army officers and other workers. The Army was already gathering donations-in-kind of other staples of life for distribution.

Of course, the condition was not confined to the Greenville scene but was prevalent all over the United States and all over the world. The ingenuity of Salvation Army workers was stretched to the maximum in every corner of the globe.

It was another solidifying moment for the "new" Salvation Army with its co-emphasis on the social and the spiritual aspects of the Gospel. "Soap, Soup, and Salvation" became firmly bonded and ingrained into the very fabric of The Salvation Army in Greenville and its outreach to the suffering poor segment of society.

1932-1933:

- CO: Commandant and Mrs. James V. Breazeale, from June 1930 (1st Appointment)
- CO: Ensign S. Patterson from 9/1931 to 1/25/1933
- S/Captain Arne Lekson from 1/25/1933
- ACO: None listed
- ABC: Assumed to be the same as last year. (No list available)
- CSM: Roland Smith

"In Kind" Donations and Distributions

The Salvation Army began to distribute surplus flour and donated garden seed to the needy people of Greenville. This was donated by the Department of Agriculture as a means to help alleviate the hunger and poverty which was rampant because of the market crash and the ensuing loss of jobs and fortunes.

According to one report, sometimes the bread lines were 500 strong at The Salvation Army when the day-old-bread was distributed.

In 1932 the community came together and built a new activity building for the Bruner Home on the Rutherford Street property. This was a completely volunteer effort to provide a place for the children living in the Bruner Home to have a safe place to play and socialize together. See the complete story in the chapter devoted to the Bruner Home for orphaned children.

Mae McIntyre was enrolled as a Senior Soldier in May 1932. She is still living. Due to age and health considerations she moved to Indiana to live with her daughter in November of 2001. She is presently the oldest living Soldier of the Greenville, South Carolina Salvation Army. Mrs. Mae McIntyre is a "Bruner Home Kid" and a lifelong member of The Salvation Army. She is not related to Commissioner William McIntyre, the first Territorial Commander of the new Southern Territory.

1933-1940:

- CO: S/Captain Arne Lekson to 6/19/1940
  Major H. P. McDonald from 6/19/1940
- ACO: Captain Thelma Giles 2/17/1934
  Lieutenant Eva Graham 6/11/1934
  Lieutenant Dorothy Tucker 8/29/34
  Captain Margaret Maultaby 8/36/1936
  Lieutenant Etta Walters 6/14/1937
  Lieutenant Robert Burchett 6/6/1938
  Lieutenant Louise Shealey 6/6/1939
  Lieutenant Fred Boyette 2/22/1939)
  Lieutenant Ben Moore 8/7/1939
  Lieutenant Mary Hajicek 2/31/1940
- ABC: James H. Price 1935
  Hugh Aiken 1936-1937
  Joseph A. (R.) Bryerson 1938
  W. W. Pate 1939-1940
- BCC: P. D. Meadows (Charter 1938)
  W.W. Pate, 11/9/1938

- LAC: Mrs. W. W. Pate (The Red Shield Auxiliary)
- CSM: Roland Smith (Deceased 8/21/1935)

A Local Salvation Army Icon Passes On

On August 21, 1935 the beloved Corps Sergeant Major, Mr. Roland Smith was promoted to Glory [died]. He had served as the CSM since the opening of the Army in 1904. CSM Roland Smith and his wife, Fannie Sizemore Smith, who died in 1961, are buried in the Conestee Cemetery, Conestee, SC. He left behind a family and descendents who are active in The Salvation Army today, some as Officers and some as Soldiers and others as employees.

Boy Power

One of the most popular places in town, The Salvation Army Red Shield Club, c1940s.

The Juvenile's Alternative to Jail

In 1938, The Salvation Army Red Shield Boys Club was formed with the aid of Mr. P. D. Meadors, a local candy manufacturer, and a group of local businessmen. In the same year a Red Shield Ladies Auxiliary was inaugurated to help support the Red Shield Boys Club. The first Chairwoman of the Red Shield Ladies Auxiliary was Mrs. W.W. Pate. On November 9, 1938, *The Greenville Daily News* reported that Lt. Commissioner Ernest I. Pugmire, Southern Territorial Commander, led a dedication service in Greenville to formally open the new program.

The particulars of the formation and other facts are found in the chapter devoted to Boys Club and Girls Club Historical progression.

Out of Many, One

The church/social related programming was going full blast at the same time the Boys Club was in formation. The Citadel program and membership was expanded to include the membership of the Boys Club and also the Bruner Home kids who desired to participate.

Outreach programs were offered to the employees and constituents of all Salvation Army units. At the same time clients of the welfare system were offered as much participation as they desired in the total Salvation Army program.

The staff membership did not change much. The new work was simply added to the workload already in progress, and the staff and employees and volunteers worked harder and longer. The citizens in the community gave more time, material, and money to support the new venture.

The epitome of the Army's methods seems to be described in the couplet, whose author is unknown to this writer, "I'd rather see a sermon than hear one any day,
I'd rather one would walk with me than merely show the way."

...And, walk with me the Army does.

Officers' Quarters

In November 1939, the Commanding Officer moved his living quarters to a new address out of the Citadel building. According to the Dispo of that time the address was 17 East Jones Street. This is apparently the first move from the Citadel as living quarters for the commanding officers. It could have been brought about by the need for more space to accommodate the addition of the Boys Club and the assignment of the Assistant Officer to operate the club. This hypothesis is not confirmed.

The Corps Officers and most of his/her assistants lived at the East Jones Street address until a change was made to Earle Street in 1961, which was closer to the new Citadel on Rutherford Street.

Note: The officers' quarters and furnishings, along with automobiles and all major equipment, are owned by The Salvation Army, and the officers move into the available quarters as they change assignments.

CHAPTER VI

1940-1949 A NEW WAR DAWNING

"I Believe We Shall Win, If We Fight in the Strength of Our King"

1940-1941:

- CO: Major H. P. MacDonald to 7/2/1941
  Major A. G. Ashby from 7/2/1941
  Brigadier James Breazeale from 3/3 1942
  [2nd Appointment]
- ACO: Captain Gordon Hyde 8/15/1941
  Captain Robert Burchett 11/19/1941
  [2nd Appointment]
  Lieutenant Sara Williams 11/19/1941
- ABC: W. W. Pate 1940
  E. L. Snipes 1941
- BCC: P. D. Meadors
- LAC: Could be Mrs. P. D. Meadors following the custom of the wife serving with the husband as leaders of the advisory group.
- CSM: Unknown (no record available)

Changes in the Wind

In 1941, a study was commencedby the local Community Chest to consider merging the Bruner Home with the Green Acres Children's Home under the supervision of The Child Care Committee of Greenville. In 1947, the Greenville Children's Center was set up with funding as a separate agency of the Community Chest. In 1949, the Bruner Home was closed. It is not clear which agency continued the program, or for how long it continued.

One of the Little Boys in "Bruner Home," Greenville

A little boy of the Bruner Home, early 1900s.

Amen Corner: The Men's Fellowship Club is Born

In the early 1940s, Major Fred Boyette, Corps Officer of Greenville, South Carolina, collaborated with Captain James Henry of Kinston, North Carolina and a group of Greenville and Kinston Corps members and others, to establish the Men's Fellowship Club movement in the Southern Territory. Mr. O. P. Fletcher was the Men's group leader in Greenville at the time.

According to Captain James Henry [Now Brigadier, Retired] the club was formed in Kinston, North Carolina as an answer to the problem of what to do with the parolees and drunks from the local jail who were released to his care and keeping. He said he formed an "Amen Corner" in the

Corps religious meetings, and the Men's Fellowship Club was born. This program became a worldwide standard program for the men of The Salvation Army.

As expansion and popularity progressed, the program was modified to include all men of the community who wanted to join the club. The MFC membership included both reformed parolees and the regular Corps members, and others in the community, in or out of The Salvation Army. Captain James Henry was the prime founder/motivator of the Men's Fellowship movement. He was not stationed in Greenville, SC.

Note: Brigadier James Henry was promoted to glory in January of 2004.

The Greenville Men's Fellowship Club and the Greenville Commanding Officer were partners in the early formulating days of the local club. Mr. O. P. Fletcher was elected founding President of the Greenville charter Men's Fellowship Club.

1941-1945:

- CO: Brigadier James Breazeale to 9/5/1945
  Captain Fred Boyette from 9/5/1945 (2nd Appt)
- ACO: Captain Ruth Jones 9/25/43
  Captain Viola Carawan 7/24/1943
  Lieutenant Madeline Sipe 5/24/1944
  Captain Dorothy Carawan 9/1/1944
  Captain Arthur Kinlaw 5/24/1944
  Captain Jack McCune 1/30/1945
- ABC: E. L. Snipes 1941
  J. Wilbur Hicks 1942
  Olin H. Spann 1943
  R. A. Jolley, Sr. 1944
  J. Kenneth Cass 1945-1946
- BCC: P. D. Meadors
- RSAC: Mrs. P. D. Meadors
- CSM: J. W Street from 1942 to 1950. (Died in 1950])

Camping for the Community Youth

Greenville Fresh Air Camp began operations in March of 1942 and continued for many years. In 1952, a Mothers and Kiddie feature was added to the programs offered. A complete report on the camping activities is found in the chapter devoted to the Boys and Girls Club program.

Additions to the Corps

In 1942, Mr. and Mrs. J. W. Street [deceased 1950] and Carrie Mae Street [deceased 1980] were enrolled as Soldiers of the Corps along with their son, Bill Street [Bill joined the Methodist Church later]. J. W. and Carrie Mae Street are the parents of Brigadier Otis Street, Major, Retired. Then Captain, Otis Street conducted their swearing-in ceremony. He was stationed at the SFOT in Atlanta at the time.

The photograph below is representative of The Salvation Army's swearing-in ceremony. This ceremony is somewhat akin to the baptism into the church.

Swearing in ceremony of the J. W. Street family, c1942.
L-R Captain Robert [Bob] Burchett, Captain Otis Street, J. W. Street, Mrs. J. W. [Carrie Mae] Street, Louise Street, William [Bill] Street, and Brigadier J. V. Breazeale, the Corps Officer.

In the 1940s, Mrs. J. W. Street was the Home League Secretary and worked as the Fresh Air Camp Dietician. Dates are unknown.

E-mail from Brigadier Otis Street, officer son of the enrollees explains his introduction to the City of Greenville:

> "I met The Salvation Army at the Atlanta Lakewood Corps in October 1938 and entered training the next September. I never attended the Greenville Corps until my parents began attending after I was an Officer. I did their enrollment while stationed at the Officers' Training College and this was my first visit. In the last years of my father's life my parents lived in the Corps building and Daddy checked in the Transients who were housed somewhere else but I am not aware of the location. Sorry that I can't supply much information. Col. Jack Waters went to Training during the time Daddy was CSM and you can probably get more from him."

In 1941, The Salvation Army closed the men's shelter on East McBee Street due to the advent of World War II. No other detail is given as to address or circumstances.There are no other records available to confirm this. The Corps record lists the address of one of the Soldier Enrollees as 309 East McBee Street.

1945-1947:

- CO: Captain Fred Boyette to 6/25/1947
  Captain Robert Burchett from 6/25/1947
- ACO: none assigned
- ABC: J. Kenneth Cass 1945-1946
  J. LaRue Hinson 1947-1948
- BCC: P. D. Meadows
- RSAC: Mrs. P. D. Meadors
- CSM: J. W. Street

Advisory Board Committee, c1940s. Members are unidentified.

Reinforcements

About 1946, a young newspaper delivery boy hung out at the Boys Club on Broad Street while waiting for his stack of newspapers to be ready. The Boys Club was just around the corner from the Greenville News and Piedmont newspaper. The young man eventually joined The Salvation Army in 1949. He enlisted in The Salvation Army School for Officers Training in 1950 and went forward to become a Divisional Leader in The Salvation Army in several Divisions. Jack T. Waters is his name. His story is featured in the chapter dedicated to the Boys and Girls Club of Greenville.

O.P. Fletcher and his Wife Montez (Mahaffey) Fletcher AKA “Smilie” were enrolled as Senior soldiers on 1/1/1946. They are the Grandparents of present day Bandmaster Michael (Mike) Fletcher.

In 1947, a young married couple named Willard and Marie Fitton Evans were soldiers of the Greenville, SC Corps while attending college. Commissioner and Mrs. Willard and Marie Fitton Evans are retired now and still active in the ranks of the Army as Officer/Soldiers after serving in a number of key leadership positions including Salvation Army Territorial Leaders for many years.

In an e-mail the Commissioners Evans related the following memories of their time in the city by the Reedy River:

"We were soldiers in Greenville from 1947-1949. At that time we were in college. Major and Mrs. Robert Burchett were the corps officers. Lt. Emily Farmer Lanier was the assistant. Mrs. Lt. Colonel Hickey was in charge of the Brunner Home. Irene Baugh Mikles was living with the Burchetts (Moleva's sister). Dorothy Lethco Rickard also lived with the Burchetts.

For a year Willard was the Bandmaster at the corps and taught music at the Bruner Home. Stokley Raines who married Captain Virginia Askey now live in Winston-Salem. I believe she was *Chairman of the Women's Republican Party of North Carolina. You may want to check this out.

Jack Waters was a member of the Boys Club. Bobby McIntyre was active in the corps and the last we heard was president of some school. More than likely the old soldiers would know where.

It was a great corps! We received excellent training. If you have any specific questions we will be happy to try and answer them.

Our best to your both,
Marie and Willard"

*Note: The Salvation Army is non-partisan. Its members exercise individual preferences.

1948-1955:

- CO: Captain Robert Burchett to 8/31/1955
  1/Lt. Mildred Gentry from 8/31/1955
- ACO: Lt. Emily Farmer 6/7/1948 [Married Colonel Rodolph Lanier]
  Lt. Ruby Cox 6/22/1949
  P/Lt. John Burgese 5/49/5/50
  2nd Lt. Violet Bivans 8/49-5/51
  2nd Lt. Betty Pittman 8/29/1951
  P/Lt. Louise Barnett 6/51-9/17/52 [Married Major Frank Gordon]
  Captain Lillian Blackburn 9/10/52-8/28/55
  Lt. Mildred Gentry 8/3/55-12/1/55 [appointed to Command]
- ABC: J. LaRue Hinson 1948
  W. Paul Bolton 1949-1950
  Charles H. Garrison 1951-1952
  J. A. Dusenberry 1953-1954
- BCC: Joe H. Britt 1954
- RSAC: Mrs. C. Henry Cranyon [1950]
  Mrs. C. B. Dawsey 1954
- CSM: Mr. J. W. Street: died in 1950

A Typical Slice of Corps Life from an Assistant Officer's Perspective

Second Lt. Violet Bivans, now Mrs. Violet Bivans Eaton of West Palm Beach, Florida, gives the following report [condensed] about her assignment as Youth Officer to Greenville in 1949-51:

> "My first Appointment as assistant Officer in Greenville, SC was in 1949.I was stationed with Captain Bob and Moleva Burchett. I lived with them on 17 Jones Avenue for two years and really enjoyed my appointment. They treated their

assistants as one of the family. We ate together, worked together, prayed together, and did all we could to help the Corps grow with the help of our lord Jesus Christ.

Mrs. Burchett informed me that one of my chief duties would be to lead the Girl Guard Troop. Although I had been raised in the Army, I had little knowledge of the program, and didn't see how I could do it. She sat me down in the dining room and went over test after test. I soon found I could pass a lot of the tests on the spot and was hooked. With her help I became a Founders Guard with all three palms. Well, that thrust me into the program and the Lord helped us to build that Troop from seven Guards to about fifty in the next two years.

I always picked up the girls for the meetings, and when we would find a girl that wanted to come we would just pile them in [into the car]. One time when we got back to the Corps, the girls were getting out, a policeman just stood there counting. He just shook his head like he knew it was a good cause. When I was transferred there were letters and poems from the girls and a good many tears from all of us. I liked the one composed by Frances Funk and Faye Rice that ended, 'there was nothing we could do but live a better life, in memory of you.'

The old building had a gymnasium and there we developed a Girl Guard basketball team and spent many hours enjoying that sport.

Our YPL [Young People's Legion] was struggling so I asked Bill Niven who had just returned from Korea to find us some [boys], and when he brought all his friends, the room was overflowing, so we had to move to the chapel. Sometimes we would have seventy-five Young People on Sunday night.

The Corps had its own camp and we enjoyed fellowship and worship there.

The old Bruner Home had been closed but we used it to pass out Christmas donations and, and other meetings when needed.

Like all Corps in those days, we spent all Saturday selling *War Crys* and collecting in surrounding towns which were *our territory. It was my job to drive the collectors.

[*Each Corps was assigned a defined area of service in which it was to operate. This generally formed a network from one Corps to the next without skipping many outlying towns and provided seamless coverage of the entire state. See also, Rural Service Units. rwk] Saturday night would find us in front of the old train station spreading the gospel on the street. Many times it was just Captain and Mrs. Burchett and myself, he on his trombone and Moleva and I on our accordions. Sunday night we had services in front of the bus station.

In those days, officers were required to do at least eight hours a week of visitation among our people. I spent many happy times during those visits, and came to know the suffering and problems around us and hope that we were of benefit. Moleva [Mrs. Captain Burchett] and I went together, and even to the Tuberculosis Sanatorium. I had been afraid to go there when I was a Cadet, as my mother was miraculously healed from that disease. But the Lord helped me to overcome my fear and I entered into the activity with joy, seeing so many that were destitute, and deserted, as their families were afraid. You just prayed that your witness helped them to gain their salvation.

During my stay there The Salvation Army tried to change over from the *tambourine to the little bucket with a shield on it for collections. The new procedure was short lived I must say and, and the old tambourine was reestablished."

Note: The old collecting scheme, using either vessel, is all but obsolete in most Corps and has been replaced by other methods of soliciting donations from the public. However, they still play the tambourine in the meetings occasionally, and, it is a collecting vessel for some Corps. (rwk)

"I do remember some of the names of the people who were coming when I was there. Such as: Judy Farmer, who later became the Guard leader, Mrs. Street and Mrs. McArthur [McCarter], Louise and Bill, Mary Ruby and Evelyn Fletcher, and Bill Nevin. Margaret Jamison was in charge of the Girls Club. Mary and Bill Widbin were students at Bob Jones University. Another student named Bruce regularly played his cornet on the street with us. Mary and Bill Widbin became missionaries and served many years on the field.

We had a big Boys Club there at that time but I was not involved in that [program].

Captain Bob Burchett brought Charlotte Palmer from Macon, Georgia along with Dorothy Lethco to the Corps. Dorothy became an Officer and later married David Rickard who was also an officer. Irene Baugh [Moleva's sister] and her husband also became officer[s]. [Colonel and Mrs. John and Irene Baugh Mikles]

Jack Waters was a soldier while I was there and he later became a Divisional Commander. I remember his first sermon. He told us that 'hell was hot.'

Charlene, Ruby and I formed a vocal trio and were able to make a contribution to our meetings.

I went on to another appointment at Kinston, NC and more Guarding work, and then became the Divisional Guard Director for the Carolinas Division. During that appointment I attended the international Girl Guard Camp in Oslo, Norway with a contingent of Guards from the Carolinas Division and around the world."

Note: This marks the end of Violet Bivans' Salvation Army Officership as reported. The narrative continues:

"I entered [employment in] the Federal Government, married, had three sons, and two grandchildren. I retired after 32 years [employment with the Federal Government].

Nothing compares with the joy I had, and am still having in The Salvation Army. It hasn't ended yet as I have been a local officer in the West Palm Beach Corps for 30 years, and now the circle goes on. My granddaughter just became a Commissioners Sunbeam. [The highest award in that category, rwk] Violet Bivans Eaton, 10 June 2003."

In November 1949, the Officers quarters address was changed in the Dispo from 17 East Jones Street to 17 Jones Avenue. (Apparently the same physical address.)

In 1949, The Salvation Army closed the Bruner Home at the request of the local Community Fund. The children were placed with relatives or other children's agencies. The sale of the equipment netted some funds that were placed in an educational trust to assist Bruner children with college expenses.

At that time plans were enacted to move The Salvation Army Corps programs from 26 East Broad Street to the

Bruner Home location on Rutherford Street. The house next door was serving as the men and women's shelter. The Women's Rescue Home Social Services Program was located in the 600 block of Rutherford Street at one time.

The Bruner Home facility was razed, and construction began on the new Corps Citadel to be occupied in 1951.

CHAPTER VII
1950-1959
A SHELTER FROM THE STORM
"He Hideth My Life in the Depth of His Love"

On November 16, 1950, The Salvation Army broke ground for the new Citadel on Rutherford Street. The cornerstone was laid in 1951. The Advisory Board Chairman was Mr. Paul Bolton. The Building Committee membership consisted of J. LaRue Hinson, Chairman of the Committee; Mr. R. A. Jolley; Mr. M. C Patterson; and Doctor W. B. Simmons. Captain Robert Burchett was the Commanding Officer.

The present offices, Corps building, social services/ homeless shelter, and CSRC are located at 417-419 Rutherford Road on the site of the old Bruner Home for children.

Over the years, additional properties in the area were added to the complex, and today it covers a large portion of the block and houses every Salvation Army program operated in the city except the Boys and Girls Club and some thrift stores.

On April 5, 1950, The Salvation Army Men's Fellowship Club named William H. Fletcher Man of the Year. Talmadge Eugene[Chuck] Fletcher was enrolled as a Junior Soldier 1/1/1946 and as a Senior Soldier on 5/25/1952. He is Michael Fletcher's dad, presently Bandmaster and Assistant Corps Treasurer.

In 1950, the Ladies Auxiliary started the doll-dressing program for Christmas gifts to little girls. This is the final year of Corps' operation in the Broad Street facility. The Boys and Girls Club continued to operate at this location until 1969. It is assumed that the doll project effectively expanded the scope of the Red Shield Auxiliary to include service to the entire Salvation Army operation in the city.

Beginning in 1951, the Corps' operations at the building on Broad Street were transferred to the new building at 417 Rutherford Street. This property has been expanded to include a complex of buildings on Rutherford Street. It has undergone several makeovers to accommodate the needs of the city's neediest citizens and to house the main program components of the Army.

The Broad Street building became the focal point for the underprivileged youth as the Boys and Girls Club. They gathered here in great numbers to enjoy a place of their own to play and reach and strive to become better citizens of the community.

The newly acquired facility for The Salvation Army Boys and Girls Club on Broad Street, c1951; the former Citadel built in 1905-07; Children waiting for the Camp Bus.

In 1951, the Broad Street building was turned over to the Boys and Girls Club to continue the work of serving the youth of the city.

In 1954, Mrs. O. P. Fletcher was named Woman of the Year by The Salvation Army Home League program.

Half a Century Long and Still Going Strong

On October 1, 1954 The Salvation Army celebrated the fiftieth anniversary of the Corps opening. Special meetings were held and the Commanding Officers distributed a booklet to the community depicting the past fifty years of progress.

Each of the major components, such as the Bruner Home program, the Women's Social program and the Emma Moss Booth Memorial Hospital program, Boys and Girls Club, playground, and camping program, and the Corps' programs were highlighted.

The playground program sponsored by the Civitan Club and operated by The Salvation Army was located on Stratham Street. This was on the property located directly behind the Citadel on Rutherford Street.

1955-1956:

- CO: 1st Lieutenant Mildred Gentry to 8/31/1956
  S/Captain Harry Gillespie from 8/31/1956
- ACO: None assigned
- ABC: Joe H. Britt (1/10/1956
- BCC: Unknown
- RSAC: Unknown
- CSM: J. Robert Friar* 1950s (according to a penciled note on his roll sheet)

*This CSM appointment cannot be confirmed by official record. There is only the note on the record sheet penciled at a later date. Judy Farmer Campbell, a long-time Soldier, employee, and local officer of the Corps confirms the service of Mr. Friar during that time period.

Mrs. J. W. Street, HLS, Dietician for Greenville Fresh Air Camps was interviewed and made the following quote to the newspaper in 1950: "I remember open air services regular on Main and Washington, and Laurens Street outside the Bus Station."

Captain Ruby Milton, a former Bruner Home officer who was in Durham North Carolina as Home and Hospital Superintendent was principal guest speaker at The Salvation Army recently at the Local Home League meeting. On October 21, 1955 Kenneth Vick was born in Greenville, South Carolina to Mr. and Mrs. Homer Leyton and Mary Summey Vick. He is one of many children of the Vick family who are directly descended from Roland Smith who is thought to be the *first Corps Sergeant Major in Greenville, beginning in 1904. Kenneth married Tammy Howe on July 7, 1984. They have two daughters, Kirby and Kari.

Captain Kenneth Vick was promoted to Glory on April 12, 2002 from The Salvation Army Dallas Texas Adult Rehabilitation Department after a long illness. He leaves behind daughters Kirby and Kari and also two sons Sam and Chris by a previous marriage. A Vick family progression from Roland Smith to the present is listed in Chapter II of this book.

1956-1962:

- CO: Sr. Captain H.M. Gillespie
- A/O: P/Lt. Kathleen Lamy (Lamp) 3/4/58-5/25/58
  P/Lt. Charles and Louise Sinclair 5/28/58-2/11/59
  Captain Annie Wylie 6/6/56-6/4/57
  P/Lt. Margie Robinson 6/4/57-1/58
- ABC: Joe H. Britt
  C. Q. Mason, 1959
- BCC: W. Marion Sanders
- RSAC: Mrs. P. E. Storey 1958
  Mrs. D. A. Boyd 1959
- CSM: Don Holcombe: late 1950s

Stewardship Reports to the Community Are Given Yearly

In the 1959 Annual Report (year 1958), the following list appeared. This report is typical up to the 1980s when the additional programs demanded a much larger staff and a much larger budget:

Captain and Mrs. H. Gillespie, Commanding Officers; Patricia Keefover, secretary and receptionist: Lindell Whitehead, Welfare Secretary: and Betty Merritt, Bookkeeper.

The Citadel was listed at 417 Rutherford Street; Red Shield Boys Club, 26 E. Broad Street; Welfare Office, 419 Rutherford Street; Men's Transient Lodge, 419 Rutherford Street; Women's Transient Lodge, 120 Buist Street.

In another report the following information appears. This is not unusual because the locations were changed around frequently to affect the better-cost effectiveness and facilities' usefulness:

The men's shelter program was reopened at 304 Pinckney Street. It had been dormant during the war years. Details are missing and no other records can be found to confirm this. The site at present is a vacant lot.

The Advisory Board of that era:

Officers: C. Q. Mason, Chairman; Raymond T. Clark, Vice Chairman; E. S. Starnes, Treasurer; Louis C. Tolleson, Secretary; Charles H. Garrison, Lifetime Member; and James A. Dusenberry, Lifetime Member.

Members: Lythgoe Wier; E. L. Snipes; Waldo N. Leslie; Joe H. Britt; Mayor J. Kenneth Case; W. Marion Sanders; W. J. Milford; J. C. Robertson; W. N. Kline, Jr.; J. LaRue Hinson; Colonel L. G. Causey; A. D. Attaway; James M. Gilifillin; Paul Beacham; and John H. Woodberry.

The same Annual Report listed the following services rendered:

Transient men: 2,289 cases; transient women: 41 cases; lodgings: 1783; meals: 4111; garments and shoes: 246; transportation: 5.

Family welfare: Applicants: 1,767; visits made: 549; consultations: 884; office interviews: 3,920; grocery orders: 989; fuel orders: 235; rent orders: 6; garments: 27,536; shoes: 1690; prescriptions filled: 106; furniture: 310; and utility bills: 12.

League of Mercy [Hospital and Nursing Home Visitation]: Number of visits: 52; individuals visited: 2,651; religious services: 12; publications/gifts: 3,855; and number of hours: 138.

Christmas and Thanksgiving welfare:
Food baskets and grocery orders: 880; number of people: 3,640; toys, garments, and candy: 1680.

Religious and Character-Building Meetings: 45 Street Corner Meetings: 577 in attendance; 301 indoor senior meetings: 7,149 in attendance; 404 youth activities: 12,944 in attendance.

Financials for the year 1958: Corps Operations, excluding Boys and Girls Club, which is included in the chapter devoted to the Boys Club: Receipts: Internal: $11,001.31; donations: $2,404.13; city and county appropriations: $1,599.96; Christmas Cheer: $7,142.59; United Fund of Greenville: $31,092.00

Total Income, $53,239.39.

Disbursements: Salaries, wages and benefits: $15,604.51; operating expenses: $12,752.14; services provided: $24,882.74. Total disbursements: $53,239.39.

Note: the above finance report is much more detailed. The author has condensed it to general areas. Also, this service and financial report format is typical of every year and is presented to the community annually as a stewardship report. The totals are correct.

In 1958, a women and children's shelter was operated at 300 Pinckney Street, next to the 304 location of the men's shelter, also at present a vacant lot. Again, details are scarce.

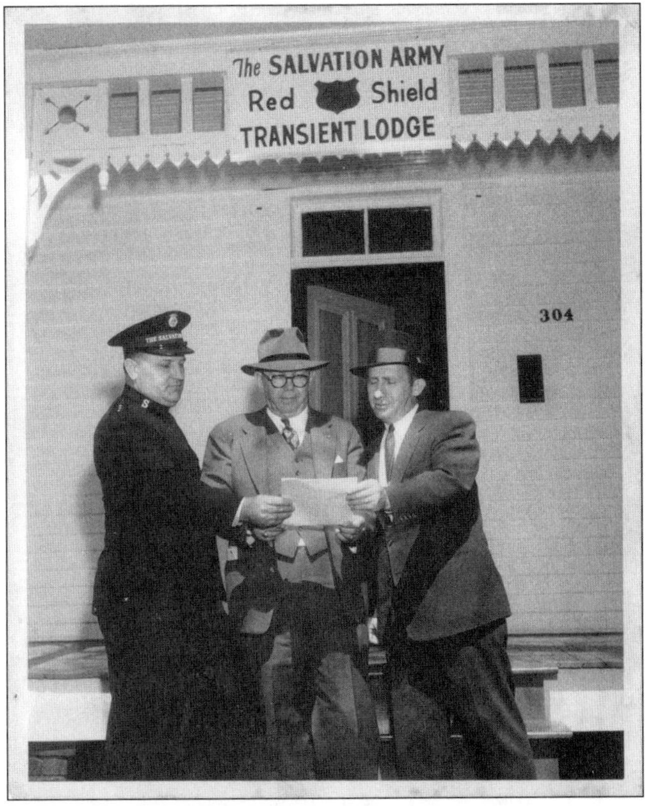

304 Pinckney Street was used as a shelter in the 1950s.

In a photo dated 1958 (not shown here), the young Vick family is pictured getting ready for the Community Camp being conducted by The Salvation Army near Cleveland, S. C. The family consists of Mrs. Mary Vick; Kenneth, age 3; Steve, age 2; Frances, age 10; and Dennis, age 4. Note: the Vick family is descended from one of the earliest families listed in The Salvation Army membership roster in Greenville. Several of the children became Officers and the others served in Local Officer positions. Some of the family members are serving the Army as Officers and others as Local Officers to this day. The Vick family is directly related to Roland Smith who served as CSM from 1904 to 1935.

- The Civitan Club sponsored the Community Camp. The Camp provided a weekly camping experience for about 1000 kids each year. It ran from June to September.
- In 1958, Mrs. Lona Crawford was crowned Queen for the night in the Home League program.
- In 1958, the Women's Auxiliary was busy raising funds and donation materials for The Salvation Army programs. The Women's Auxiliary worked tirelessly from 1938 (Red Shield Club Auxiliary) to 1998 in behalf of the boys and girls of the community and made a marked difference in the quality of service provided for our youth.

There is also a photo we were unable to show here of Mrs. O. P. Fletcher in a period costume representing the Ladies Home League for the Ladies Auxiliary Garden party. The Garden Party was a fund raising event sponsored by the Auxiliary. This fund raising program and other activities gave opportunity for hundreds of local citizens who were prominent in the community to participate in the work of serving the community through The Salvation Army programs, while not, strictly speaking, being members of The Salvation Army.

Every Salvation Army unit benefited greatly by having such a cadre of devoted and dedicated women as the foundation of the public representation for The Salvation Army. In most large and successful Salvation Army operations today there is a group such as this providing support and service for the community.

A Shelter from the Storm

The "shelter from the storm" provided by The Salvation Army covers a vast area of geography and an unbounded range of human needs. It is open to all who have needs of any sort. It also provides a multitude of avenues for service for community leaders who desire to help hold the umbrella up. It is available in any storm. The Women's Auxiliary is one such group of dedicated citizens.

Moving Across Town

In November 1961, the Officers' Quarters was moved to 125 East Earle Street from 17 Jones Avenue in order to be near the Rutherford Street Citadel. In November 1961, the Assistant Officers' Quarters was listed for the first time. This address was 318 West Stone Avenue.

CHAPTER VIII
1960-1969
SECOND TIME AROUND
"I'll Go Where You Want Me to Go, Dear Lord"

1962-1964:

- CO: S/Captain and Mrs. Henry and Bernice Lyons Gillespie to 6/27/1962
  Captain James and Mary Lou Hipps from 6/27/1962
- ACO: Lt. Don and Virginia Wolfe 2/11/59-6/27/62
  Cadet Lt. Don and Doreen Watts 11/21/62-6/6/63
  Lt. Ben and Sandra Dennis Walters 6/6/63-8/25/63
  Cadet Lt. Robert and Joanna Swyers 9/1/63-10/29/63
  Lt. Larry Price 11/1/63
- ABC: Unknown
- BCC: Unknown
- LAC: Mrs. Alvin G. Cox, 1963-1964
- CSM: Unknown

In November 1963, the Assistant Officers' Quarters was listed as 221-B Croft Street.

Mrs. Joanna Swyers Norris gave the following report. She is a former officer stationed in Greenville from 1963-64, then married to Cadet Lt. Robert Swyers [deceased), and later married to Mike Norris who is also a former officer.

> "Bob and I were assisting in Greenville as Cadet Lt. - Sept. 1963. (Captains) Jim and Mary Lou Hipps were the COs. On October 31, 1993, they were farewelled and we became the acting COs. Cadets Patsy and Tom Cundiff were sent to us for their Christmas assignment and Capt. Larry Price was the assisting Officer. In January 1994, Major Loren Boone became the commanding officer and I believe

it was late February of 1994, Bob and I as Cadet Lts. were farewelled to Anderson, SC. We only served there 7 months.

I remember the Cranford family, the Vicks were young kids attending the Corps, Tom, Linda, Ken, I particularly remember. Smiley Fletcher was HL Secy."

-Joanna Swyers Norris

Additional Roster and Eyewitness History

Following is the summary of a report by Mrs. Mary Summey to an unknown person about 1963: [replicated as nearly as possible]

OFFICERS

Ensign and Mrs. J. W. McSheehan; Captain & Mrs. Hanna; Captain & Mrs. Brown; Ensign Mamie Patterson; Captain & Mrs. Pringle; Captain & Mrs. Purdue; Captain & Mrs. Crook, Stayed 7 Years; Adjutant & Mrs. Story; Adjutant & Mrs. Price; Commandant & Mrs. Baker; Captain & Mrs. Burnell; Captain Eva Bivans; Captain Bertha Sanders; Adjutant & Mrs. Turkington; Captain & Mrs. Matteson; Commandant & Mrs. Breazeale; Ensign & Mrs. Patterson; Major & Mrs. Lekson, stayed 7½ Years; Major & Mrs. McDonald; Major & Mrs. Ashby; Brigadier & Mrs. Breazeale; Captain & Mrs. Robert Burchett, stayed 12 Years; Major & Mrs. Gillespie, stayed 6 Years; Captain & Mrs. Hipps; and Cadet-Lieutenant & Mrs. Robert Swyers.

- Ensign McSheehan came to Greenville in 1903.
- Ensign McSheehan held the first meeting in a tent on East Court Street.
- Open-air meeting-corner of Main and Washington and in front of the Old Mansion House [Now the Poinsett Hotel] and a meeting in a hall on Falls Street.

- They lived on Manley Street until the hall was ready.
- Captain Hanna lived three weeks from the day the hall was dedicated.
- The cornerstone was laid in 1906 and the hall was dedicated in 1907.
- The cornerstone was erected: FOR THE GLORY OF GOD AND THE WELFARE OF MANKIND 1906.
- The Army building was the first in the South owned by the Army.

1964-1966:

- CO: Captain and Mrs. James and Mary Lou Hipps to 6/29/1964
  Major and Mrs. Loren and Joy Moyer Boone from 6/29/1964
- ACO: Cadet Lt. Thomas and Mary Holz Jones 6/9/64-5/29/65
  Captain Bodell and Sondra Heath 9/65-1/30/66
  C/Lieutenant Thomas Jones 5/31/1964
  Captain Bodell Heath 9/1/1065
  Captain Jacqueline Campbell YO /2/2/1966
- ABC: J. B. Aiken to 1966
- BCC: E. A. Ramsaur, 1966
- LAC: Mrs. Alvin Cox, 1964
- CSM: Unknown

In a newspaper report in 1965, Captain Loren Boone gave the following account of the historical Salvation Army story:

> "On February 1, 1964, after leaving Georgia, North Carolina, and Texas, to name a few, he became headmaster of the Greenville Mission, "the oldest in the State."
>
> Captain Boone and his wife [Joy Moyer Boone], who holds equal rank, were the 24th husband and wife team to direct the local mission.

"Salvation Army activities, 'love in motion, Christianity in action' began activities on October 1, 1904 with Ensign and Mrs. J. W. McSheehan conducting open air crusades at 317 N, Manley Street. Services were soon moved inside a tent at E. Washington and Brown Streets.

The first cornerstone for a Salvation Army building in the South was laid in 1906 at 26 East Broad Street, now the Red Shield Boy's Club, and was dedicated 'to the Glory of God and the welfare of Mankind.'

Following the mobile pattern, which seems to be inherent with the Army, Headquarters here have been located on E. Court Street, Laurens Street, Falls Street, W. McBee Avenue, E. Broad Street, and presently at 417 Rutherford Street.

DURING THESE CHANGES THE 'SOLDIERS' AND THEIR 'OFFICERS' RECEIVED AND CARRIED THEIR CREED FROM A TENT NEXT TO A CIGAR FACTORY AND FROM A LOFT OVER A LIVERY STABLE.

The Salvation Army Uniform on Parade

In 1965 there is a photo of several Salvation Army ladies modeling the appropriate uniforms of the Salvation Army Officers and lay members at a Ladies Auxiliary meeting in Greenville. They are as follows:

Mrs. O. P. Fletcher was wearing a regulation stand-up collar in a white uniform for ladies. Mrs. Melva Crawford wore a new "laid down" collar uniform. Mrs. Don Campbell modeled a Guard leaders uniform. Mrs. Cadet Lt. T. E. Jones displayed a Salvation Army Officers regulation uniform. Mrs. Talmadge Fletcher wore a Grey uniform, Miss Pat Habin wore a Sunbeam Uniform with sash and Miss Crawford wore a guard uniform with sash.

A group of Cadets in regulation uniform from the Salvation Army School for officers training c1960's.

Also, in 1965 Mrs. Peggy Winslow was elected the "Textile Queen" of the Home League program.

Note: One of the most viable and active lay groups in the Salvation Army is the Ladies Home League. It consists of thousands of ladies worldwide. In every Salvaton Army unit, these ladies, who meet weekly, form the backbone of the Salvation Army's membership outside the Soldier-roster. Salvation Army membership is not required for admission to this ladies' group.

Young Girls and Boys Program

Judy Farmer Campbell was the commissioned Guard Leader and Mary Brock was the Sunbeam leader. The photo shown below is representative of the the Guard and Sunbeam program. The standard program for girls in the Salvation Army, it is an ongoing vehicle for training and equipping girls for adult life. The age range is 6 years for Sunbeams to 12 years for Girl Guards.

Don Campbell was the unofficial leader of the boy's program along with the Corps Officers and several of the other lay leaders.

A singing group consisting of Guards, Sunbeams and boys club members perform for Commissioner William Dray and the Advisory Board, and Ladies Auxiliary c1952.

1966-1975:

- CO: Captain and Mrs. Loren and Joy Moyer Boone to 8/31/1966
- CO: Major and Mrs. Fred and Sadie Boyette from 8/31/1966 (Second Appointment)

- A/O: Lt. and Mrs., Alvin Smith, 6/67-6/68
  Lt. Charles R. Feld, 6/9/1968-?
  Lt. Cathy Carter, 6/5/69-70
  Captain Robert Melton 9/1/71-?
  Lt. Michael McDonald 6/9/1974
  Lt. Carl Simmons, 2/2/1972-?
- ABC: Waldo Leslie, 1966
  Ben Leonard, 1968
  Joe E. Hayes, 1971
- BCC: Rex Osteen, 1965
  E. A. Ramsaur, 1966
  J. Austin Griffith, 1967
  Russell C. Ashmore, SR, 1968
- LAC: Mrs. Jerry Gleits, 1968
  Mrs. Sue Ashmore, 1972
  Mrs. W. H. Miller. 1973
  Mrs. Dorothy Gleits, 1975
- CSM: unknown

Recycling-Salvation Army Style

This multi-appointment city has hosted several officers for more than one appointment as commanding officer. Major and Mrs. Fred and Sadie Boyette began their second appointment in 1966.

Other Officers who have served multiple terms in Greenville are:

- S/Captain J. Rivers Lebby, served two terms, including his home service as a soldier.
- Major and Mrs. J. V. and Emma Breazeale served three terms, including their home service as soldiers.
- Major and Mrs. Loren and joy Moyer Boone served two terms.
- Major and Mrs. Robert Burchett served three terms.
- Major and Mrs. George and Ethel Graves served two terms at the Bruner Home.

Several Officers served more than one term in the Women's Social Service Department and the Emma Moss Booth Memorial Hospital system.

Selecting a Hometown

Additionally, a number of retired and former officers have made Greenville their homes and served as soldiers and employees of the Salvation Army in this city. They are as follows:

Linda Vick Griffin, Roscoe and Frances Kitchen Hines, Benjamin and Phyllis Kitchen Anderson, Charles and Sharon Anderson Mason, Alfred and Virginia Kitchen Davies, Robert and Myrtle Beasley Kitchen, Harmon and Ruby Wood Anderson, Raymond and Hope Casarez Kitchen, Marie Kitchen, Michelle Norris Robbins (re-entered Training in 2002), James and Elizabeth Robbins, David and Jeanette Lane Jones

Random Scenes in a Concerned Community

- In 1966 a fund drive was commenced to construct the Boy's Club and the transient lodge. This was a reactivation of the 1959 plan. The goal was $450,000.00. In 1968 the groundbreaking ceremony to construct the Boys Club on Owens Street was celebrated. Target completion date was February 1969.
- In 1969 Mrs. O. P. Fletcher was Salvation Army Representative at World Day of Prayer. She is shown in a Newspaper photo wearing a Salvation Army uniform.
- In 1968 Brigadier James V. Breazeale was promoted to Glory from his retirement home in Little Rock Arkansas. He was a native of Greenville and was stationed here in 1930-31 and again in 1942-1945 as the Commanding Officer. He was the son of Mr. and Mrs. James and Ella Simpson Breazeale of Greenville.

- In 1968 the Home League Program elected Mrs. Frank Wingfield Woman of the Year.
- In 1969 Captain Roscoe and Mrs. Frances Kitchen Hines moved to Greenville with their children, Sharon Denise and Howard Thomas Hines. They resigned their officer commission after having served in seven corps in the Southern Territory. They did not attend the Greenville Corps but instead joined the First Church of the Nazarene. Roscoe opened and operated three vacuum and sewing stores until his retirement. The stores are still doing business in Greenville. Frances became an educator on the college level teaching business and management courses. Ultimately, she was appointed Dean of the Business School at Greenville Technical College. In June 2002, Frances was hired as Director of the Greenville Corps Social Services Department.
- In 1969 a young man named William Madison showed up at the lodge to receive rehabilitation. He later joined the Salvation Army as a soldier and was recommended to the School for Officers Training in 1971. He was commissioned in 1973. Today he is married to the former Mary Lewis and they are stationed, as Majors William and Mary Madison, in the Adult Rehabilitation Center as administrators.
- In 1971, the former Emma Moss Booth Memorial Hospital Building on McBee Street (now Kirk Boulevard) and Patton Street (now St. Francis Street) was razed to make way for the St. Francis Hospital expansion. The Salvation Army Women's Social Service Department ceased operation of the hospital due to budget constraints in November 1931. The hospital was purchased and rededicated by the Order of Saint Francis (The Little Sisters of the Poor) in 1932 to be a catholic church sponsored hospital. The name changed to St Francis Hospital. The actual site of the Salvation Army

Hospital is now a parking lot next to the St Francis Hospital Emergency Entrance. There is a building sitting on part of the site. The Saint Francis Hospital complex stands on the same spot in Vardry Heights today.

Additions to the Rutherford Street Campus

SALVATION ARMY DEDICATION—Taking part at Sunday's dedication of the new Administration and Social Welfare building of the Salvation Army in Greenville are, from left, Brig. Fred Boyette, commander; Col. Paul S. Thornburg, field secretary of the Southern Territory, Atlanta, speaker; Marvin P. Cannon Jr., chairman of the SA advisory board; and Congressman James R. Mann, who brought a flag which has been flown over the nation's capitol for the new building.

In 1967-69, a capital campaign was commenced with a goal of $364,840.00 to build a transient and administrative building on the Rutherford Street property. A total of $279,251.98 was realized. This was a continuation of the previous effort.

In 1968, Mrs. Jamie Horn was serving as welfare secretary for the Salvation Army. The welfare secretary is employed to oversee the distribution of aid to the community. Often, though not always, this position is filled by a member of the organization and is a salaried position.

Mrs. Horn is a long-time Salvationist and employee of the Salvation Army.

A Local Plank Owner Speaks

In 1968, Mrs. Norean Willbanks McCarter, who was a Salvation Army member for 50 years, filed this report for *The Greenville Daily News.* She came to Greenville in 1903. She stated that she had held every lay position available to a Salvation Army member up to that time.

- The first meetings were held in a tent where the old cigar factory stood on Court Street, behind Carpenter Brothers.
- There were also street meetings in front of the old "Mansion House." (Now the Poinsett Hotel)

A Little Mystery

As a note of interest (but not necessarily fact) the family of a J. J. McCarter lived in the 200 block of Manley Street at the time the McSheehans came to town. Since there is no 317 block of Manley Street they could have taken up residence with the McCarter family. Developed Manley Street was only one block long in 1904 and numbered in the 200s.

Norean Willbanks McCarter may have been the first youth convert. Her first address in the roll book is 1605 East North Street, which is around the corner from Manley Street.

The problem existing in the roll book is that Norean is listed as Mrs. Norean McCarter, even as a Junior Soldier enrollee. No other maiden name is given. She was married to a Mr. A. B. McCarter in 1914 and is in the photograph of the original Salvation Army group beside the cigar factory in 1903-04 as Noreen Willbanks. (I learned later from Mrs. Judy Farmer Campbell that Mrs. Norean McCarter is actually Norean Willbanks who married into the McCarter family.)

A Hometown Champion

Mrs. Judy Farmer Campbell was brought up and nurtured in The Salvation Army under the ministry of Captain and Mrs. Robert Burchett and other officers who followed (1949-1981). Her mentor and role model was at that time (age 8), Lt. Violet Bivans, Youth Officer in Greenville in 1949. Later, when Captain Lillian Blackburn was assigned to the Greenville Corps as Youth Officer, she played an important and lasting role in molding and shaping the sweet spirit and highly energetic leadership Judy Campbell displays today.

She was active as a Jr. Soldier (1950) and a Senior Soldier (1955) also holding commissions as Company Guard (Sunday school Teacher), Corps Cadet, Musician, Songster, and many others. She was also a member of the Boys' and Girls' Club. She was a War Cry (Army Publication) seller and later the bookkeeper for the Corps.

She was a member of the Salvation Army from 1949 to 1981 when she resigned to join the Brushy Creek Baptist Church in Taylors, SC along with her husband, Don Campbell.

Both Don and Judy were deeply involved in leadership positions in the Army programs with Judy holding very strong and successful leadership positions in the Girl Guard program for seventeen years. Both served as leaders and mentors for the young people who attended the army youth meetings.

She has detailed knowledge of the Salvation Army of that era and keeps voluminous records including photos, newspaper clippings and reports of progress in the Army up to this date.

Following, in Judy Farmer Campbell's own words, is her testimonial of the impact the Salvation Army made on her at an early age:

Hello

Just wanted to tell you that we didn't make it to Major Reagan's funeral. I wanted to go but things came up and Debbie couldn't make it and I wasn't feeling well so we didn't go. You spoke of me knowing a lot of people in the Army and keeping up with as many as possible. I had no brothers and sisters (well, one half brother and sister but I never lived in the same house with them.) I had a stepmother and after she left it was just my Dad and me so the Army was MY LIFE. I loved the Army and everyone in it. I was very involved and spent most of my time there doing something even if it was only washing dishes or helping Ma Street (Mother of Otis) prepare food for canning. It amazes me as to how many people I knew in the Army. But then I was there from age 8 until a short time after we moved into this house (1949-1981).

The Army and it's people meant so very much to me and I will always cherish all the wonderful memories that I continue to hold in my heart even until today. It is such a thrill when I hear news from an Army acquaintance. Speaking of which - I received another nice letter yesterday and the program from the Merrifields Retirement Dinner. Would you believe I knew some of the people listed on the program? Through the years when we have been on vacations and out of town on trips we usually would find the Army and attend church there thinking we wouldn't know anyone. Wrong! It always turned out that I always knew someone there. Don would say, "I don't believe this!!!" I always attended camps, Y.P. Councils, Div. Band Practice, Congresses and anything that came along - therefore I always made wonderful friends from out of town too. Corresponded with many even way back then. Through the years occasionally run into one of them - always feels sooooo good to see them again. If I could make a list of all the people I've known through the Army no telling how many pages it would be.

You were right - I probably would have known just about everybody at that funeral and would have been able to renew lots of old friendships. Am so sorry we did not get to go for many reasons. Would have loved putting my arms around Becky, Melody and Mrs. Reagan again.

Salute and Go Forward

Active Salvation Army officers are pledged to go where and when they are assigned by the Command structure. At times they are needed to build upon the foundation laid down by either themselves or others and going back to an appointment for a second or third assignment was not too unusual at that time.

Retired and resigned officers are free to choose where they will settle after active service. They are not assigned. The exception is that they may, by mutual consent, do consulting or extra-retirement services where they are needed.

Soldiers and adherents in “good standing” may transfer their membership, by request, to any Salvation Army unit in the city where they make their home.

CHAPTER IX
1970-1979
CONSOLIDATING
"Bringing in the Sheaves"

Advisory Board Meeting c1959-62.

In 1971 the Citadel building on Broad Street, which was being used for the Boys and Girls Club operation until 1969, was sold for $30,000.00 and a capital campaign was commenced to raise $200,000.00 (including the sale of the Broad Street property) to complete a new Boys and Girls Club. The Boys and Girls Club moved into a new facility on Owens Street.

In 1972 the men's transient lodge was located on 208 Stall Street along the northern side of the Rutherford Street property.

In 1973, Mrs. W. H. Miller was elected as Ladies Auxiliary president succeeding Mrs. John Ashcroft.

Transplanted Reinforcements

In 1973, Major and Mrs. Benjamin and Phyllis Kitchen Anderson moved to Greenville along with their five sons. Two were in the United States Army in Germany at the time. Ben served as Director of Financial Services for the City of Greenville while Phyllis became Director of Congregate Dining for Urban Ministries. She also served as Director of Pickens and Oconee Counties Service Unit for the Salvation Army and Bookkeeper for Greenville Corps and the Boys and Girls Club. They attended the Salvation Army as soldiers. Both are presently in leadership positions in The Salvation Army. Ben is the Corps Sergeant Major and Phyllis is serving as Corps pianist.

On March 2, 1974, Brigadier and Mrs. Alfred and Virginia Kitchen Carey Davie moved to Greenville as retired officers. They were later divorced and Brigadier Alfred Davie moved back to New York to live with his Son. Virginia Carey served as a non-officer for a time but regained her rank of Brigadier, and her first married name, Carey.

She lived and worked in Greenville and worshipped at the methodist church for a time. She later rejoined the Salvation Army and was active in many programs as her health allowed. She is presently residing in an Assisted Living Facility as a retired officer.

She worked for many years as a personal care giver to senior citizens all around Greenville. Some of her children and grandchildren are living in Greenville, also.

In 1974, Mr. and Mrs. Sam and Ilene Wentz Knowlton transferred in as Soldiers from Greensboro, NC. They brought with them two sons, Randall and Troy, and immediately offered themselves for service to the community through the Salvation Army organization. Both are multigenerational Salvationists. Sam is from the Eastern Territory and Ilene is from the Southern Territory. Both have lived and served in several different cities in their respective territories. Both have been active in several local officer positions especially in the youth and music departments of the Corps. Their two sons were Junior Soldiers. When they grew up they married and joined a church.

New Living Quarters for Officers

In 1974, new living quarters for the officers were purchased on 6 Overton drive at a cost of $38,302.75.

The old Officers quarters at 125 E. Earle Street were sold and the money realized was applied to the cost of the new quarters. The Earle and Bennett Street location is now certified as a Historic District of the City of Greenville.

Also in November 1974, the Assistant Officer's quarters were listed as 419 Rutherford Street.

Service Units

Brigadier Alfred Davey, who was retired, initiated the Service Unit program in Seneca, South Carolina under the command of the Greenville Corps. (See year 1928-29 for details.) He was employed by the Salvation Army of Greenville to administer the programs in that area. This unit was commissioned as a full-fledged Corps in 1994. (See the story at the 1994 dateline.)

1975-1984:

- CO: Major Fred Boyette to 8/27/1975
- CO: Major John V. Cole from 8/27/1975
- ACO: Lt. Larry Broome 6/7/77-8/21/78
  Lt. Henry and Cheryl Hunter 6/14/79-1/27/80
  Lt. Allison Williams 8/24/82-1/1/84
- ABC: Harrison Marshall 1978-1980
  James Cooksey 1981-1982
  James Sheppard 1983-1984

- BCC: Unknown
- LAC: Mrs. Mary Frances Bigby, 1976
  Mrs. Maude Cashion, 1977, 1978, 1979
  Mrs. Ellen Brady, 1980,1981
  Mrs. Lila Ruth Godfrey, 1982, 1983
- CSM: unknown

An Officer's Watch

In the evolution of the Salvation Army in every community the Corps Officer who is presently assigned to command the Corps sets the tone and substance of the programming. Certain functions are mandated by the Divisional/Territorial and International Command but wide latitude is given to the Corps Officer for organization and implementation of specialized programs on the local front.

Needless to say, every command is a different command and this adds to the attractiveness and effectiveness of the local Salvation Army from year to year.

The core work of the Army is not generally affected, and in fact, is often enhanced by the changes in style and content as the officer strives to put his personal stamp on "his watch" of leadership.

It is a part of the romantic mystique of the world's attraction to the Army's unique nature.

Likewise, the Advisory Board rotates one-third of its members and, the chairman and the other board officers change from year to year. The same is true of the several councils and auxiliaries.

The Corps local leadership is changed from year to year as circumstances dictate, as well.

Thus, in any given decade the leadership of the Army will wax and wane and be subject to the effective strength of the prevailing cadre of leadership.

The effectiveness of the local Salvation Army is thus strengthened and unified to meet current needs in any given community in the aura of the present time.

There are always new members added with new and different views on the needs of the community and methods to address those needs. The Army is thus able to address current and emerging needs as they arise.

The replaced leaders usually remain in contact with the Army and often take on added assignments in special situations.

Life membership classification is given to Advisory Board members, who serve for a number of years and render outstanding service to the community before retiring from the board.

Thus, over the years literally thousands of local citizens in each community are aligned with the passion and purpose of the Salvation Army. This is especially so in passing the one hundred-year mark of service in the community.

Passing Through

In the middle 1970s a young lady named Elizabeth Fowler was engaged for a short time as a “Corps helper” for the Greenville Corps. After being commissioned as an officer, she served several years in Corps, Divisional, and Territorial appointments. (At the time of this writing, Major Elizabeth Fowler Duracher was serving at Territorial Headquarters in the recruiting department. Her husband Major Frank Duracher is assistant editor of the *Southern Spirit.*)

A Local Hero Returns Home

Major Jack T. Waters, Boys Club member to 1949 and Mr. Norman Eoute, Director of the Boys and Girls Club in Greenville from 1955 to 1990.

In 1978 Major Jack T. Waters returned to his hometown of Greenville, South Carolina to receive the Distinguished Service Medallion for outstanding work in the Salvation Army. At that time, Major Waters was serving as the Southern Territorial Community Relations and Development Secretary. Mr. Norman Eoute, was the Boys Club executive director.

In 1979 Brigadier and Mrs. Harmon and Ruby Wood Anderson moved to Greenville from their retirement home in Mobile, Alabama after many years of service as officers in the Salvation Army. They are the parents of Mr. Benjamin Anderson, CSM of the Greenville Corps.

Brigadier Harmon Anderson was afflicted with Alzheimer's disease and spent his last days in an acute-care nursing home. Mrs. Brigadier Ruby Anderson lived alone for many years. She was active in Corps work for a number of years before becoming housebound and eventually succumbing at the age of 94. Ben was their caregiver for many years. Both are buried in The Salvation Army Cemetery in Atlanta, Ga.

New Construction

In 1981 a new Thrift Store with a loading dock was constructed on the Rutherford Street property behind the Bruner Chapel.

The cost of construction was $37,873.00. Change orders added another $7207.60, making the total cost of the facility $45,080.60 dollars.

Teach a Kid to Blow a Horn and He'll Never "Blow" a Safe

Major John V. Cole brought a renewed appreciation of brass band music to Greenville.

He was a member of the North and South Carolina Divisional Band and his keen interest in brass music led him to re-establish a working brass section to accompany the singing of hymns in the meetings.

Here excerpted from a copy of The Greenville Daily News is an interview with Major Cole on November 4, 1978.

BRASS BAND CARRIES ON TRADITION

This is the place where the major can put to use one of his loves-brass music. The divisional band usually has 15 members. The instruments are generally provided but all musicians volunteer their time.

"They play every Sunday", Cole said. "Because if you miss (practice) with a brass instrument you can hang it up."

[NOTE: In the very most rigid circles of Salvation Army regulations the Bandmaster has the right to exclude a band member on Sunday if he does not attend the weekly practice, it doesn't happen very often at all these days. rwk]

The kettle and brass band are natural associations with the Salvation Army. The band plays for services and on the streets around the kettles at Christmas time.

Why brass? Cole said the Founder of the Salvation Army—General William Booth—started the brass ensemble because people seemed to pay more attention to loud music. A crowd could be kept under control and he found that brass instruments weathered the elements and stayed in tune better.

(Historical Note) Charles Fry and his three grown sons, who were musicians, initiated Salvation Army brass music in 1878 in Salisbury, England. They had come to the rescue of Captain Arthur Watts and his group who were having trouble with hooligans at an open-air service.

Learning that they were expert musicians, Captain Watts invited them to come along and help with the music. They brought their instruments to the open-air ring to provide music. Their music somehow subdued the crowd and the hooligans were quieted. This pleased the Fry family so much that they joined the Army and dedicated their music making to God.

> Thus started the sojourn of the brass band as the principal mode of music in the Salvation Army. The founder, not willing to let any opportunity to go unexploited, seized on the novel idea and it took off.
>
> —Sallie Chesham, *Born to Battle*

A portion of the same article in the Greenville News of that day mentioned the following information: Mrs. Gladys Whitehead was celebrating her 20th year as a social service worker with the Salvation Army.

- Mr. Fred DeMott was in charge of the transient program and Larry Morgan, who had just returned to Greenville from California, was the houseman.
- The men's dormitory was located in the basement of the administration building.

There was also an announcement posted that Major James Hipps of Richmond, Virginia was scheduled to conduct revival services at the Citadel November 5-12, 1978. Major and Mrs. Hipps are former Corps Officers of the Greenville, SC operation. (1962-1964)

Good Capacity Service

The 1970s and part of the 1980s saw the Salvation Army in Greenville serving in good capacity and making plans for future advances as challenge presented the opportunities.

The Boys and Girls Club building was completed on Owens Street and occupied in 1969. In 1971 the Citadel on Main Street was razed to make way for the Greenville News' expansion project.

In 1975 Cadet Hilda Howell was assigned to Greenville as a summer assignment assistant.

Today Major Hilda Howell is the Retired Officers' Territorial Headquarters representative. She has also served as Divisional Guard Director and Territorial Guard leader before coming to her present position.

Note: Being close enough to the Officers Training School in Atlanta to make day trips, Greenville, SC is often host to a group of Cadets on a “field training” mission. Many future leaders of the Salvation Army have visited here in such capacity. One notable example is Major Vernon Jewett, present Divisional Commander of the North and South Carolina Division.

CHAPTER X
1980-1989
THE QUASI-CENTENNIAL YEAR
"Rouse then Soldiers, Rally 'Round the Banner"

Major and Mrs. John and Alyce Cole continued to serve as Commanding officers to 1984. See previous chapter for the history line 1980-1984.

1984-1988:

- CO: Major John V. and Alyce Cole to June 1984
  Majors Evans (Chief), and Catherine Colbert from June, 1984
- ACO: Lt. and Mrs. Cedric W. McClure 6/15/84-11/7/84
  Lt. Kimberley Smith 6/5/85-1/12/86
- ABC: Earl Stall 1985
  Curtis Kelly 1986
  Hansell Simpson 1987-1989
- BCC: Wally Mullinax, 1987-1989
- LAC: Mrs. Gail Knops, 1984, 1985, 1986, and 1987
- CSM: Charles (Chuck) Mason, appointed 4/19/1988

Note: Since the death of CSM J. W. Street in 1950, the author could find no available official record of an appointed CSM up to this time. Charles (Chuck) Mason was appointed to the position in 1988.

In 1987 Major and Mrs. Robert and Myrtle Beasley Kitchen retired on medical leave from the Salvation Army and subsequently moved to Greenville.

Both resumed activities as members of the Salvation Army as both employees and volunteers for the Army in many capacities. Robert is a real estate owner and Myrtle works in planning and decorating businesses in the city. Two of their children moved to Greenville and are active in the Salvation Army.

Both Robert and Myrtle teach Sunday school classes and Myrtle teaches craft classes at the Boys and Girls Club during the summer season.

Homeless Shelter

Major Evans Colbert reports that during his stay as Corps Officer (1984-1988) the city of Greenville helped him establish, fund, and operate the Salvation Army's overnight homeless shelter in the city.

This was effectively a new program, necessitated by the escalating numbers of the homeless, street-people population at that time.

The regular transient and CSRC facilities were overflowing and there was no room to house the new influx of homeless people.

Following the successful completion of the new and larger facilities, this program was absorbed into the regular social service program and the facilities were used for other programs.

The building is now in use as the youth meeting place and for social programs. It is located just behind the old Bruner recreational building.

1988-1991:

- CO: Majors Evans (Chief) and Catherine Colbert, to June 1988
  Majors Cecil and Elma Blackwell Brodgen, From 6/1988
- ACO: Lieutenant Jacqueline Marie Guillary, 6/4/1989
- ABC: Hansel Simpson 1988
  Harrison Marshall 1989
  Wally Mulinax 1990
- BCC: Jack Watson, 1990-1992
- LAC: Mrs. Elizabeth Gaynor, 1989
- CSM: Charles (Chuck) Mason, appointed 4/19/88

Whereas the year 1988 may have been deemed by some to be the more proper year to officially celebrate the centennial of the opening of the work in Greenville by Captain Fielding and Lieutenant Kaiser in 1888 (January-April), it is doubtful that a celebration was effected at that time. Because 1988 was also a split year for incoming and outgoing commanding officers, a centennial celebration would have been very difficult to plan and execute properly.

Logistical and Tactical Changes

Changes in downtown Greenville made it difficult for the Army to conduct street meetings, and the distance from the new facility on Rutherford Street presented transportation and logistical problems.

Gradually the "street meeting" program began to wane and the Army held its "open air" meetings less often. The new location on Rutherford Street presented new challenges for outreach and service to the community but the Army was hard at work solving the problems and servicing the people with a new set of effective programs.

The complex at Rutherford Street became a venue for new methods of reaching out to the needy. The location change from Broad to Rutherford that started in the fifties was completed in the 70s and 80s.

In 1969, the Boys and Girls Club had moved from Broad Street downtown to a handsome new facility on Owens Street. By the 80s, the Army in Greenville was well on its way to new heights of service to the needy.

The Salvation Army clientele was shifting in all directions from downtown to the outlying districts while the downtown district was taking on a decidedly business-like atmosphere. Office, government, and commercial buildings were replacing residential and manufacturing structures at a rapid rate.

New street traffic and local ordinances hindered the street-meeting program so that it was both dangerous and difficult to conduct open-air services.

Therefore, it was time once again for the Army to fold its tents and go to the area where their services could most benefit the clients and the community at large.

...On they marched.

CHAPTER XI
1990-1999
THE LAST DECADE OF THE TWENTITH CENTURY
"Marching on in the light of God"

Changing the Guard in the Boys and Girls Club

In 1990, Mike Foss transferred from Charlotte, North Carolina as the Executive Director of the Boys Club to the same position with the Greenville Boys Club. He replaced Norman Eoute, who retired from the Club to continue his pastoral ministry.

The name was changed to The Salvation Army Boys and Girls Club to coincide with the name of the Boys and Girls Club of America.

Local Advisors and Other Volunteers

At the beginning of the last decade in the twentieth century, the advisory board roster and the Boys and Girls Club Council consisted of the following:

OFFICERS

Harrison Marshall, Chairman; Mrs. Nancy Sibley, Vice Chairman; U. J. Thompson, Secretary; George Short Jr., Treasurer.

MEMBERS

George Balentine Jr., Robert Booth, Dr. Richard Branyon Jr., James F. Burgess, Mrs. Bobbie Clinkscale, James Cooksey, Richard Eckstrom, Mrs. Elizabeth Gaynor, James M. Gilfillin Sr., Richard Hallyburton, J. Wright Horton, C. Dan Joyner, Curtis Kelly, Mrs. Grace Kisner, Waldo N. Leslie, John Marshall, Ray Michael, Robert Patterson, J. D. Plowden, Elbert Ray, James Sheppard, Raymond Schroeder, A. L. Snipes, Rev. Zoel A. Taylor, Leslie Timms, and Mrs. Betty Walker.

THE BOYS AND GIRLS CLUB OFFICERS

Jack A. Watson, Chairman; James O. Seel Jr., Vice Chairman; Robert Tiedeman Jr., Secretary; Wallace Mullinax Jr., Treasurer.

MEMBERS

John Ashmore Jr., Terry Cooper, Charles Groves, Douglas Harper, Ben Harvey, Walter Heape, James F. Harrison Jr., Thomas Henderson, Gardner Hendrix, Ron Jones, Harold Lollis, William Norris, Reginald Person, Mrs. Alva R. Phillips, Samuel T. Piper, Leroy Shelton, E. Roy Stone, Jr., and Joe Watson.

1991-1998

- CO: Captain and Mrs. Cecil and Elma Blackwell Brogden, to June 1991
  Captain and Mrs. R. Curtis and Gail Mikles Fleeman, from June, 1991
- ACO: None Appointed
- ABC: Harrison Marshall, 1991
  Elbert Ray, 1993
- BCC: Sam Piper, 1993-1995
  Al Phillips, 1996-1997
  Carlisle Rogers, 1998-1999
- LAC: Mrs. Evelyn Brady, 1992
- CSM: Charles (Chuck) Mason

In June of 1991, Ray Patro was sworn in as a Soldier of the Salvation Army. He came through the CSRC program and married Patricia Dunn, a Soldier since 1979 and an employee since 1988. Patricia was sworn-in as a soldier in Wilmington, North Carolina and moved to Greenville to work for Major Cecil Brodgen who was the Corps officer in Greenville at that time. Ray was the thrift store warehouse supervisor and had been president of the Men's Fellowship Club. Both were active in the corps as volunteer leaders.

In 2003 Mr. and Mrs. Patro moved to Wilmington, North Carolina and took up similar positions in the Salvation Army there.

Training for Officership

Although not listed as being assigned in the official register as assistants, the following Cadets and Corps Helpers sojourned here for a short time according to Majors R. C. and Gail Fleeman who were the Corps Officers during that time.

According to Major Fleeman, the following Cadets were stationed in Greenville during the summers they were Officers: George Hackbarth, 1991; Greg and Sylvia Franks, 1992; Tom and Julie Louden, 1993; Phil Heath, 1996.

Additionally, Tianne Mull served as a Corps helper from 1994-1995, and Bernice Knott as a Corps Helper in 1997.

(Major Fleeman added that although Gail's mother, Irene Baugh Mikles, never served in Greenville as an appointed officer, she lived with her sister and brother-in-law, Captain and Mrs. Robert Burchett, and graduated from Greenville High School in 1946 or 1947.)

Shifting the Nuance/Keeping the Substance

With the arrival of the new Salvation Army Corps Officers in 1991, the Army in Greenville began to take on a decidedly quasi-modernistic religious mode of programming in the hopes of attracting contemporary and youthful membership. Both Captain R. C. and Gail Fleeman were talented musicians and leaders.

Blending with the standard Salvation Army methods, this new system both enhanced the new and reinforced the old traditional Salvation Army meetings.

Community Relations

The Salvation Army's social service and community work grew and gained favor with the local leaders.

Under the leadership of the Advisory Board and the Commanding Officer, great strides were made to enlarge and enhance the service capacity of The Salvation Army.

In the middle 1990s, the Greenville Salvation Army Corps Band, under the direction of Bandmaster Mike Fletcher provided preliminary music for the annual Greenville Symphony Orchestra Christmas concert on West Broad and South Main Streets.

The band assembled outside the Peace Center for the Performing Arts at Broad and Main Streets and provided an outdoor Christmas carol musical concert as the patrons entered the building for the main concert.

Ninety Years Strong

In 1994 the Corps Officers, Captain and Mrs. R. C. and Gail Fleeman, and others commemorated the 90th year of continuous operation of the Salvation Army in Greenville.

A celebration was planned and memorabilia, including coffee mugs with the 90th year inscription, was distributed. Special emphasis was given to the Bruner Home program. A number of former "Bruners" were assembled and honored by the Corps during the annual Corps homecoming celebration.

The "grown-up" Bruners in 1994/Captain and Mrs. R. C. Fleeman and their children right center.

Building up the Temple of the Lord

- In 1997 a new dining building was constructed on the Rutherford Street property at a cost of $175,000.00. This building was dedicated to the memory of Mary C. Davidson and bears her name on the outside and on a plaque in the dining area.
- A new lodging facility for men was completed at a cost of $620,000.00 along with renovations of the women's shelter at a cost of $432,000.00.
- Additionally, in the same year a new thrift store and warehouse were completed on Rutherford Street in front and Buncombe Street in the rear in the 200 block of Rutherford Street. The total cost of this facility was $689,200.00.
- The existing facilities of the thrift store and warehouse were converted to a senior citizen program facility at a cost of $432.000.00.
- Construction was begun on the men's dormitory building on the West End of the Rutherford Street property.

Note: The funds to construct these new and renovated facilities was raised by the Advisory Board, Auxiliaries, and Councils, and by endowments provided by the citizens of Greenville over a several year period. There are no outstanding property mortgages.

Major R. C. Fleeman was elected president of the Homeless Coalition of Greenville. This organization is made up of service providers to the homeless and advocates for better care of the homeless in the metropolitan area of upstate South Carolina.

A "Calling to Service"

Early in the the 1990s, one of the promising young members of the Corps was moved to apply for admission to the Salvation Army's College for officers' training.

Mr. Robert (Robbie) Davis was accepted as an officer candidate (Cadet) and attended the College for Officers' Training in Atlanta, GA and is now a Salvation Army officer serving in the North and South Carolina Division.

In 1993 Major and Mrs. Raymond and Hope Casarez Kitchen retired to Greenville, SC and joined the Corps as Soldiers. Both served as musicians and taught Soldiership Classes for recruits and prospective Soldiers.

At the present time both are active in the Salvation Army. Both serve on the Corps Council and Raymond serves as an Advisory Board member.

A New Corps is Born

On November 13,1994 the Service Unit in Seneca, SC was dedicated as a full fledged Corps operation. From 1974 to 1994 the Service unit was operated under the direction of the Greenville, South Carolina Corps.

The Corps Officer in Seneca was Sergeant Henry F. Houston. Local Officers were Frances Mobley, Home league secretary and Sunday school teacher; Bonnie Mobley, Welcome Sergeant; Irma Lane, League of Mercy secretary; Carolyn Schmidt, Corps pianist; and Heather Slaza, Sunday school teacher. All were sworn in as Soldiers and commissioned as Local Officers.

Junior Soldiers added were Brittany Houston, Kahley Houston, and Whitney Houston.

Mr. Charles Oglesby served as Chairman of the Advisory Board and Mr. Norman Crain, County Supervisor, represented the community leadership at the installation.

The Greenville, SC Corps Officers were Captains R. C. and Gail Fleeman.

The Divisional Commander who conducted the installation and opening ceremony was Lt. Colonel David Mikles. He is descended from Captain Eva Bivans (Later, Mikles), 1924 CO of Greenville.

Following is the historical progression of this Service Unit-to-Corps journey.

HISTORY OF SENECA, SOUTH CAROLINA CORPS

Brigadier Alfred Davey, Retired, opened the work of the Salvation Army in Seneca, SC in 1974 by organizing a Service Unit that operated under the Greenville South Carolina Corps.

The work continued under Mrs. Phyllis Kitchen Anderson until June 1991. In June 1991 Major Glenna West was appointed to open a new Service Center responsible for Oconee County and Pickens County, South Carolina. During the tenure of Major Glenna West, facilities were secured at 625 East North First Street.

In June 1992 Captain and Mrs. Frank Ross were appointed as the Commanding Officers of the Seneca, South Carolina Service Unit.

In November, Major and Mrs. John (Genelle) Sipe, retired, were appointed pro-tem in command of the work.

In January 1993, Sergeant Henry Ford Houston was appointed as the Corps Administrator for Oconee and Pickens County with headquarters in Seneca.

In October 1993, the old thrift store on 625 East North First Street was moved to its present location at 304 East North First Street. The Service Center continued to grow and as a result, the Seneca and Easley organizations were separated in January, 1994 with new officers being placed in charge of the work in Pickens County (Easley).

New living quarters were purchased for the Corps Administrator and his family in September 1994.

An Advisory Board was organized on October 5, 1994 with Charles Oglesby as Chairman. The Territorial Commander approved the opening of the Seneca Corps on October 3, 1994.

Reinforcements

- In 1995 Mrs. Ozella Beckford (Becky) joined the Salvation Army as a Soldier. Her husband Kenneth remained with the Baptist church. She is presently serving as a Thrift Store operator and leader of youth and senior units.
- Mr. James Todd was enrolled on the same date and is presently serving as a truck driver and is active in the Salvation Army as an usher in the services and a volunteer worker.
- A number of young people who were Junior Soldiers were transferred to the senior soldier rolls and added to the strength of the Army in Greenville over the years. Additional Junior Soldier recruits were added yearly.
- Additional adult recruits were enrolled, and some dropped out as the Army grew and prospered in the city.

The "swearing in" of new soldiers and recruits is an ongoing process in every city and it adds depth and strength to the Army's profile and scope of service.

The soldier-membership roster in Greenville hovers around 100-150 from year to year.

The outreach program volunteers number in the thousands in most major and mid-size cities. It is not unusual for nearly the entire community to join with the Salvation Army in relief efforts at certain times of the year and when disaster strikes.

In 1997 Miss Bernice Knott came to Greenville from England. She transferred her membership to the Greenville

Corps. She came to the United States on a work visa as a nanny for a family living in Greenville. She entered the College for Officers Training in 1998 and is now Captain Bernice Knott.

After serving in several appointments in the USA, she was transferred back to England and is now serving in that country as a United States Officer on loan in her native land.

Steve and Kathryn (Kathi) Kazimer moved to Greenville from the Eastern Territory and were accepted as Soldiers in Greenville in 1996.

Steve transferred and Kathi attended the Soldiers' class and was enrolled at that time and sworn-in as a Soldier. Kathi became employed as the Corps Welfare Secretary and Steve volunteered in the Corps in the music Department and the Men's Fellowship Club as well as doing the youth work. Both added new dynamics to the Corps program, especially in the religious/music/youth section. In 2002 the Kazimer family transferred to the Anderson, South Carolina Corps.

In 1998 Brigadier Marie Kitchen moved to Greenville as a retired officer. Her health prevented her from being active in the Army's work in Greenville. She was promoted to Glory (died) in 2001.

FAREWELL, OLD FRIEND, YOU HAVE SERVED YOUR COMMUNITY WELL

In this decade the Women's Auxiliary, which was formed in 1938 as the Red Shield Auxiliary, was disbanded due to the changing scene of services and programming of the Boys and Girls Club and the Corps Youth Programs.

The new array of services in Greenville did not lend themselves well to the huge citywide programming provided so effectively by the Auxiliary in years past.

It is noted that the Advisory Board and the Boys and Girls Club Council have been expanded to include women from all walks of life in leadership positions in the Army's civilian volunteer boards.

During the lifetime of the Greenville Salvation Army Women's Auxiliary organization literally hundreds of Greenville's finest female citizens gave forceful credence to the Founder's claim, "Some of my best men are women."

The Salvation Army in Greenville will eternally owe a debt of gratitude to the women who served in the Women's Auxiliary so effectively and faithfully to provide unique and attractive venues of service to the youth of our community in the years from 1938 to 1998.

Women's Auxiliary of Greenville c.1953/representative of sixty years of auxiliary service in Greenville-1938-1998.

In June 1998 when Major and Mrs. R. C. and Gail Mikles Fleeman and their children were transferred to Florida, a huge crowd gathered to bid them a sad, yet fond, farewell.

Amateur videotape was produced to record the event and to show appreciation to the Corps officers who had given so much and extracted so little from the community.

In November 1998 the Assistant Officer's quarters were listed as 1608 Pinecroft Drive, Taylors, SC.

CHAPTER XII
2000-2004
THE DAWN OF A NEW CENTURY and CELEBRATION
"Come, Oh Come with Me, Where Love is Beaming"

1998-2001:

- CO: Major and Mrs. R. Curtis and Gail Mikles Fleeman, to June 1998
  Captain and Mrs. Michael and Judy O'Bryan Vincent, From June 1998
- ACO: Lieutenant and Mrs. Dean and Pamela Mortez, 6/1999-6/2000
- ABC: Graham Profitt 2000-2001
  Ben Crider 2001
- BCC: John Baker 2000-2001
  Duke McCall, Jr. 2001
- CSM: Charles (Chuck) Mason

During this recorded partial decade (2000-2004) the International Officer ranking system has begun to change by order of the General.

All Cadets are now to be commissioned with the rank of Captain (instead of Lieutenant).

The rank of Lieutenant is reserved for short time and part time "field commissioned" officers. The rank can also lead to full Officer rank in some cases.

This change effectively does away with the previous ranks of Auxiliary Captain and other designations. Provisions are made for Soldiers in good standing, if desired, to apply and be accepted for temporary officership and married people can now be commissioned separately from their spouses, if desired. (Special considerations are necessary.)

There are other changes in the structure to simplify the ranking system and allow for ease of assignment and transfer of officers to and from the field and between the field and non-officer status.

In 2002 the "Board" memberships of the Corps "church" programs were changed to reflect more accurately the duties and responsibilities of the (church) boards and Councils.

The Corps Council membership roster and scope was changed to reflect the addition of ex-officio members and related duties involved in the Council.

The "Senior Census Board" was renamed the "Senior Pastoral Care Council" to reflect broader duties and responsibilities of the group. Membership was changed to reflect the added qualifications of membership and responsibilities.

The Young Peoples Census Board was changed to the Young People's Pastoral Care Council to address added responsibilities in dealing with youth memberships.

Changes and Renovations in Greenville

On the local front some finishing touches were added to the social service buildings in the compound on Rutherford Street.

- Some parking and walking areas were paved and new fences built.
- The men's dormitory, which was started in the previous administration, was completed and occupied. Additions and improvements were made to the Officers' living quarters.
- The Administration building was upgraded and outfitted to allow for more efficient traffic and control of employees and clients.
- The old Bruner Home recreational building (built in 1932) was transformed and upgraded in appearance inside and out to provide a church-like operation to accommodate the evolving religious model being introduced to the Corps families and young people.

- New staff members were hired and new program directors were engaged to lead the newly instituted order of service.
- Some new thrift stores were established and operated in several outlying areas.

A new plan for a women's dormitory began to take shape as a part of the overall master plan developed by the long range planning committee of the Advisory Board and the Corps Officers. This addition was to be constructed on an unused portion of the compound on Rutherford Street.

The Women and Children's shelter is presently housed in the lower level of the Administration building where the dining area was recently located.

There are no addresses listed as Assistant Officer's quarters. As of 2003, there are no Assistant Officers assigned to Greenville, although "Corps Helpers" and program employees are engaged as needed to carry on the work inside and outside the compound.

2001-Present

- CO: Captain and Mrs. Michael and Judy O'Bryan Vincent to June 2001; Major and Mrs. Stanley and Carlene Cox Melton from June 2001
- ABC: Ben Crider
- BCC: Duke McCall
- CSM: Charles (Chuck) Mason to January 2002
Benjamin (Ben) Anderson, from January 2002

In January 2002 the Corps Sergeant Major Charles (Chuck) Mason was honorably retired from that position because of illness. Chuck is a leader of men and an example of sterling Salvationism at the lay level.

Having grown up in the Salvation Army and participated in most of the programs he is uniquely suited to command the respect and admiration of both the Social Service/ rehabilitation participants and the Corps Community Center section of operations.

His love for the Army is exceeded only by his love for his Lord. He is the husband of Mrs. Sharon Anderson Mason, a descendent of the original CSM, Roland Smith. Chuck now enjoys the title of the "retired" Corps Sergeant Major. He has served as Corps Sergeant Major since 1988. Benjamin Anderson replaced him.

The newly appointed Corps Sergeant Major is a former Salvation Army Officer who has lived in Greenville more than twenty years and has been a faithful Soldier and leader of Army programs both as a Soldier and a commissioned Officer for many years. He is a retired employee from The City of Greenville's budget and finance division.

Stewardship Report (Annual Civic Salute)

At this Annual Report meeting Wendy Willis, Miss South Carolina, 1998 gave the principal address. According the program notes, she has a love for God and a desire to make a difference for Jesus Christ. Wendy has a Bachelor of Arts degree in speech and communications with a music minor from Clemson University.

Current Command Structure

Following is the listed USA Salvation Army Territorial commands and a partial listing of operational centers:

International Headquarters, London, England
International Commander, Rank General

National Headquarters, Alexandria, Virginia
National Commander, Rank Commissioner

Western Territorial Headqtrs, Long Beach, California
Territorial Commander, Rank Commissioner

Central Territorial Headquarters, Des Plaines, Illinois
Territorial Commander, Rank Commissioner

Eastern Territorial Headquarters, West Nyack, NY

Territorial Commander, Rank Commissioner

Southern Territorial Headquarters, Atlanta, Georgia

Territorial Commander, Rank Commissioner

North and South Carolina Divisional Headquarters

Charlotte, North Carolina

Divisional Commander, Rank varies

Divisional Corps/CSRC centers

All major and secondary Cities in the Division

Corps Officer, Rank varies

The Army Surrounding the Salvation Army

The Salvation Army Advisory Board membership roster in the year 2001-2002 listed in the Annual Report to the community of 2001 (dated May 14, 2002)

Greenville Advisory Board Officers' Roster

Graham Profitt, Chairman; Ben Crider, Vice Chairman; Robert Jones, Secretary; Judy Powell, Assistant Secretary; and Roy Chamlee, Treasurer.

Advisory Board Members

Tim Brett, Chuck Brewer, Janice Butler, Claire Carter, Roy Chamlee III, Dave Chesson, Melvin Davis, Judge Ralph Drake, Monty DuPuy, Dan Foster, Elizabeth Gaynor, Earle T. Harding, Granville Hicks, Matt Hunt, Robert Jones, Curtis Kelly, Earl Lewers, Alvin McCall, Hap Marshall, Paulette Murphy, Joe Pearce, Judy Powell, Elbert Ray, Rex Rice, Jane Shaw, Jim Sheppard, Arthur Snipes, Jim Stovall, Gary Strickland, Zoel Taylor, Mike Thomason, U. J. Thompson, Elton Todd

NOTE: The Boys and Girls Club Council roster is listed in the Chapter dedicated to that unit of Greenville Salvation Army operation.

In 2001-02 a balanced Salvation Army Corps program was in operation. Mainstream Salvation Army programs and ideological models were established both in the religious and the social programming.

Educationally and spiritually qualified employees and religious leaders were hired and engaged to work with the social service programs and religious/character-building programs.

Neighborhood family participation was encouraged and young people from the community were invited to participate in the operation of the Army's programs.

The religious meetings took on traditionally modeled content identified with the church services of the day and The Salvation Army oriented operational methods.

In 2002, Major and Mrs. David and Jeanette Lane Jones retired from divisional headquarters appointments and moved to Greenville as their retirement home.

Both Majors David and Jeanette Lane Jones are active in the Corps programs and in divisional functions. Both serve on the *Corps Council and David serves on the **Advisory Board.

They are the parents of Chana Jones Fletcher (Corps Cadet Counselor and Corps Pianist) who is the wife of Michael Fletcher (Bandmaster of the Corps band and Assistant Corps Treasurer).

*Corps Council

Briefly, this body consists of certain members of the Salvation Army religious/character-building community of leaders and the Corps Officers. Its function is to advise the Corps Officer on matters concerning the religious and character-building activities carried on within the Corps center.

** Advisory Board

Generally speaking, this is a body of local business and professional community leaders who advise the Salvation Army Corps Officer on all matters pertaining to the operation of The Salvation Army in the community. They represent the Army's operations to the public and work for the overall good of the community through the Salvation Army.

PLANNING FOR THE FUTURE

In 2002 and 2003 several significant ventures were initiated and began to grow into viable building blocks within the community.

- The 2025 vision initiative was undertaken by the Greenville Chamber of Commerce and the citizens under the chairmanship of Dr. David Shi, President of Furman University. This is a follow-up of *Max Heller's plan of twenty-five years ago which has produced most of the catalyst for growth of the city up to this time.
- Max Heller arrived in Greenville in 1938 as a refugee from the persecution in Europe. He became Mayor of the city and is credited as the driving force of the revitalization of downtown Greenville.
- United Way of Greenville County, under the chairmanship of Mrs. Susan Shi, wife of Dr. David Shi instituted its new Initiatives plan to design a new method of assessing needs and allocating funds to member agencies.
- Under the Chairmanship of Ben Crider, The Advisory Board of The Salvation Army in an ongoing needs assessment study began to formulate plans for expansion and improving its methods and scope of providing relief assistance to the community in light of changing demographic and population trends.
- A needs assessment study was begun by Walter Coles Consultants to determine the area and scope of services needed by the Salvation Army in the community.
- As a result of the study by the Walter Coles group and in light of several fast-breaking events involving the main properties of the Salvation Army in Greenville a new feasibility initiative is scheduled for the near future. This initiative will determine the plan and direction of a more effective Salvation Army operation in the community.

The Chamber of Commerce, the United Way, and the Salvation Army initiatives, although independent of each other, are in the formative stage and committees are working to increase and enhance the delivery of services to the community on a countywide plane.

The Centennial Stewardship Report

On May 13, 2003 The Salvation Army presented its annual report to the community of activities conducted in 2002.

The principal speaker was Commissioner Fred Ruth, the Salvation Army's representative to the United Nations since January 1, 2001.

Commissioner Ruth has been elected the United Nations NGO (Non-Government Organizations) Executive Board and heads the resources committee. He is a retired Salvation Army Officer. During his 45 years as an Officer in The Salvation Army his United States appointments included Columbus, Georgia; Charlotte, North Carolina; Atlanta, Georgia; Washington, D. C.; and Los Angeles, California. His overseas appointments included Seoul, Korea; London, England; Singapore, and Sydney, Australia.

The Civilian Arm of the Salvation Army

The Advisory Board roster going into the year 2003 and the last to be listed in this century of service is as follows:

Officers

Ben Crider, Chairman; Roy Chamlee III, Vice Chairman; Robert Jones, Secretary; Judy Powell, Assistant Secretary; and Earl Harding, Treasurer.

Members

Tim Brett, Charles Brewer Jr., Janice Butler, Claire Carter, Melvin Davis, Judge Ralph Drake (Recently deceased), Monty Dupuy, Don foster, Bill Fuller, Clark Gaston, Elizabeth Gaynor, Matt Good, Kevin Hatch, Betty Hedgepath, Granville Hicks, Reid Hipp, Brian Holden, J. Wright Horton, Mat Hunt, Curtis Kelly, Earl Lewers, Alvin McCall, Harrison Marshall, Paulette Murphy, Joe Pearce, Graham Proffitt, Elbert Ray, Rex Rice, Jane Shaw, James Sheppard, Arthur Snipes, James Stovall, Gary Strickland, Zoel Taylor, U. J. Thompson, and Elton Todd

The Salvation Army Boys and Girls Club Council Roster

Duke McCall Jr., Chairman; Greg Jansen, Vice Chairman; Amber Richards, Secretary; and Jack H. Watson, Treasurer

Members

John E. Austin, John Baker, Tony Barnhill, Brodie Brigman, Johnny Mack Brown, Richard L. Crain, Jim Freeland, Alva Phillips, Sam Piper, Labarbara Sampson, Linda Kelly, Rita Smith, and Mike Spivey.

Advisory Board members assigned to the Boys/Girls Club Council: Janice Butler, Ben Crider, Earle Harding

Ex-Officio Members: Ben Crider

Salvation Army Personnel attached to the Council: Major Stanley Melton/Captain Greg Davis, Corps Officer, Major Pete Costas, Jr.

Divisional Boys and Girls Club/Community Centers Director: Thomas Michael Foss, Boys and Girls Club Director

The annual report listed services provided as:

43,567 nights shelter
100,568 meals
330 items of furniture and household items given
13,599 items of clothing given
46 medicine prescriptions
65 rental assistance
1,513 referrals for long term assistance
5,276 food boxes...
860 utilities paid...
159 transportation assistance
40,336 toys...
662 worship services with 22,659 in attendance...
468 visits to nursing homes with 4,672 persons for 1.394 hours...
96 campers and 70 days camping time...
644 youth and adult session of character building with 24,347 attending.
3,409 volunteers gave a total of 9,833 hours of service.

The Boys and Girls Club reported 1,907 children enrolled and in attendance at the club and 555 children enrolled in the smart centers.

The Annual Financial Report

The total budget for the Salvation Army in Greenville in 2002 was as follows:

PREVIOUS BALANCE FORWARD	**$520,030**
INCOME	
Public Support	**$1,290,989**
Internal Support	**$255,752**
Government	**$61,438**
United Way	**$268,521**
TOTAL EXPENSE	**$4,090,323**
Excess (Deficiency) of Revenue & Expense	**($54,088)**
END OF YEAR FUND BALANCE	**$465,942**

PREVIOUS BALANCE FORWARD	**$520,030**
INCOME	
CSRC	**$1,620,559**
Boys & Girls Clubs (incl $362,016 from the United Way)	**$538,976**
TOTAL INCOME	**$3,991,469**
EXPENSE	
Programs and Supporting Services	
Staff Compensation/Professional Fees	**$686,725**
Other Programs/General Expenses	**$1,256,871**
Payment to Supervising Headquarters	**$107,235**
CSRC	**$1,398,517**
Boys & Girls Club	**$640,975**
TOTAL EXPENSE	**$4,090,323**
Excess (Deficiency) of Revenue & Expense	**($54,088)**
END OF YEAR FUND BALANCE	**$465,942**

The Annual Report from any year contains pertinent and informative information including photographs of current activities of the program participants and new or updated facilities or special accomplishments.

It also lists names of volunteers and others that have given outstanding service to the community in the past year through the medium of the Salvation Army. It is the Salvation Army's method of keeping the general public appraised of the current work in the community.

A general statement of thanksgiving is given on behalf of the needy citizens who have been served through the great heart of the public.

The Fletcher Family

The Fletcher family name goes back to the early 1930s in Greenville Salvation Army circles.

Mike Fletcher is an entrepreneurial businessman, who seves on the Territorial Soldiers Advisory Committee and is a member of the Territorial Songster Brigade. His wife, Chana Jones Fletcher is a schoolteacher and businesswoman, as well as the Corps Cadet Counselor, Sunday school teacher, and Corps pianist. She is the "official greeter" of all new incoming officers to the City.

Moiedna Fletcher was born in 1871 but was not enrolled as a Salvation Army Soldier until 1930. The Fletcher family has been in the area from before the beginning of the SA in Greenville (1888) but it is uncertain if they were connected to the Corps at that early date.

Following is the family tree of the Fletcher family who were/are members of the Greenville Corps:

Children of Michael and Chana Jones Fletcher: Generation VI

Caleb Fletcher: Born March 28, 1988-J/S-S/S
Caitlin Fletcher: Born March 25, 1990-J/S
Zachary Fletcher: Born February 3, 1993-J/S

Children of David and Cathy Fletcher Smith: Generation VI:

Clayton Allen Smith: Born June 11, 1983-J/S, S/S
Haley Catherine Smith; Born July 2, 1986-J/S, S/S
Logan Hunter Smith: Born March 30, 1993-Cradle Roll

Fletcher Generation V

Michael Fletcher: Born November 12, 1957-J/S, S/S, L/O
Married/Chana Jones Fletcher: Born July 30, 1961-J/S, S/S, L/O

Catherine Fletcher Smith: Born January 18, 1961-J/S, S/S, L/O
Married/David Allen Smith (Not a Soldier)

Fletcher Generation IV

Talmadge Eugene (Chuck) Fletcher: Born 7/14/37, J/S 1/1/46, S/S 5/25/52.PTG 5/6/91

Ruby Fletcher McCoin: Born 3/2/36, J/S 9/26/43, S/S 4/15/51, Ex/S 10/75

William Fletcher: Born 10/14/33, J/S 4/20/43. S/S 5/5/49 Ex/S 4/23/84

Evelyn Mae Fletcher Estep: Born 8/15/32, J/S 4/23/43, S/S 4/4/49, ex/S 2/9/56

Fletcher Generation III

Alice Rebecca Fletcher Craft: Born 9/14/15, S/S 11/16/30, PTG 2/11/91

O. P. Fletcher: Born 1/29/04, S/S 1/1/46 Married/Montez (Smilie)

Mahaffey Fletcher: Born 2/14/07, S/S, 1/1/46. She served as the Corps YPSM for many years.

Fletcher Generation II

William Harrison Fletcher: Born 8/5/1895, S/S 1/1/46, Soldiership transferred to St Petersburg, FL 1/28/59 Married/Mary L. Atkison Fletcher: Born, 10/4/1912, S/S 8/4/1929, Company Guard/YPSM 1930, Soldiership transferred to St Petersburg FL 1/28/59

Fletcher Generation I

Mrs. Moiedna Fletcher: Born 7/21/1871, S/S, 1/16/30, (S&G 12/16/57, PTG Date unknown)

TERROR FROM THE SKIES

September 11, 2001 will undoubtedly be the sounding date for Americans for years to come. It is the date of a massive and deadly terrorist attack on America. A group of terrorists hijacked airliners and crashed two of them into the twin towers of the World Trade Center in New York killing 2823 people.

At the same time, terrorists flew another plane into the Pentagon in Washington, DC killing a total of 125 people. In a third attack, passengers on another flight managed to overtake the hijackers crashing the plane into a field in Pennsylvania to abort another planned attack on Washington. This action resulted in the civilized world's declaration of a war on terror around the globe.

Defining Moment for The Salvation Army

It was another defining moment in the ability of The Salvation Army to provide massive and instant service to the citizens of our great country.

Almost from the start, the Army was on the scene of each location with spiritual aid and comfort for the thousands of victims and volunteer workers on site. Major Stanley Melton, Corps Officer of Greenville, SC immediately went to the Washington DC area where he served with other Salvation Army personnel as a crisis counselor for the rescue workers and victims at the Pentagon. He remained at that post for nearly two weeks before being relieved by other Salvation Army personnel.

Hundreds of Salvation Army workers and counselors worked long, hard hours dealing with the horrible aftermath of the attacks.

High Praise, Indeed

A police Officer from Greenville, SC was among the volunteer rescue workers. Rita Seaborn, the victim/witness coordinator for the Greenville Police Department filed the following report in the *National Salvation Army War Cry* on July 8, 2002.

> "I am a law enforcement Officer with the Greenville police Department in South Carolina. Because of my training with the National Organization of Victim Assistance (NOVA), I spent a week working at Ground Zero in New York. The work was difficult and very sad. But the uplifting moments came at the hands of many Salvation Army workers assigned there. I have never before been so privileged as to be among so many dedicated kind and caring people as those representing the Salvation Army.
>
> Many times I found myself watching them move among the devastation and embedded sorrow with such peace and commitment. I would be wishing that I 'had what they had.'
>
> I have long come to depend on our local Salvation army shelter for assistance with those whose lives are disrupted due to crime or their own mistakes. I know that through them help and advice is always available.
>
> But I never realized how far-reaching the generosity of the Salvation army is until I first walked into the ground zero dome and saw hundreds of police officers firemen, paramedics, and construction workers eating a much needed hot meal served up by smiling Salvation army workers. At the 'Hard Hat Café' I witnessed workers continually enter for dry socks, bandages, or bottled water and mostly for a kind and supportive word.
>
> Once when my own heart had been broken completely by a particularly sorrowful story, two Salvation Army volunteers recognized my deep sadness, and I was on the receiving end of their soft, gentle words, their compassion and courage. It was a good and comforting place to be.
>
> These men and women from the Salvation army whom I was honored to meet came from all across the United States and Canada to help everyone at ground zero. They put their lives on hold for awhile to make the lives of strangers a little better. Although surely they

> were tired and sad and longing for their own homes, I never saw a frown or heard a sharp word from anyone. They were simply the best in all that they did.
>
> When a rumor (that proved to be false) surfaced that The Army would be leaving, the recovery teams, the police and fire personnel and the workers were extremely hurt and worried. The tent had become their home away from home, a refuge amid the ruins, and the Salvation army workers their family and support.
>
> My stay at ground zero was far too brief and I sadly left knowing there was much more to be done. But I hugged so many new friends and whispered through my tears my good-byes, and just before I took that final step from the door of the tent, I took one last look back. There, just as when I had arrived, I saw tired men and women eating a hot meal and wonderful men and women wearing red jackets moved among them offering encouragement, nourishment, supportive words and a smile. And I wondered, just what is it that they have?"[iii]

This scenario of emergency service which is replicated hundreds of times throughout the world in greater or smaller measure from year to year gives dramatic impact to the presence and purpose of The Salvation Army in the eyes of the public.

"Go Ye into All the World and Preach the Gospel to Every Creature"

In 2001 prospective officer candidates Matthew and Rebecca Steadham Trayler were appointed to the Greenville Corps by the Divisional Commander as "Corps Helpers" to prepare for training at the College for Officers Training (CFOT). They were accepted as Candidates for Officership on February 20, 2002. This is the preliminary stage of training of Salvation Army Officers.

Officer Candidates Matthew and Rebecca Trayler
with baby Trayler.

Michele and John Robbins and their children/Majors Robbins
(parents) and Melton (Corps Officers) in background.

At about the same time another couple, Mr. and Mrs. John and Michelle Norris Robbins were preparing for entry into the CFOT.

Michelle is a native of Greenville and a former officer who resigned her commission to marry John. John will attend the CFOT and Michelle will assist in the Army's programming system until his commissioning. John's residence is in Greenwood, SC with his retired Salvation Army parents, Major and Mrs. James and Patricia Smith Robbins. Michelle's home is in Greenville.

Visions of the Future

Presently, the Advisory Board's Needs Assessment Committee, an ongoing committee, is studying the current work of Greenville with an eye on a new capital campaign to expand and improve the Social Service and Corps/Religious-character building programs.

Centennial Celebration

On January 11, 2002 the Centennial Celebration Committee was formed with Major Raymond Kitchen, retired, as chairman to draw up a plan for the 2004 Centennial Celebration

On June 30, 2002 a final report and suggested plan for the centennial celebration was delivered for further study and implementation or revision. A copy of that report can be found in the appendix.

Replacements for Candidates Sent to Training

In August 2002 Mr. and Mrs. Rob and Monica Barber were engaged to work as Corps helpers and Youth Leaders in the Greenville, South Carolina operation. Both are Salvation Army soldiers who formally attended the College for Officers Training.

September of 2002 saw yet another Soldier transferee to the Greenville Corps. Mr. and Mrs. Ronald, Jr. and

Terri Green became active and Ronald's Soldiership was transferred. He is active in the Corps band program. Terri is not a Soldier but joined the fellowship of the Corps and was employed in the accounting department.

Ronald Green is the son of Major and Mrs. Ronald, Sr. and Doris Green who are retired and living in Florida.

Horror Revisited

On September 11, 2002 the City of Greenville held a memorial service to commemorate the terrorist attack on America. The Greenville Daily News filed a report under the heading, "Tears, cheers, remember victims, terror war with troops."'

A part of the article includes an interview with Mr. William Kapp, a crisis counselor with the Salvation Army. It follows:

> Salvation army crisis counselor William Kapp, who spent 10 days at ground zero with New York City firemen, was there because he needed closure.
>
> They were among the thousands of upstate residents who filled more than half the stadium in Greenville Wednesday night to mark the one-year anniversary of the terrorist attack on America.
>
> Kapp and those who took blood to New York City were thanked by the crowd for their volunteer service after the attack.
>
> Kapp, who has traveled around the nation and the world helping in disaster relief for 31 years with the Salvation Army, sat with firefighters from the South Greenville Fire Department.
>
> "I'm sitting with these guys because they represent the best America's got", he said.
>
> As tears welled up in his eyes, he said "remembering what he saw at ground zero has been hard for him during the past year. He still has nightmares and becomes emotional when he passes a local fireman on the street.

It goes without saying that on that day, there were commemorative services all around the City of Greenville and, in fact, all around the nation and the entire civilized world. The theme "We Will Never Forget" aptly describes the mood of the people remembering the tragic event and heroes, who were many and varied on that day and the days to follow, as well as the challenge to the perpetrators of the cowardly attack upon our nation.

In addition to the extraordinary service after the disaster of 9/11, The Salvation Army never missed a beat in the ongoing programs of service to the communities all around the world. Such is the heart of the hundreds of thousands of Salvation Army Officers, Laypersons, employees, and volunteers that serve humanity in every corner of the globe under the red, yellow, and blue banner.

Bonds Uniting Americans Grow Stronger Each Day

Appearing in *The Greenville News* on Saturday September 23, 2001 was a moving tribute by Mr. Knapp to the heroes and heroines of the September 11 tragedy and the unity and courageous resilience of the American people. The article ended with, "We are strong, free, a united nation, a nation under God."

Another Corps is Born

The creation of the Service Unit program in 1928 (see timeline 1928) provided Salvation Army programming to rural communities all over the United States of America. It has spawned the establishment of full time Corps Centers in some of the communities.

Two notable examples in the Greenville area are Easley and Seneca, South Carolina. Both are now functional Corps centers serving their respective communities with Officers appointed to administer the work, Advisory Boards, and Soldiers.

Seneca, SC was captioned a Corps on Sunday November 13, 1994.

On Sunday, December 1, 2002, the Salvation Army Service Unit in Easley, South Carolina dedicated the Official Corps building at 501 Old Liberty Road as a full-fledged Corps.

In keeping with the updated terminology the Corps building is referred to as "The Center of Worship and Service" denoting the duality of the program of The Salvation Army.

The Service Unit program has operated since early 1974 under the leadership of the Greenville Corps and the Divisional Office.

In 1998 A/Captain and Mrs. Gene and Minnie Harrell were appointed to the Service Unit as Commanding Officers.

They set to work creating the Corps operation as a bona-fide Salvation Army entity.

The Dedication Program was as follows:

Band Ensemble: NSC Division Music Department
B/M David Dawes and Major Pete D. Costas. Jr.
Vocal Offering: "Find us Faithful": Major Alice Bell,
Associate Director Women's Ministries NASCD.
Leader: Major Mark Bell General Secretary NASC DIVISION
Speaker: Lt. Colonel Stanley Jaynes Divisional Commander
Welcome: A/Captain Gene Harrell, Corps Officer
Opening Song: "How Firm a Foundation"
Prayer: A/ Captain Minnie Harrell
Congregational Song: "The mission"
Dedicatory Vocal Offering: "Near the Heart of God"
Jennifer Miller
The Message of Dedication: Lt. Colonel Stanley Jaynes,
Divisional Commander North and South Carolina Division
Prayer of Dedication: Lt. Colonel Jean Jaynes
Closing Song: "Joy to the World"

A social and fellowship time was celebrated in the Youth Hall, which was located in an adjoining building.

INNOVATIVE METHODS OF RECRUITING AND TRAINING OFFICERS AND LEADERS

According to an article by Major Frank Duracher in the Southern Spirit dated February 6, 2003 a new system of training and ranking of Officers has been in place in the Southern Territory since May 2002. This is in addition to the standard two year "in residence" requirements for training of cadets. The title of the article is "Flex Training Provides Valuable Options for Cadets in Unusual Circumstances."

He quoted the then Training Principal of the College for Officers Training of the present day North and South Carolina Divisional Commander, Major Vern Jewett.

> "The rank of lieutenant would be bestowed on personnel who are non-commissioned officers by definition, who are serving on the field in positions where they are 'authorized by their territorial commander to fulfill all responsibilities usually undertaken by a commissioned officer insofar as this is legally acceptable.'"
>
> —Orders and Regulations for Lieutenants in the United States of America

Eleanor Southerlan ready to serve c1994.

UNREMARKABLY REMARKABLE

Ellie died...The banner draping the Holiness Table in the chapel at Eleanor Southerlan's memorial service at the Corps read "Promoted to Glory." It may well be the only "promotion" she had ever received.

The congregation was not the usual Sunday congregation. It was made up of Ellie's family and some outside friends who exhibited unusual love and genuine feelings of loss for this frail soldier-saint. A few Soldiers of the Corps were there as well.

Ben Anderson, the CSM, conducted the service and retired Officer Major Myrtle Beasley Kitchen gave the eulogy and comforted the family. She was a most unremarkably remarkable woman. She was seventy-five years of age.

She lived out her final years in a nursing home and in and out of hospitals, often in great pain and distress.

She was materially very poor but she shared all that she received with whomever was in need.

Eleanor Southerlan was sworn in as a Soldier of the Greenville Corps in the 1970s at the age of 42 years.

The program announcement said that Ellie was a faithful Soldier and listed her volunteer participation in the operation of the Corps over the past thirty or more years. Among them were, Sunbeam leader, Sunday school teacher, Home League local officer, welcome and greeting sergeant, League of Mercy participant, and other service filled duties.

One would not have known that Ellie was in the house unless he was the recipient of one of those hugs or that whispered "I love you" and the genuine radiance of the spirit of Christ that emanated from her heart both in and out of the meetings.

She spent much of her life caring for her children and grandchildren and some of her neighbors, always with a quiet and sincere spirit of service-love. Ellie was the epitome of the song the Army sings,

"I have not much to give thee lord,
For that great love which made thee mine.
I have not much to give thee Lord,
But all I have is thine."

Truly, she bore the "cup of cold water in His name," and served it up well. Ellie is the living example of the spirit of the many members of the Salvation Army, both in and out of uniform, who have rallied around the cause of the Army in the entire world in the name of Christ.

Now her ashes are in an urn but her name is on the roll of the Lamb's Book of Life, and she is hugging the Savior, whispering in His ear, "I love you."

Well done, Ellie. You are truly "Promoted to Glory."

One Service, One Spirit, Two Different Worlds

The Greenville Journal reported the following in an article in the December, 27 2002-January 2, 2003 edition:

CIVITANS AND SALVATION ARMY PAY TRIBUTE TO RALPH DRAKE

The Civitan Club of Greenville recently rang the bells at the Salvation Army kettles at Kmart on Wade Hampton Boulevard to honor Judge Ralph Drake. Drake, a former Greenville Probate judge, has been a Civitan member for 44 years and served on the Board of Directors (sic) of the Salvation Army for more than 45 years. To honor his contributions, the Greenville Civitans and The Salvation Army Band paid a tribute to Drake with a ceremony on December 21 and rang the bells in his honor from 10 a.m. to 8 p.m.

A NEW CENTURY - A NEW CHALLENGE

The events of the world have placed its inhabitants into the throes of dilemma. We find that we must run faster and faster just to remain in the same place.

So it is with The Salvation Army and its vast array of services and programs to benefit the needy. It is doubtful if they will ever resolve the problems of wholesale sin and Salvation, poverty, want, and need, but they must certainly try...and try they will.

Even in the year of the Greenville, South Carolina centennial, plans are being effected to expand and grow and improve upon the quality and quantity of services to the needy in Greenville.

The final chapter will not be written until the end of time, as we know it. One can be confident that the Salvation Army will be there to usher in that final day. They will be still looking for more and, greater responsibilities in the ongoing war against sin and poverty.

Such is the spirit of William Booth and the early pioneers of the Army, and it has infected and motivated every generation of the Salvation Army members up to the present. It will do so right through the end of time.

It is evident that, while the past has been defined and crystallized, the future is a shimmering beacon that requires much work and forward planning to assess the answer to the future anticipated and unknown events of the entire community.

The nascent century in the new millennium is dawning... we must anticipate it with proactive minds.

Services to All the World - At Home

The Salvation Army is "at home" in the entire world as missionary and native-grown operators of services to humanity.

However in the United States there is a growing demand for these other world programs right here at home. Although the Salvation Army has been at the forefront of services to incoming aliens since the beginning of their existence, the mounting tides of new immigrants has shifted. The influx of new citizens with traditions and values ingrained from their native land dictates a new and radical approach to services to the needy.

Taking note of this new direction, the Salvation Army has increasingly made accommodations to embrace the new cultures. A *Spanish edition of the Southern Spirit was launched in 2003 in Atlanta, Georgia, and social and religious services in the languages of the minorities have been instituted in many major cities around the United States.

*Note: The Salvation Army yearbook (official report) of 1958 records the following statistic on page 152: "El Grito de Guerra has entered its fourth year of publication, and is also being used throughout the United states in Corps where there are Mexican and other Spanish-speaking adherents. Salvation Army Senior and Y. P. activities continue to develop in Mexico. Capacity crowds and souls at the Mercy seat characterize every meeting"

The Spanish edition of the Salvation Army Radio broadcasting program, "Wonderful Words of Life" was begun in order to reach and enlighten the masses of Spanish-speaking citizens and immigrants.

Corps centers were established in some cities to attract and serve other cultures being integrated into the mainstream of the United States.

The Army's world is truly shrinking but its vision is expanding without limits.

It is not uncommon for the Salvation Army to cross-train officers by assigning them to various overseas posts for special work, and to entertain foreign officers as administrators, workers, and employees in the United States.

This practice fosters the Army's mandate to be compatible with the universe of service to the masses of humanity.

The Salvation Army is truly at home in any land.

Additions to Staff

Early in 2002 several additions were made to the administrative staff of The Salvation Army in Greenville. Mrs. Frances Hines was engaged as the Social service Director. Mr. Benjamin Anderson was hired to oversee the financial section and Mr. David Guy was placed on the CSRC administrative staff. Major Myrtle Kitchen, a retired officer, was given responsibility for general Corps special programming.

At a later date Major Jeannette Jones was employed in the finance department and in 2004, Major David Jones was hired as special events coordinator.

Other changes were made in the staff to enhance and improve the effectiveness and productivity of the rapidly growing operation.

Swearing-in ceremony of new Senior Soldiers and transfer from the young Soldiers' roll c2003.

On April 13, 2003 a swearing-in* ceremony was held at the Corps Building Chapel in Greenville.

The following new Soldiers were admitted to membership in the Salvation Army:

Junior Soldiers (age fourteen and under): Lisa O'Neal, Cameron Whitten, Corey Whitten, Brandon Mason, Dorian Mason, Aissa Seaborn.

Brandon Brogden was sworn-in at a later date by his grandparents, Majors Cecil and Elma Brodgen, former Corps officers.

The following young people were sworn-in and transferred from the Junior Soldier's roll to the Senior Soldiers** roll: Tiliza Whitner, and Treyona Wright

The following adults were sworn-in and transferred from the recruit's roll to the Senior Soldier's roll: Michael Criswell, Mattie Nell Hudson, Mr. and Mrs. Shane and Jodi Timmerman.

The following members to be transferred (from Junior to Senior rolls) at a later date by a relative***: Caleb Fletcher, Gilbert Kapp, Kenny Brogden

Soldiers in good standing transferred from another Corps: These members are transferred at their request upon recommendation of the Corps Officer: Vincent William Wallace from the Columbia, South Carolina Corps.

All senior soldier enrollees have completed the Soldiership indoctrination class and the junior enrollees have completed the Junior Soldiers class requirements.

*Note: Swearing-in is tantamount to baptism into the Church. The Salvation Army flag, the Articles of War (Soldier's Covenant) and, for children, the Jr. soldier's pledge are used. Water baptism is not used. In 2004, the term "swearing in" and "Articles of War" were replaced with "enrollment"'and "he Soldiers covenant"' in order to more adequately define the membership process.

**Senior Soldiers, Age 14 and older: The Salvation Army Flag and the 'Articles of War/Soldier's Covenant' are used.

***Relatives: Only a Salvation Army Officer may conduct the swearing-in ceremony and often the event is arranged for a relative who is an officer to do the service as a courtesy to the family.

CHANGING OF THE GUARD IN THE SALVATION ARMY (No Trooping of the Colors)

In June of 2002 the Southern Territorial Commander and President of the Women's Ministries Department, Commissioners Raymond and Merlyn Wishon Cooper were honorably retired and were replaced by Commissioners Phil and Keitha Holz Needham in the Atlanta, Georgia Territorial Command.

Early in 2003 the North and South Carolina Divisional leaders Lt. Colonels Stanley and Jean Browning Jaynes entered into honored retirement and were replaced by Majors Vern and Martha Brewer Jewett in the Charlotte, NC

Divisional Headquarters.

On May 5, 2003 a list of changes of officers in the Southern Territory was posted in the official publications and on the Internet. Each officer was contacted prior to the listing by his/her immediate supervisor to advise them of the change relating to him or her.

This is a normal order of reassignment of Officers each year. Other transfers are dispersed throughout the year as authorized by the several Territorial Commanders and the General.

The three other Territorial commands issue the same style change of commands, also.

There were about 164 commands and corps changes in the South involving an estimated average of 274 officers considering married officers being transferred as a unit. Of these, 33 were in the North and South Carolina Division involving 55 Officers.

Most transfers are effective in the latter part of June and some are at other times to effect a smooth change of command.

Hail and Farewell, Salvation Army Style

Greenville, SC commanding officers Majors Stanley and Carlene Cox Melton were included in the list to be transferred to Montgomery, AL as Corps officers and Captains Gregory and Tammy Robinson Davis of Goldsboro, NC were assigned to Greenville, SC as Corps officers effective June 25, 2003.

Thus begins a new administrative initiative for the Greenville, South Carolina Corps to carry it into the second century of service to the community.

2003-Onward

CO: Majors Stanley and Carlene Cox Melton to 6/25/2003
Captains Gregory and Tammy Robinson Davis from 6/21/2003

All other local leaders', employees', and volunteers' rosters in Greenville remained the same.

In keeping with standard, unwritten protocol, the Advisory Board hosted a private farewell reception for Majors Stanley and Carlene Cox Melton. Thank-you and good-byes were exchanged.

On Sunday June 21, 2003, a public farewell was held in the Greenville, South Carolina Corps Chapel. Members, clients, friends and well-wishers were present to bid farewell to the Meltons who had served two years as the Corps Officers. This standard is set by the Salvation Army in all Corps appointments; Generally, farewell on Sunday and report to your new appointment the following Wednesday.

During the summer months of June, July, and August the Salvation Army Camping program is in full round-robin swing. Each new week ends one camping session and begins another. This is in addition to the normal routines of ongoing operations of Salvation Army programs in the community.

It is a fast-paced and sometimes hectic time for officers, who are required to serve on various camp staffs, and Divisional and Territorial Committees, as well as get their vacations in, and learn new Corps' routine almost simultaneously.

On Wednesday June 25, in keeping with standard welcoming protocol, Captains Gregory and Tammy Robinson Davis arrived to take command of the Greenville, South Carolina Corps. Their children, Joshua Lamar (age 11) and Zachary Wayne (age 6) accompanied them to the new assignment.

A public welcome meeting was held in the Chapel at the Corps on Sunday June 29, 2003. Major Pete D. Costas, Jr. of the NSCDH conducted the public installation service

The Advisory Board conducted a private welcome service during the regular Advisory Board meeting in June. Major Vernon Jewett, NASC Divisional Commander, conducted the installation service.

The Newest Member

On August 4, 2003 baby Brennan Trey Davis was born in Greenville Memorial Hospital and took his place in the Corps cradle roll roster. He is the newest baby member to be enrolled to date (as of this writing). Captain and Mrs. Greg and Tammy Robinson Davis are the parents.

Transition and Flux

- In September 2003 a young lady from Canada named Kathy Smith was engaged as Corps Pianist and later listed as Youth Music and Arts Director. She married Mr. Jason Stock shortly thereafter. Both have been employed at Camp Walter Johnson for the past two years. Jason Stock is a Senior Soldier of Goldsboro, North Carolina via Upstate New York. Kathy Stock was enrolled as a senior soldier on Sunday July 4, 2004.
- In October, 2003 Senior Soldiers Mr. and Mrs. Ray and Pat Patro transferred to Wilmington, North Carolina to take up positions in that Corps.
- At about the same time Senior Soldiers Mr. and Mrs. Bonnie and James Todd left Greenville and took up positions in the same City.
- On November 9, 2003 Junior Soldier Caleb Fletcher was transferred to the Senior Soldier's roll and sworn-in by his grandparents, Major and Mrs. David and Jeannette Lane Jones.
- On November 16, 2003 the following Junior Soldiers were transferred to the Senior Soldier's roll and sworn-in by Captain and Mrs. Greg and Tammy Davis the Corps Officers: Gilbert Kapp, Robdrgust Maddox, Tiliza Whitner, and Brian Wright.
- Mrs. Shirley Robinson transferred from her church and was sworn-in and added to the Senior Soldier's roll during the same ceremony.
- In the summer of 2003, according to the Church Bulletin, Mr. And Mrs. Rob and Monica Barber

were listed as Prospective Candidates (P/C). Shortly thereafter, Mr. And Mrs. Shane and Jodi Timmerman also were listed as Prospective Candidates. (The term Prospective Candidates denotes a person who has offered himself for Salvation Army Officership and is considered to be in training to apply for the position while serving in a local Corps Center as a volunteer or employee. rwk)

- On January 18, 2004 a special Sunday service was conducted by Captains Greg and Tammy Davis, Greenville Corps Officers, honoring Mrs. Mary Vick with an additional 'Silver Star' for her children who are serving as Officers in the Salvation Army. Each of the children of Mary Vick were present and took part in the meeting. The Vick family is descended from Mr. Roland Smith, the first Corps Sergeant Major of the Greenville Corps 1904-1935. The special speaker and the Silver Star presenter were Major and Mrs. William Madison. Major Madison entered training from Greenville in 1971 and was commissioned in 1973. Thus began the 2004 Centennial Celebration of the Greenville, SC Corps.
- On May 13, 2004, The Salvation Army in Greenville lead by Captains Greg and Tammy Davis, Corps Officers, and Mr. Ben Crider, Advisory Board Chairman, held its final Annual Civic Salute and report to the community for the century (1904-2004). Commissioners Phil and Keitha Holz Needham were the principal guests and speakers. Commissioner and Mrs. Needham are the Territorial Commander and Director of Women's Services for the Southern Territory. In that capacity, they are responsible for the operation of the Salvation Army in the entire region of the Southern United states. (Note: One of the daughters of Commissioner and Mrs. Phil Needham attended Furman University several years ago and they often visited the school and took part in the activities associated with parents-pupil events.)

- Music and entertainment was provided by various participants of Salvation Army units. Commissioner Keitha Needham, an accomplished vocalist, performed flawless classical selections in keeping with the theme of the meeting.
- Awards were given to representative volunteers, donors, supporters, and others for outstanding service during the year 2003.
- The complete list of participants in the 2003 Christmas program and the sponsorship of the Annual Meeting expense is as follows: Taylors First Baptist Church, Greenville Breakfast Rotary Club, Mauldin First Baptist Church, David and Audrey Gay, Joan Adams, Kelly and Bob Duff, Target Stores, Wal-Mart Woodruff Road, Kmart Church Street, The Salvation Army Board of Advisors, Boys and Girls Clubs Advisory Council, Greenville Civitan Club, Edwards Road Baptist Church, Greenville East Rotary Club, Malden High School Honor Society, Porsche Club of America, Riverside High School Key Club, Salvation Army Youth Group, Salvation Army Employees, Wade Hampton High School Honor Society, Chris Allsap, Susan Beduct, Carolyn Brown, John Bush, Greg and Josh Davis, Tim Driscoll, Marshall Femster, George Hetrick, Nell Hudson, Jim Hunter, Evelyn Jones, C. Munson, David Nigh, Donna Qualls, Tina Verba, Mike Wait, Kmart at Sulphur Springs Road, Butler Road-Maudlin, Wade Hampton Blvd., Wal-Mart at White Horse Road-Greenvilleand Simpsonville and Taylors, Sam's Clubs, Lowe's at Greenville, Simpsonville, and Greer, Belks at Simpsonville and Haywood Mall, Green's Beer and Wine, Stax Omega, Palmetto Center, Bi-Lo Stores.
- Annual Meeting Sponsors: Lewis Barker, Behavior Resources, Bi-Lo LLC, Brett Public Relations, Dr. Charles Brewer, Elizabeth Coley, Richard Crain Sr.,

Ben Crider, Custom Development Solutions, Elliot Davis, Daniel Foster, Clark Gaston Jr., Greenville Tech Northwest campus, Reverend and Mrs. Carey Hedgepath, Greg Jensen, Harrison Marshall, Robert McCauley, Ed Patterson, State Farm Insurance, Palmetto Bank, Samuel Piper, M. Graham Profitt Sr., Rosenfeld Einstein, James Sheppard, Shaw Resource. Inc., Arthur Snipes, James Stovall.

NOTE: The previous lists of names represent just a fraction of the local citizens and businesses that rally around the Salvation Army throughout the year. To list all of them would take far more space than can be allocated in this book.

- Mr. Ben Crider received an award for outstanding leadership, as Chairman of the Advisory Board in Greenville for the past three years.
- The Boys and Girls Club was the featured program as the theme of the annual Civic Salute. Participant members present a musical program. The "Smart Centers" - A special program operated in the public school system by the club to keep students on track to complete the courses - was honored as the principal program of the year.
- The following new Advisory Board members were welcomed and installed by Major Vern Jewett, Divisional Commander, North and South Carolina Division. They will serve three year terms as volunteer advisors to The Salvation Army in Greenville. They are the last to be so honored in this centennial cycle of the Salvation Army in Greenville: Pete Byford, Bob McCauley, Rex Meade, Richard Osborne, John Puckett, Frank Richards, and Joyce Smart.
- Boys and Girls Club Council changes and additions in 2004 are Brodie Brigman, who replaced Jack Watson as Treasurer of the council.

- New Council members inducted in 2004: Lewis Barker, Jennifer Barr, Elizabeth Coley, Linda Kelly, and Sheriff Steve Loftis.
- All other Advisory Board members and Boys and Girls Club Council members in the previous year remain.

"Marching Along, Marching Along, The Salvation Army is Marching Along..." (From a marching song sung in Salvation Army meetings.)

Transitional events (2003-2004) that may impact the future of the Salvation Army in Greenville and in all the world.

- In late 2003 the announcement was made via International, National, and regional publications that the Salvation Army has entered into "bilateral dialogues" with theologians of the World Methodist Council. According to the definition, "bilateral dialogues" is the phrase used to describe theological conversations between representatives from two Christian denominations. The discussions have led to another meeting in January 2005 at the World Methodist Council Headquarters at Lake Junaluska, NC.
- The year 2003 saw two innovative beginnings into the cyber-world for the Salvation Army. The general public was invited to contribute to the annual "Red Kettle Campaign" and become an on-line bell ringer for the fund raiser via the Internet. The "Angel Giving Tree" for the Christmas program could also be accessed via cyberspace for the first time in The Salvation Army's history.
- In 2003 the newly elected General of the Salvation Army, John Larsson reminded the international rank and file of the purpose and mission of the Salvation Army with these words, "A Corps is meant to be a mission team, a force led by a Captain and not a flock led by a Pastor."

- On January 20,2004 an announcement was made in national news media that The Salvation Army was set to receive a legacy from the estate of Joan Kroc, the McDonalds heiress. The total will exceed 1.5 billion dollars. The legacy will be used to construct and finance operations for Community Centers around the United States. Mrs. Joan Kroc was the widow of Mr. Ray Kroc, founder of the McDonalds fast food chain of restaurants, who was an ardent supporter of The Salvation Army, as was his wife. In 2002 the Ray and Joan Kroc Corps Community Center was opened in San Diego, California thanks to a gift of ninety-two million dollars by Mr. and Mrs. Kroc.
- On January 15th, 2004 the Greenville, SC Salvation Army Advisory Board under the leadership of Chairman Ben Crider, Corps Officers Captains Greg and Tammy Davis, and the Divisional and Territorial Leaders launched a campaign to upgrade and enhance the public's appreciation of, and information about, the Salvation Army in the community. A feasibility study and, possibly, a fund-drive will follow. The feasibility study will be conducted by Custom Development Solutions (CDS), Patricia H. McAbee, Study Director. The final report was due March 25, 2004.
- Note: At the March 25, 2004 Advisory board meeting the feasibility report was presented as a positive project. A proposal to proceed immediately with the Capital Campaign with a target amount to be selected later was recommended by the study group. Custom Development Solutions (CDS) will be the directors of the Capital Campaign with Patricia H. McAbee as the director of operations at the local level. The proposal was approved by the Advisory Board.
- In 2004, an Annual Review by the Salvation Army in the United Kingdom (the birthplace of the Salvation

Army) with the Republic of Ireland dropped the words, "Branch of the Christian Church" and declared, "The Salvation Army is an International Christian Church working in 109 countries worldwide as a registered charity. The Salvation army demonstrates its Christian principles through social welfare provision." The official publication of January 17, 2004 and January 24, 2004, *The Salvationist* requested feedback from the readers. (Speculative Note: Such a change in designation would require official action by the General to make it an authorized statement of the Salvation Army's descriptive literature.)

- In the January 17, 2004 issue of *The Salvationist* a book about General William Booth was reviewed and the question begged, "Why another biography about the founding General of The Salvation Army? Could it be that the timeless statement the general posed at the outset of the ministry, 'People will say, What is the Salvation Army, and who is William Booth' is no closer to being fully answered in this dawning new millennium than it was in the early days?" It is always a fascinating question to Salvation Army historians and to Salvationists and followers everywhere.
- Early in 2004, The Salvation Army "Roots-South" leadership team of The Southern Territory-USA announced a Roots gathering in Atlanta, Georgia for the dates June 3-6, 2004 in connection with the Commissioning of new Cadet/Captain graduates.

  (NOTE: Roots South has its origin in the Roots movement within the Salvation army. This movement was begun in the United Kingdom ten years ago to call the Salvation Army to its roots of, among others, Biblical Christianity. The mission statement states that, "Roots exists to call Salvationists to Biblical Christianity, radical discipleship, contemporary communication of the Gospel and a passion for the lost, which are at the root of the Salvation Army & the Christian Church.")

- In March of 2004 the International Chief Secretary of the Salvation Army issued a minute on behalf of the General that stated that The Salvation Army will no longer use the term "Articles of War" on its membership certificate. Substituted will be the term "The Soldiers Covenant". The body of the document is not changed.
- The term "swearing in" is dropped from the platform ceremony of membership acceptance and the new term "enrollment" is substituted. The ceremony remains the same.
- In the *Salvationist* of March 6, 2004 reports adherency has been redefined. The General clarifies Adherency membership status and introduces a personal statement of faith. This revised document requires that all adherents adhere also to minimum standards of the Christian faith—a confession of Salvation through Jesus Christ. The official designation is now "Adherent Member." All other requirements in the original document remain unchanged.
- The *War Cry* of March 13, 2004 announced that the Salvation Army and Adventists met to discuss common ground for ministry. The opening paragraph of the article declares, "Culminating 25 years of informal contacts, theologians from the Seventh-Day Adventist Church and the Salvation Army met for four days of theological dialogue in January." The final paragraph states that the dialogue will continue in 2005 at the Salvation Army Sunbury Court Conference Center near London.
- In an article introducing the newly revised Spring 2004 Issue of Priority magazine published by the Eastern Territory of the Salvation Army, and describing the Corps Community Center in San Diego, CA donated by Mr. And Mrs. Ray and Joan Croc the following is quoted: "At one end of the Center, the new University Avenue Christian Fellowship meets for Sunday morning worship

and midweek activities. Joan Croc knew full well that The Salvation Army is not just a charitable organization, but also an Evangelical Church denomination."

The end of 2003 and the early months of 2004 concludes the historical record of the first century of continuous service by The Salvation Army in Greenville, South Carolina. There is much work yet to be done, and planning is already underway for the century of tomorrow, and the millennium to come. God is still adding to the International Movement, The Salvation Army Citadel He began in 1865.

FIRE A VOLLEY! AMEN! AND ANOTHER! HALLELUJAH!

(A traditional early Salvation Army exclamation used in religious meetings.)

SALARMIANA*: The Meeting

"Fire a volley!" Cried the leader,
"Amen," fired the happy throng.
"And another, even louder",
"'Hallelujah' loud and strong.
"Fix your bay'nets, and another!"
Up went right hand straight and high,
"Amen! Fire another volley,"
"Straight into the devil's eye".

"Rise, salute, you valiant warriors!"
Fingers point to Heaven's door.
Sing a happy, joyful greeting,
We'll regroup upon that shore.
"Who will witness for the Savior?"
"Hallelujah, saved by grace."
"Amen, fire another volley,
Wield for Christ the Holy Mace."

*SALARMIANA - From a series of descriptive poems emphasizing Salvation Army programs, services and religious meetings

"Rally soldiers for the knee-drill,
From your bench to mercy seat!
'Ere we march to field of battle,
Pray for strength sin's test to meet.
Sing your song, you sainted warriors,
Clap your 'ten strings,' beat the drum.
Fill the hall and ring the rafters,
Call the sinner forth to come.

Hear the message straight from Heaven,
God is love and Christ is life.
Who will feel the grand conviction,
Leave the road of sinful strife?
Draw the 'net-string' with persuasion,
Urge the broken heart to come.
He alone can heal the sorrow,
Found in palace, flat or slum.

Ring the 'Hall' with drum and banner!
Sing the Angels' joyful song.
"Amen!" "Fire another volley",
As God's 'ocean' rolls along.
March the 'hallelujah windup',
Clap and sing of power and grace.
Onward! March! Salvation Army,
Christ, the Captain, sets the pace."
—Raymond W. Kitchen-1971

CHAPTER XIII
1904-1906-1914-1917-1949
GREENVILLE, SC BRUNER HOME HISTORICAL PROGRESSION
"When mothers of Salem their children brought to Jesus"

Group of Little Boys and Girls of the "Brüner Home," Greenville, S. C., Ensign and Mrs. George Graves in Charge

Children at the Bruner Home c1921-1926 with Ensign and Mrs. George Graves.

The Bruner Home for Children adds another phase of The Salvation Army's unique and varied programs to the landscape of service in Greenville, SC.

Operated under the auspices of the Salvation Army's Women's Social Service Department but as a separate program, this children's home concentrated on the care and nurturing of children who were orphaned, discarded, or otherwise without adult support.

The Bruner Home has an interesting and productive humanitarian history even before the Salvation Army was asked to take over as the operator in 1917, and owner in

1927. The Army operated the Bruner Home from 1917 to 1949. The founding year of the Bruner Home is 1906.

In 1927, at the time of the official formation of the Salvation Army Southern Territory as the fourth Territorial command in the United States, ownership of the property and plant passed from the Bruner Industrial Home, Inc. to The Salvation Army.

Bruner Home Origin and Development

In 1904 the Southern Baptist Missionary Society established a home for children of active missionary parents. Greenville was chosen as the location of this home because of the city's splendid schools and colleges.

This Missionaries' children's home continued in use until 1914 when conditions on the foreign fields changed and schools for English and American children were established.

Next Door Neighbors

In 1906 Miss Sarah Davis, a splendid Christian woman, established a home for dependent children of Greenville a little north of the Baptist's Missionary Children's home on Rutherford Street. She felt she was lead by God for this work and started on her faith. Her first building was a small three-room house located in the 500 block of Rutherford Street. Donations of vegetables from farmer friends helped to feed the children and she worked without salary. The first person to give a substantial sum was a young woman named Nell Bruner. I quote from an article in the Greenville News dated 12/28/1930:

"A Miss Davis started the Bruner Home. A Mrs. Bruner gave the first $500 for the work and that is why it is named for her. Miss Davis was sent to Florida for her health and a Salvation Army officer, who had been in charge of the State Child placing Bureau, was asked to come here and take over the home."

As Miss Bruner continued to give of her time and money, Miss Davis honored her by naming the orphanage Bruner Home for Children.

Miss Davis labored faithfully and soon had the interest of a number of prominent citizens of Greenville who gave not only of their money, but also of their time, and she was able to form a Board of Trustees.

Through the efforts of the Board, she was able to secure a building.

This building was purchased in 1914 from the Southern Baptist Church, who had used the building for a home for missionaries' children. (Note: This would have been the Southern Baptist Missionary Children's home next door to the Bruner home for Orphans on Rutherford Street. rwk)

In December 1916 Miss Davis felt that the work was growing too large for her to continue as its head for she was then sixty years of age.

She wrote The Salvation Army Headquarters asking that they take over the work.

In reply to this request, the Army stated that because of a shortage of officers, they would not be able to undertake the responsibility of the Bruner Home for at least six months.

In May 1917 the request was considered again, and in August 1917 the Salvation Army took over the operation of the Bruner Home.

Commandant Mary Bebout was the administrator of the Women's Social Service Department (Rescue Home for Women) in Greenville at the time so the supervision of the Bruner Home fell to her responsibility. The Women's and Children's rescue home operated by the Salvation Army was located in the 600 block of Rutherford Street.

The address of the Bruner Home for Children at this time is listed as 515 Rutherford Street. (Note: this could have been the original three-room house of the first Bruner Home mentioned above. However, this is not confirmed.)

This is one block from the Women and Children's rescue home operation of the Salvation Army, which is listed as 617 Rutherford Street.

Captain and Mrs. George and Ethel Graves were added to the staff in that year.

In the year 1919 Captain Stella Smith and Lieutenant Lillian Myers were added to the staff.

In 1920 Envoy Mrs. Pertain added and Lieutenant Lillian Myers transferred.

The year 1921 lists Captain and Mrs. Alfred Graves as in command, but I suspect that this is the aforementioned George Graves because the name flips back to George Graves later that year. Commandant Mary Bebout is shown as transferred to the Emma Moss Booth Hospital in Vardry Heights. Also Lieutenant Etta Russell was added in December of that year and Captain Stella Smith was transferred. In 1922 Envoy Florence Kebby, Ensign Lucy Melzer, and Captain Christina Sundstrom reported for duty. Captain Stella Smith, Envoy Mrs. Pertain, and Lieutenant Etta Russell were transferred.

In 1923 Lieutenant Dottie Myers, Envoy A. Shultz, and Envoy Mary DeDarrie were added. Envoy Florence Kebby was transferred.

In 1924 Lieutenant Elizabeth Young, and Envoy Rowena Smith were added and Envoy Mary DeDarrie was transferred.

In 1925 Lieutenant Ida Ackley was added and Envoy Rowena Smith was transferred. In 1926 Captain Edith Fisher, Envoy Addie Sills, and Captain Alta Salisbury were added and Lieutenant Ida Ackley and Adjutant Lucy Melzer were transferred.

In 1927 Adjutant Ella Dean and Lieutenant Vera Black were added and Captain Lottie Myers, Captain Edith Fisher, and Envoy Addie Sills were transferred.

The Bruner Industrial Home, Inc. deeded the property to The Salvation Army in 1927. That same year the Southern Territory was formed as the fourth Territory in the United States. In 1928 Captain Agnes Hagen was added. Lieutenant Vera Black was transferred.

In 1928 the address of the Bruner Home changed to 417 Rutherford Street. (Dispo listing)

In 1929 Lieutenant Opal Dean, Ensign Ada Trembath, Captain Ethel Graves, and Ensign Agnes Coon were added. Captain Agnes Hagen, Captain Ethel Graves, and Lieutenant Ethel Dean were transferred.

In 1930 Envoy Rowena Smith (2nd appointment) Commandant, Mrs. Rex Munselle (Commanding Officer), Captain Florence Hare, Lieutenant Grace Bishop, and Lieutenant Lora Nelson were added. Adjutant and Mrs. George Graves, Adjutant Ada Trembath, and Ensign Agnes Coon were transferred.

In 1931 Captain Evelyn Alisea was added. Captain Florence Hare was transferred.

In 1932 no one was added. Envoy Rowena Smith was transferred (3rd appointment).

In 1933 Commandant Ida Anderson, and Captain Madeline Shaw were added. Lieutenant Grace Bishop was transferred.

In 1934 no changes were recorded. In 1935 Adjutant Lottie Myers, Captain Eva Gunn, and Envoy Rowena Smith (4th appointment) were added. Commandant Ida Anderson, and Captain Madeline Shaw were transferred.

In 1936 no changes were recorded. In 1937 Major Alfred Graves (Commanding Officer, 2nd appointment, Captain Elizabeth Rowland, Captain Pearl Huffman, Lieutenant Florence Clay, and Captain Nellie McCauley were added. Captain and Mrs. Rex Munselle, Adjutant Lottie Myers, Lieutenant Laura Nelson, Envoy Rowena Smith and Captain Eva Gunn were transferred.

In 1938 Lieutenant Lenora Crenshaw and Lieutenant Eleanor Murgitroyde were added. No one transferred.

In 1939 Adjutant Ima McMillan and Adjutant Lulu Deck were added. Lieutenant Lenora Crenshaw and Lieutenant Florence Clay were transferred.

In 1940 Major Frances Roberts (Commanding Officer) and Captain Alma Agee were added. No one was transferred.

In 1941 Captain Ethel Wells was added. Lieutenant Eleanor Murgitroyde was transferred.

In 1942 Adjutant Mary Porteous and Lieutenant Katherine Gibson were added. Adjutant Lulu Deck, Adjutant Ima McMillan, Captain Elizabeth Rowland, and Captain Ethel Wells were transferred.

In 1943 Captain Minnie Douglas and Captain Eleanor Swearingen were added. Lieutenant Katherine Gibson was transferred.

In 1944 Major Lisle Shackelford, Major Emma Camidge, and Lieutenant Marjorie Harris were added. Captain Minnie Douglas, Captain Alma Agee, Captain Eleanor Swearington, Major Emma Camidge, and Lieutenant marjie Harris were transferred.

In 1945 Captain James Handley (Commanding Officer)and adjutant Catherine Stimler were added. Major Lisle Shackelford, Adjutant Mary Porteous, and Captain Nellie McCauley were transferred.

In 1946 Captain Carl Ferrell and Captain Lillian Gardner were added. No one was transferred.

In 1947 Captain Letha Montgomery and Captain Earl Short were addedCaptain Carl Ferrell and Captain Lillian Gardner were transferred.

In 1948 Mrs. Lieutenant Colonel Hickey was added. Captain Earl Short and Adjutant James Handley were transferred.

In 1949 Major Ruth Houston was added. Lieutenant Bernettie Willerton, Lieutenant Colonel Edith Hickey, and Major Ruth Houston were transferred.

All officers were transferred out. The Bruner Home was closed in 1949.

A True "Home" for Children

The actual day-to-day operation of the home was designed to foster good citizenship and to prepare the children for life as productive adults.

To this end daily routines were established such as work schedules, recreation time, study periods, recreational activities and worship and praise services. Of course, there was plenty of free time and free-play time as well as time for socializing.

In Playground of the Bruner Children's Home, Greenville, S. C.

Playground at the Bruner Home on Rutherford street c1925.

There was close association with the Salvation Army Citadel program as well. Several youth groups were formed at the home that mirrored the standard Salvation Army programs. One such group is the Girl Guarding program.

The picture below was provided by 2nd lieutenant Violet Bivans from Captain Eva Bivans' personal album circa 1920s.

Bruner Home Girl Guard Program c. 1920s/Officers Captain and Mrs. George Graves. Others unidentified.

The general public was solidly supportive of the Salvation Army's Bruner home and donated significant amounts of tangible support to the cause.

According to an article in a newspaper on September 18, 1932 (The date is not clearly visible in the article, nor is the name of the newspaper) volunteer workers from several construction firms in the city constructed the Recreation Building.

Community Building Project

> *THIRTY WORKERS COMPLETE STRUCTURE ON SECOND DAY AS HUNDREDS WATCH.*
>
> "The Bruner Home orphans now have another place to play 'horsie'.
>
> The recreation building, which was to have been erected Friday, but which was not completed because of delay in an order of lumber, was finished at noon

yesterday, and the children will daily be turned loose in the 'palace of play'.

Gymnastic equipment, perhaps including a wooden or leather 'horsie', will be installed in the structure as soon as Major Rex Munselle (appointed 1930), in charge of the Bruner home, can raise the necessary funds.

The building was erected largely through the aid of the Edwin Gould Foundation for Children.

Hundreds of visitors were present yesterday morning to watch approximately 30 workers complete the project, which has yet to receive a dab or two of paint.

Citizens and firms of Greenville offered their services free of charge in the construction of the house.

The skilled laborers of the project follows:

S. L. Williams, F. E. McDaniels, F. H. Pollard, B. F. Lee, W. G. Owens, Pink Davis, Hubert Howard, W. A. Lee, R. F. Cox, J. B. Green, C. J. Moody, Bob Jones, F. F. Coleman, W. W. Burns, J. T. Dempsey, T. A. Armstrong, C. D. Cantrell, Mr. Moody, S. J. Kilgore, P. H. McDaniels, R. T. Cantrell, V. A. Dacus, C. H. Cantrell, T. B. Rickard, E. M. Smith, R. J. Westmoreland, E. E. Sullivan, T. B. Wickliffe, Ed. Loftus, W. C. Owens, C. H. Campbell, J. E. Chalmers, C. F. Long, A. P. Williams, W. P. Smith, E. F. Vanadore, W. B. Keller, N. C. Wooten, L. P. Hollis, G. M. Cox, W. O. Jones, Herbert White, L. O. Wade, W. E. Heath, A. G. Vaughn, L. T. Lane, Thos. Kelly, E. M. Messengale, W. C. Matttox, Clarence Williams, C. W. Brown, E. J. Barton, Fred McMahon, Clarence Castles, C. J. Burns, W.C. Eskew."

Note: This building is the only facility still standing and is the only one from the original Bruner Home program. The present Citadel stands on the property where the housing unit stood and the recreation building is where the old playground was previously located. Later on, the playground was moved to the back of the property and became a Civitan Club-sponsored facility operated by the Salvation Army. Presently that area is used for warehousing and living facilities for the men clients.

Among the workmen were the following: Fred Brothers-four painters; George Davis-a squad of electricians; Cox and Hodgens-twelve carpenters; Morris-McKay-five carpenters; and Ramseur Roofing and McDaniel Roofing Company.

In keeping with the dated protocol, a contingent of African American workers was also listed as volunteers on the project. These are Willie Taylor, Calvin Blakley, Walter Smith, Donnie Bonaparte, L. C. Carter, Arthur Blakley, Sam Abercombe, Chef.

A FAMILY OF GOD'S CHILDREN

The children were divided into age groups in the boys and girls sections. The older children were to help care for and model good behavior for the younger children and the officers and staff gave oversight and stability to the group in a family setting.

Capt. James R. Handley, superintendent of the Bruner home, on Rutherford street, is shown above with several of the home's approximately 40 children characteristically crowded around him. The home is operated by the Salvation Army and is a member agency of the Greater Greenville Community Chest. Bruner home children are orphans, half-orphans or products of otherwise broken homes.

The 'Bruners' as a family c1945/Captain James E. Handley.

Everything possible was done to salvage the children from the distressful circumstances that brought them to the Bruner Home.

Effort was made to reunite them with their families or relatives and get them back into a family care situation within their own natural surroundings.

A family situation was fostered in the home at all times. The Bruner Home became home to some of them and the other members became their family circle. It remains so to this day. (Literally, the Bruners, now all senior citizens, still consider themselves to be one family.)

A group of Bruner children at play c1945.

In addition to seeing that each child attended the public school system, officers arranged extra classes within the home for homemaking, occupational study and moral and ethical character development.

76 Trombones...110 Cornets?

As a part of the program of character building the Salvation Army taught the children to play musical instruments. At one time the Bruner Home had a fine brass band that added a great deal of religious emphasis and musical training to the home.

In 1946 the band consisted of at least 31 members and included, among other instruments, a glockenspiel.

The director of the band was Mr. Pat Garnet who was the band teacher for Parker High School at the time. He volunteered his time to teach the children to play musical instruments

In 1948-49 a young college student and Soldier of the corps named Willard Evans was the bandmaster at the Corps. He also taught the children in the Bruner Home to play musical instruments. Commissioner Willard Evans and his wife, Commissioner Marie Fitton Evans are now retired after years of service as distinguished officers in high leadership positions in The Salvation Army.

Note: Community program and service volunteers are the lifeblood of the many Salvation Army programs.

In almost every character-building initiative and in some of the church program there are literally hundreds of community citizens giving of time and substance to assist the Army in its humanitarian work.

The result is well-rounded, community-spirited co-operation between the Army and the community at large.

The Salvation Army Corps band with Bruner Home children c1920s.

The children of the Bruner Home (They called themselves "Bruners") were also involved in other regular Salvation Army activities. A brigade of Corps Cadets (a disciplined Bible Study Group) was in operation within the home setting and several youngsters excelled in the curriculum.

The Corps Cadet Brigade membership requires Salvation Army membership so these youngsters were Salvation Army Soldiers.

A Bruner Corps Cadet Brigade of the Salvation Army.

"Bruners" who were enrolled as Soldiers of the Salvation Army:

Reba Brack, 1/1/1934, JS
Larry Brendon, 1/13/1934, JS
Mamie Brown, 1/13/1934, JS
Eunice Ellis, 1/12/1919, JS
Mrs. Gertrude Howard, 1/123/1919, SS
Lillian James, 1/3/1943, JS
Helen Justice, 11/16/1930, JS, 1/12/1939, SS
(One of the triplets)
Florence Kebby, (date uncertain, 1922) SS
Mamie Bell Lea, 4/11/1920, SS
Martha Lyda, 1/3/1943, JS
Evelyn Justice Madden, 11/16/1930 JS, 1/12/1939, SS
(One of the triplets)
Ellen Justice Perkins, 11/16/1930 JS, 1/12/1939, SS
(One of the triplets)
Doris Mobley, 12/4/1938, JS
Elizabeth Pate, 1/13/1934, JS

Several of the Bruners were accepted into the Salvation Army's School for Officers Training and went on to become productive Officers serving in the Officer Ranks as leaders. Some who attended the SFOT changed careers and did not remain as officers.

The known listing of Bruners who attended the Salvation Army Training College is:

Envoy Florence Kebby (1922)
Major Doris Henry Jones (1940s)
Captain Ruby Milton (unknown)

The Justice Triplets:
Ellen Justice Perkins, RN (1930s)
Helen Justice, RN (1930s)
Evelyn Justice Madden, RN (1930s)

One of the rosters of the Bruner Home Kids from an undated listing assembled in 1994 using updated names and positions is listed below:

Helen Adams, Minnie Benson, Ilene Blanton, Billy Boling, Zenus Boling, Zinn Boling, Mary Lou Bridges, Azalee J. Brookshire, Fred Burriss, Patsy Miller Calderone, Mrs. Lonnie Coleman, Crystal Collins, Fred J. Collins Jr., Beatrice Davis, Kathleen B. Grimes, Geneva Gosnell, Doris Green, J. B. Heatherly, Mrs. Major Doris Jones, Helen Justice, Mrs. Lorraine Kelley, Mrs. Edna Lankford, Maureen Lewis, Mrs. Helen Loftis, Mrs. Evelyn Madden, Harry Mansfield (1930-36), Robert Mansfield, Mrs. Mae McIntyre, Ruby Milton, Mrs. Alice Moon, Rev. Thomas L. Painter, Mrs. Ellen Parkins, Catherine Pinnix, Stokely Raines, Mrs. Ruby Redman Foster, George Rushton, Mrs. Myrtle Sanchez, Mrs. Ellen M. Mansfield Shelton (1930-36), Mr. Wandell Smith, Mrs. Elizabeth Stewart, Mrs. Helen B. Taylor, Ellen Tramble, and Frank Tramble.

(The above list is just a sampling of the known record. Most of the rosters have been lost or otherwise unobtainable.)

Over the course of years of operation of the Bruner Home and its predecessor institutions literally hundreds of children passed through the doors and were helped to become good, upright citizens of our state and the country.

The children who were admitted to the Bruner Home came from many different, stressful, often debilitating, and dangerous situations.

As an example, this is the story of one of the children that was placed in the home by the local welfare system. She began to write an article for publication but it was cut short by her death as an adult. Mrs. Major Doris Henry Jones was promoted to Glory in 2001. Her husband, Major Jesse Jones, submited this quoted material. Major Jesse Jones was also promoted to Glory in September of 2003.

I quote as accurately as possible:

PRESTO RIDICULO
By Major Doris Henry Jones

PREFACE

How much of what you remember do you remember? Are many of the memories yours or another's?

Supposedly, my earliest memory is of a fight between my mother and father. I, in my memory as a child younger than three, am the heroine of this drama. The certainty of being younger or just three is that when my father left his family I was three. Of course, my father was well supplied with families. It is my understanding from a cousin that 'good ole dad' married five times. I am told my mother was wife number three. Supposedly, wife number four told him she would kill him if he left. I guess he believed her and simply outlived her. Otherwise, I am sure a man of his energy and initiative would have generously sacrificed himself and made every effort to marry at least ten times. A man of his talent could do no less.

My mother suffered a mental breakdown and was committed to a state hospital two months before I was six. Thus, I learned early that I was not easy to live with. Had I only been able to reason, I could have saved my parents a lot of heartache and simply presented myself to the orphanage, where I went after my mother's illness and commitment, before they took such drastic steps to distance themselves from me. The orphanage was a godsend.

I remember telling a coworker about my supposedly dysfunctional childhood. Her response was, "How did you turn out to be so normal?" My secret was and is now that I, at 61, have no idea what normal is. As Popeye proclaimed, "I yam what I yam."

Life, despite its problems and my inadequacies, is good. I have been blessed with a Heavenly Father who is much more efficient and proficient then any earthly father could be. I have been blessed with a husband who loves me. He doesn't like me at times, but he loves me. I am blessed with children who love me. I am blessed with grandchildren who love me and permit me to love them. I am blessed with friends who love me. Perhaps a better question than my former co-worker posed would be, "How, with all you have been given, can you not be normal?"

Perhaps the memories I shall present are factual and unadorned. Perhaps they are colored by time and distance. A few of them, perhaps, may be the memories of others. I am just happy to have them.

CHAPTER 0NE

Weak and foolish would have been an apt description for the five-year-old who was to have some stressful changes in her young life. However, the age of five is characterized by resilience, also. Part of this is due, I am sure, to not having learned to be possession-minded, or social class-minded, or physical beauty-minded. She had no deep philosophical beliefs or doubts.

At five years of age, children do not understand adults. They accept them unconditionally, but they do not understand them. Thus when I was presented with a situation where I had no explanation, I invented one.

I had been sent to the orphanage as a 'latch-key' kid. Of course this term had not appeared in the mid-thirties. I was taken to the orphanage after school and sent home each afternoon so that I would arrive when my mother had come home. My mother was a "single parent", another term not in use at that time. She, in the middle of the "great depression," walked each day looking for work. Someone, considering my welfare I am certain did not want me to go home each day to an empty house. Thus, the after school arrangement.

On this particular day, I started home. There was so much to interest me and I received regular spankings because I never managed to reach home at the designated time. However, they were not particular tortuous and I suppose I reasoned that enjoying the walk home was worth the trade off of receiving a few minutes of unpleasantness. On this day, however, I reached home to find no one there. The door was locked and so I sat on the front stoop and waited. I waited for

> what seemed to be a long time and no explanation for the situation appeared. Yet-something appeared-a vehicle from the orphanage with a worker came to transport me back over the road I had only recently traveled, to the orphanage. Formally, I was not sent to the orphanage permanently. Yet, in reality, that day was the first of all the days of eleven years when the orphanage was my home, Again, no explained to me why my mother was not home or where she had gone.
>
> The other children in the home were curious. No surprise there, but since I had no explanation, I simply invented one. I could not conceive that my mother might simply chosen not to return (she Didn't). So I concocted a story of intrigue and kidnap. I had gone home and found the house ransacked (I did not know that word and have no idea what word I knew and used in its place), signs of a great struggle everywhere, and my mother missing. I was certain she would return when she could escape those individuals who were preventing her from being with her child. The other children, some of whom believed and some, I am sure who scoffed, simply accepted me from that time on as one of them. After all, all of them were consigned to the orphanage due to unusual circumstances. They saw nothing unusual in one more kid who needed a home..." (This is the end of the narrative. It was never finished. rwk)

One of the sad and unforgettable facts of this story is that the father was living just a few miles from the Bruner Home and never visited or made any attempt to contact his child.

In this poignant and all too true account are found the elements of the main reasons that children are lead to orphanages and institutions of temporary care all around the world.

The circumstances change and the differences are as varied as the number of human beings who inhabit the earth, but the hurt and confusion is always there to haunt the child even through adulthood and beyond.

The story of the Justice Triplets, Ellen, Helen, and Evelyn is another example. They were born in Rutherfordton, NC on October 4, 1921. After their mother died they were taken to the Emma Moss Booth Memorial Hospital where they remained until they were three years old.

They were then transferred to the Bruner Home and remained there until they graduated from high school. They went on to become registered nurses and Salvation Army officers. All have reentered civilian life and now live in different parts of the country. Love finds a way of healing

At least one wedding took place in the Bruner Home and produced a Salvation Army Officer couple. On June 11, 1947, Doris Henry, a Bruner Home resident, and Jesse Jones, who had been at times an employee of the Bruner Home, the Salvation Army Corps, and an employee of the Cash and Carry Grocery store, were married in the front room in front of the fireplace. Major Fred Boyette conducted the ceremony.

Jesse was a Salvation Army Soldier from Durham, NC who was attending college in central South Carolina and commuting to Greenville on Sundays.

Both attended the Salvation Army School for Officer's Training in Atlanta, GA and were commissioned as Salvation Army Officers.

Mrs. Major Doris Henry Jones is deceased. Major Jesse Jones was promoted to Glory in September 2003. They had three children.

Disbanded in Fact but Always Together

At the request of the local Community Chest organization the Salvation Army operation of the Bruner Home was phased out in 1949 and merged with another children's home. Both eventually disappeared into the pages of history.

However, some of the members of this elite group, grateful for the "helping hand" of the community in their youths, are still active and involved in the community as senior citizens and productive workers in their chosen fields. They still remain as a family and stay in touch with each other.

The Ever Evolving but Ongoing Army

In 1949 the Bruner Home was closed and preparations were made to construct the new Corps Community Center/ Social Welfare operation on Rutherford Street.

The Farewell Salute

On November 27, 1949 Lt. Commissioner Albert E. Chesham, Southern Territorial Commander presided at the closing ceremony of the Bruner Home for Children in Greenville, S C.

Assisting him in the program were the following members:

Captain Robert Burchett and the Corps Band
Mr. Paul Bolton, Chairman, Advisory Board
Brigadier William Groom, Property Secretary, Atlanta
Greenville Mayor Kenneth Cass, Chairman, Bruner Home Council
Mrs. C.H. Branyon, President, Bruner Women's Auxiliary
Major George Graves, Opening Superintendent of Bruner Home
Mrs. Lt. Colonel Edith Hickey, Then Current Superintendent
Citadel Songsters
Lt. Colonel May Wilmer, Territorial Women's Social Svc Secretary
Major Ethel Graves, Registrar

THE ARMY BEHIND THE ARMY

Listed below as a matter of record to emphasise the community involvement in the Salvation Army over the years are the community-spirited citizens who made up the "Army behind the Army" in 1949. This is representative of the vast support of the community in every Salvation Army endeavor.

There are groups of like-minded citizens still serving today in the Army all around the globe. This list does not include the Boys and Girls club council and the Ladies Auxiliary. They are listed elsewhere in this book.

The Salvation Army Advisory Board, 1949

Paul Bolton (Chairman), M. C. Patton (Vice-Chairman), La Rue Hinson, J. Kenneth Cass, J. B. Orders, W. B. Grayard, E. L. Snipes, Olin H. Spann, R. A. Jolley, J. H. Cannon, Thomas Miller, Major R. F. Watson, Charles H. Garrison, Lawson Scott, Dr. W. B. Simmons.

Bruner Home Council, 1949

Mayor J. Kenneth Cass (Chairman), M. C. Patton (V. Chairman), C. C. Pierce, Sapp Funderburk, Mrs. L. Wayne Brock, Mrs. Kelly Sisk, Mrs. Redford Laney, Kirby Hammond, J. Robert Lindsay, L. B. Bowers, Ed Petit, L. W. Hazelwood, Mrs. Joe Piper, J. P. Batson, Alan Suttles, Andy Thornton, Clarence H. Thomas, G. H. Cleveland, Robert Hunter.

Bruner Home Women's Auxiliary, 1949

Mrs. C. H. Branyon (President), Mrs. Mattie Able, Mrs. E. S. Adams, Mrs. J. W. Adams, Mrs. John P. Ashmore, Mrs. Thomas Anderson, Mrs. R. R. Bishop, Mrs. D. A. Boyd, Mrs. John Carter, Mrs. George S. Coleman, Mrs. Otho Crain, Mrs. Charlotte Crouch, Mrs. Frank Ferguson, Mrs. E. W. Giles, Mrs. E. A. Gillfillin, Mrs. Joseph Gimburg,

Mrs. William Goldsmith, Mrs. Judson Graves, Mrs. W. R. Gregory, Mrs. Kirby Hammond, Mrs. S. Howie, Mrs. Jesse Locke, Miss Caroline Miller, Mrs. E. E. Neese, Mrs. Fred Osteen, Mrs. M. Ousley, Mrs. J. W. Powell, Mrs. Frank Raysor, Mrs. Winona Reid, Mrs. George Rieseifield, Mrs. C. H. Roper, Mrs. A. F. Rude, Mrs. Sallie Shannonhouse, Mrs. S. C. Shelton, Jr., Mrs. W. B. Simmons, Mrs. King Thackston, Mrs. J. R. Thompson, Mrs. K A. Traynham, Mrs. T. J. Veazey, Mrs. H. M. Weeks, Mrs. J. F. Welborn, Mrs. H. P. Williams, Mrs. Mamie Wilson, Mrs. W. C. Woodward, Mrs. R. D. Wooten, Mrs. Sol Zaglin, Mrs. Hugh Cunningham, Mrs. Harry S. Abrams, Mrs. Douglas Doan, Mrs. Edgar Jones, Mrs. Matterson, Mrs. S. H. Brown, Mrs. Virginia Simkins, Mrs. J. L. Garlington.

The Duke Endowment Trust established by James B. Duke in Charlotte, North Carolina has shared generously in the program for orphans who lived in the Bruner Home.

The Bruner Home was not listed in the Disposition of Forces from 1950 onward. The Citadel Program was moved to the Bruner Home location in 1951 into a new building constructed for the Salvation Army. This paved the way for the Citadel at 26 East Broad Street to be turned over to the Boys and Girls Club as their exclusive home.

CHAPTER XIV
1908-1931
WOMEN'S SOCIAL SERVICES HISTORICAL PROGRESSION AND EMMA MOSS BOOTH MEMORIAL HOSPITAL
"Touch me with thy healing hand, Lord"

The Emma Moss Booth Memorial Hospital c1921-31.

"Out upon a hill just within the City limits, yet standing on it's own grounds which are the dimensions of a park, is what Dr. Hart describes as the best and most complete Hospital of it's class in the United States..."

—Greenville S. C. Rescue Home for Women and Children

That was the name of the first Salvation Army Women and Children's shelter program in Greenville. It started in May 1908 when the Women's Social Services Department of the Salvation Army assigned Captain Mary A. Minton and A. Palmer (no rank given).

The work centered on relief for homeless women and children and a home and hospital program for pregnant, unmarried and abused girls and women. According to the National Archives listing of officers, the location was Rutherford Street. The street number is not given here but is listed elsewhere as 617 Rutherford Street.

When the responsibility of the Bruner Home was transferred to the Salvation Army, The *War Cry* of 1917 indicated that the Women's Rescue Home was located about a block from the Bruner Home. This would verify the 617 Rutherford Street location of the Women's Rescue Home.

In July of 1908, Captain Ida McNary was assigned to Greenville and in November Adjutant L. Higham and Ensign Mary Bebout came aboard. This was the Women's Social Service Staff of the Greenville, South Carolina Rescue Home in 1908.

In April 1909, Lieutenant Minnie Lester was added to the staff. Captain Minton, A. Palmer, and Adjutant Higham were reassigned to another city.

The succession of officers was fast and furious in the Women's Social Department. They arrived and departed almost monthly with some serving just a month before moving on to other cities. The Disposition of Forces lists the changes quarterly.

Between the years 1908 and 1932, when the Woman's Social Work closed out in Greenville, a very large number of officers and assignees had sojourned in this place.

Nursing staff of the Emma Moss Booth memorial Hospital, Greenville, SC c1925.

Below is the chronology of Officers who came through the Greenville Rescue Home and later through the EMBMH program:

1908: Captain Mary A. Minton, A. Palmer, Captain Ida McNary, Adjutant L. Higham, and Captain Mary E. Bebout.

1909: Lieutenant Minnie Lester, Captain Jennie Stewart, Lieutenant Caroline Hetzel, and Adjutant Anna Franklin.

1910: Captain Alma Bestall, Lieutenant Alice Suttle, Lieutenant Florence Davis, Ensign Cora Beetle, Captain Ethel Newham, and Lieutenant Isabel L. Davie.

1911: Lieutenant Edith M. Lord.

1912: Ensign Ellen Jones, Lieutenant Eliza Bean, Lieutenant Fannie Bean, and Captain Helma Swanson.

1913: Lieutenant Elizabeth Hutchinson and Lieutenant Elizabeth Jackson.

1914: Lieutenant Ethel Foxhall and Lieutenant Agnes Huband.

1915: Captain Ina Depew.

1916: Lieutenant Lucinda Wolstagle, (mentioned as a heroic worker in a *War Cry* report on the opening of the new hospital in Vardry Heights.)

1917: Captain Anna Work

1918: Major Mary Wagner

1919: Lieutenant Gertrude Worthy

1920: No assignments (last year on Rutherford Street)

1921: (The operation was moved to the new hospital in Vardry Heights.) Ensign Elizabeth Orr, Ensign Jennie Wicklund, Lieutenant Etta Russell, Captain Margaret Vanderburg, and Captain Mary Daley.

1922: Adjutant Harriet Speelman, Captain Margaret McIntyre, Captain Bertha Stanford, and Lieutenant Vera Hammell, RN.

1923: Envoy Rowena Smith, Katherine Lord, RN, Lieutenant Anna Westborn, and Lieutenant Irene Menger.

1924: Adjutant Augusta Peterson, Captain Ollie Smith, Captain Grace Fitzgerald, Ensign Myrtle Marshall, Ensign Johanna Keller, Lieutenant Anna Graves, Captain Florence Turkington, RN, Captain Harriet Todhunter, Lieutenant Rutherford, and Lieutenant Ida Blackman.

1925: Lieutenant Mary Johnston, Lieutenant Ford, Lieutenant Gladys Wilder, Lieutenant, and May Helwig.

1926: No new assignees.

1927: No new assignees. This is the first listing of nurses in training school.

1928: No new assignees.

1929: Miss Balentine and Miss Price.

1930: No new assignees.

1931: Commandant George Lewis (Superintendent), Captain Annie Harrison (Bookkeeper).

1932: Not listed in Disposition of Forces. The hospital was closed and the Women's Social Service in Greenville was discontinued.

The Saint Francine Little Sisters of the Poor began operation of the hospital under the name of Saint Francis Hospital in 1932. The expanded and upgraded Saint Francis Hospital is a major provider of health care today.

Social Services operations were remanded to the Salvation Army Corps program and operated as the Corps Social Program at the Citadel on Broad Street. It is operating as such today.

Commandant Mary E. Bebout and Staff of the Home and Hospital at Greenville, S. C.

The first lady of service to the needy in Greenville.

In the Greenville Salvation Army Social Services field, the name Commandant Mary E. Bebout is the constant.

Having progressed through the ranks in Greenville to Commandant, she commanded the program from start to completion.

The exception is the first year when Captain Mary A. Minton initiated the work, and the first three months of 1909 when Adjutant L. Higham was apparently the Lead Officer.

Commandant Mary E. Bebout effected the transfer of the Bruner home for Children from the Bruner Industrial Home Incorporated to the Salvation Army in 1917. This program was the mainstay of the Women's Social Services program during the construction of the hospital in Vardry Heights.

At that time, the Women's Social Program was operated in three sections, the Women's Shelter, the home and hospital, and the Bruner Home Program.

Adjutant and Mrs. George Graves were appointed to the Bruner Home in 1917. In 1921 they assumed command of the Bruner Home program.

Commandant Bebout concentrated on the new Emma Moss Booth Memorial Hospital program as the superintendent.

She oversaw, locally, the design and construction of the hospital from 1917 to 1921 when it was dedicated and placed into operation. The hospital operated from 1921 to 1931 when it was closed due to indebtedness and high operating costs

It was sold to the St. Francis Little Sisters of the Poor in 1932. They began renovations and operation of the St. Francis Hospital in that year.

It is not clear where the responsibility for the homeless shelter for women lay during this time. It could have been in either the command of the Bruner Home, or the hospital programs, or shared by both. There was room set aside in the citadel to house homeless persons at one time.

The evidence of officer assignment indicates that the shelter program was vested in the Rescue Home Program under that administrator.

(Another possibility is that the Women's Shelter could have been located at the 517 Rutherford Street address, but no proof is offered. rwk)

There also may have been an arrangement with the local Corps Officer to house the Women and Children's home in the Corps Building on Broad Street. Commandant J. V. Breazeale verifies this fact in an article in the Piedmont newspaper in 1930.

THE COMMANDER ARRIVES IN GREENVILLE

Following is a condensed quotation from the Salvation Army Southern *War Cry* dated February 12, 1921. I have attempted to use the original language and form of the article.

> THE EMMA MOSS BOOTH MEMORIAL HOSPITAL
>
> Named for one who gave her life when serving the people of this country, this institution in not only a monument to that life and service, but an embodiment, alike of the community spirit of the South and of Greenville. Of desire for the welfare of the operatives on the part of local corporations, and of the willingness and capacity of the Salvation Army to be, in the footsteps of its great Captain, the servant of all.
>
> Representing the last word in hospital construction, the Emma Moss Booth Memorial hospital is complete from basement to roof with every appliance needed by medical men and tender-hearted nurses to alleviate human suffering.
>
> The building of this Salvation Army Hospital is the greatest single effort ever made in Greenville in behalf of the women and children of this community who are in need of physical, moral and spiritual help...
>
> Leading Moral and Spiritual Effort
>
> This is a great Christian effort in which all our churches and all our people and our corporations are joining with The Salvation Army...
>
> The new building is one of the handsomest and costly in Greenville, being faced with stucco and having tasteful brickwork as coining. It has cost, with equipment, $250,000. Half of which has been paid by

the following corporations of Greenville and vicinity in proportion to their sizes: American Spinning Company, Alice Mills, Brandon Mills, Camperdown Mills, Cone-tee Mills, Dunean Mills, Easley Mills No, 1, 2, and 3. Enoree Mills, F. W. Poe Manufacturing Company, Franklin Mills, Judson Mills, Poinsett Mills, Mills Mill, Piedmont Manufacturing Company, Saluda Manufacturing Company, Union Bleaching and Finishing Company, Victor-Monaghan Company, Woodside Cotton Mills, and Woodruff Cotton Mills.

Greenville has a reputation for public spirit, but also for investing it's money carefully and choosing its agents wisely, and the public may be sure that it's business leaders formed their estimate of The Salvation Army from its hard-earned record at home and abroad before contributing for their corporations over $125,000...

The hospital medical staff is as follows: Surgery-Dr. T. B. Reeves, Obstetrics-Dr. W. M. Bennett, Urology-Dr. T. M. Davis, Pediatrics-Dr. F. Jordan, Internal Medicine-Dr. George R. Wilkinson, Eye, Ear and Throat-Dr. E. W. Carpenter.

The hospital will also have on its consulting staff the following well-known physicians: Dr. Hobart Ashley Royster, Raleigh, N.C.; Dr. Charles M. Minor, Asheville, N. C.; Dr. Norman N. Heggie, Jacksonville, Fla.; Dr. William Weston, Columbia. The Women's Auxiliary, headed by Mrs. David Cardwell has done yeoman works in numerous directions.

The institution will be divided into the medical department, the home department, an outdoor patient department, a clinic, and training school for nurses (with state license).

Built primarily for women and girls who have been led astray, and for babies who come into the world without names, the hospital flings wide its doors to whomever comes to it in sickness and in need. The spirit of service which is to reign supremely there knows no limitations...

The Army hopes to meet one of the urgent needs of the state as is being pointed out by Dr. J. Adams Hayne, Secretary, State Board of health. For instance, South Carolina has one of the largest infant and maternity mortality rates of any state in the union...

Doctors who served in the
Emma Moss Booth
Memorial Hospital
1921-1931
Dr. G. R. Wilkinson, Greenville, S. C.
Dr. J. B. Reeves, Greenville, S. C.
Dr. T. M. Davis, Greenville, S. C.
Dr. E. W. Carpenter, Greenville, S. C.
Dr. Fletcher Jordan, Greenville, S. C.
Dr. W. M. Burnett, Greenville, S. C.

PHYSICIANS WHO ARE REPRESENTATIVE OF VERY MANY MORE WHO GIVE THEIR SERVICES TO THE SALVATION ARMY HOMES AND HOSPITALS

DEPARTMENTS AND OBJECTS OF HOSPITAL

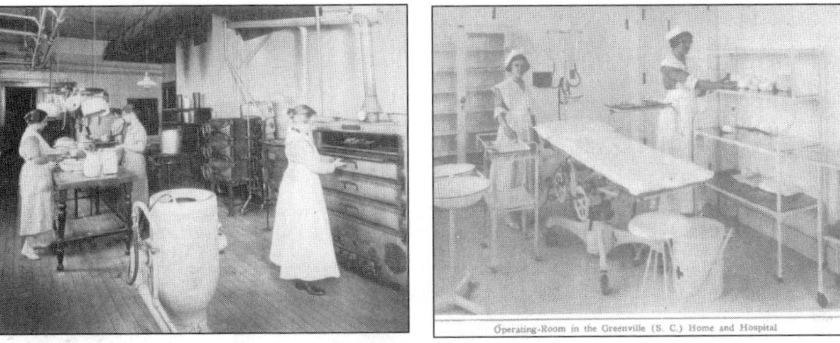

Operating-Room in the Greenville (S. C.) Home and Hospital

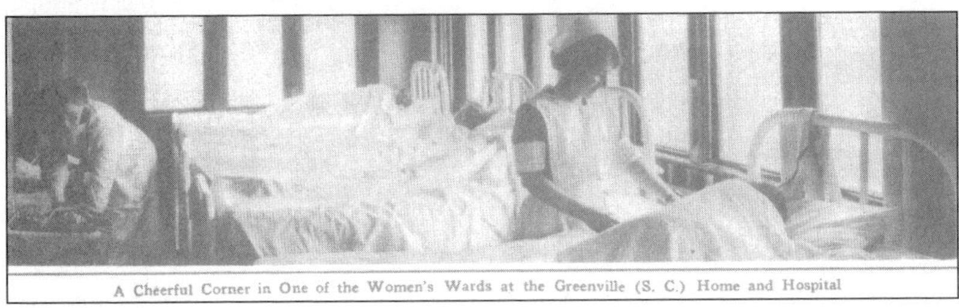

A Cheerful Corner in One of the Women's Wards at the Greenville (S. C.) Home and Hospital

Departments of the EMBMH hospital Greenville, SC c1921-31.

There can be no doubt that the spirit, which permeates the workers of the Salvation Army, and has contributed so much to their usefulness, will follow them into this new world. A typical example of this was shown recently when Captain Woleslegle who now has charge of the children in the home department of the E. M. B. H., with a few untrained assistants took good care of over thirty children. At one time sitting by the bedside of one seriously ill through the entire night....

EQUIPPED WITH EVERY KNOWN DEVICE

The hospital in its physical aspect is worthy of the great organization with the greater cause, which it is to serve. Three stories and a basement, built of brick and cement, and equipped with every device known to medical science for the alleviation of suffering and the healing of the sick, it stands upon a wooded knoll, a magnificent monument to the army of devoted men and women who have made its erection possible.

The general plan of design is in the shape of a large "T", with the halls running down the center in each direction.

On the first floor are the quarters and office of the Superintendent, Commandant (Mary E.) Bebout, a reception room, a sun parlor, which is to be used as a schoolroom for the student nurses, a dormitory for children from four years of age up, a maternity ward and a children's ward. The second floor contains many rooms for private patients, in addition to the maternity and infants wards. The third floor is set apart largely for the nurses quarters, operating rooms and surgical patients...

Perhaps the most interesting of the many features are the infant's wards. There are a half-dozen of these scattered on all three floors, and they are all on the north side of the building in large rooms, glass-enclosed and opening into the maternity wards. The babies will be placed in little white-enameled bassinets arranged

In the foreground left is the T shaped former Emma Moss Booth Memorial Hospital surrounded by the site work of the new Saint Francis Hospital and the new construction. Photo taken from a photograph of the picture hung in the present Saint Francis Hospital in Vardry Heights. c1970s.

around the sides of the walls, just below the windows and swung three-at-a-time on trucks that can be shifted at will. There are a total of fifty-six of these little baskets, besides regulation crib-beds for the lager children.

The plan is that the mothers of the babies will be placed in wards next to the infant's wards and the babies will be taken to their mothers for food and drink...

The main kitchen is in the basement and is a perfect marvel of steam and electrical appliances. The three huge ranges are heated by high-pressure steam supplied from the main boiler, which also supplies the heat. ...In addition to the main kitchen, which will supply food for the large majority of patients and staff, each floor will have a smaller diet kitchen.

On the third floor located in the south wing one finds the operating-rooms and those several rooms that are appendages to every modern operating-room. Across the hall is the X-ray room although there is yet no X-ray machine, and then the anesthetizing room in which the patients will receive ether before being rolled into the operating-room proper.

ALL POSSIBLE RELIEF FROM NOISE

Connecting all floors is a silent electric elevator, and in addition, there is a stair-tower. Each room and hall is as near sound-proof as can be assuring each patient all possible relief from the usual hospital noises.

Light has been another factor that has received considerable attention, and there is not a room or a hallway in which old sol does not throw his rays through during the day. Fresh air, which is so essential in the treatment of all ailments of the human family, is also to be in abundance, and the person viewing the building is impressed with the number and size of the windows.

The contractor for the building was E. A. Fonda of this city, while the building committee consisted of Thomas F. Parker, Chairman W. E. Beattie, Augustus W. Smith, B. E. Geer, A. O. Lawton, Lieut. Colonel J. Atkinson, and Commandant Mary E. Bebout.

A note in small print at the bottom of the article stated:

"Two registered nurses are wanted for the Emma Moss Booth Hospital in Greenville, S. C. one for the position of Supervisor of Training School and one to take the supervision of the operating room. Salvationists will be preferred but young women of Christian character, though not connected with the Army, if able to teach, will be considered. Regulation nurse's salary will be paid."

In the credit box on the page was written in small print:

"Reports of the opening of this institution were contained in last week's War Cry. The Chief Secretary (Colonel Holz) and the Secretary for Women's Social Work (Colonel Mrs. Bovill) represented the commander (Commander Eva Booth, the daughter of the Founder, rwk) at the official ceremony. Mr. B. E. Geer of the

> Judson Coffee Mills, presided, and others taking part were Rev. H. H. Hart (Russell Sage Foundation) and Congressman J. J. McSwain. Special mention was made of Mr. Thomas F. Parker, to whom we owe a very large share of the credit for the establishment of the hospital, and not only this but a veritable large multitude of enterprises.
>
> Both the Greenville News and the Piedmont devoted most generous space to the event. From the excellent description of the hospital printed by both we have compiled that information given on this page.

The Women's and Children's Shelter and later the Emma Moss Booth Memorial Hospital program was operated by the Women's Social Service Department of the Salvation Army and administered by the Salvation Army National Headquarters, Eastern Territorial command.

Officers, Assistant Officers, trainees, employees, and volunteers were allocated and maintained by those offices and were not, generally, parts of the local Corps Citadel program.

In addition, a separate Board of Advisors was recruited to maintain community support and guidance for the operation of the hospital.

The Officers who were assigned to the hospital were sometimes listed as members (Soldiers) of the Citadel and as such participated as leaders and teachers in the ongoing religious, character-building, and social welfare work within the community in their spare time.

Following is a listing of the administrative staff of the hospital, and the progress of the hospital until it was closed some years later, in November 1931.

1908-1919: The Salvation Army in Greenville operated a rescue home for women under the leadership of Brigadier Mary E. Bebout. The first known address of the facility is 617 Rutherford Street just outside of the Greenville city limits.

In 1917 Adjutant and Mrs. George Graves were assigned to the Rescue Home for Women, which had just added the Bruner Home for Children to its scope of responsibility.

Brigadier Bebout apparently was assigned to the Women's Home and Hospital program as commander that same year.

An effort was launched to construct the new hospital to be named Emma Moss Booth Memorial Hospital. The location of this facility was to be in Vardry Heights close to the Judson mill. The rationale for this location is unknown to the author.

After the EMBMH was operational, the Bruner Home for children apparently became a freestanding separate operation under the command of the Women's Social Service Department until 1949 when it closed due to consolidation of programs by the local Community Chest in order to save funds. (The Bruner Home program is highlighted in a separate chater of this book.)

Following is the progression of the Emma Moss Booth Hospital from its inception:

In 1919 the Superintendent was Commandant Mary E. Bebout and the ASO was Captain Woleslegle. The EMBMH was completed, dedicated, and opened for business inJanuary 1921.

Mr. B. E. Geer of the Judson Coffee Mills presided. Colonel Holz, Chief Secretary, and Colonel Mrs. Bovill, Secretary for Women's Social Work represented the Salvation Army.

The Southern Salvation Army *War Cry* gave a report of the event in the early February issues.

The report included the long awaited visit of the Commander, Eva Booth, who was the daughter of the founder, General William Booth.

Commissioner Eva Booth, National Commander, or as she preferred, "The Commander," was quite ill when she undertook this trip through the southland to promote and inspect the Army's programs. By the time she arrived in Greenville, she was so ill that she was not able to attend the dedication of the hospital.

The next day she was well enough to be able to speak to a large audience in the Downtown Presbyterian Church.

I quote, in condensed segments, from the *Salvation Army Southern War Cry* dated February 5, 1921.

> *WELCOMED TO GREENVILLE, S. C. BY CHEERING THRONG - OPENING THE EMMA MOSS BOOTH MEMORIAL HOSPITAL A NOTABLE FUNCTION- "THE SALVATION ARMY CHALLENGES THE BEST," SAYS CONGRESSMAN AT GREAT MEETING - THE COMMANDER INSISTS ON DELIVERING MESSAGES OF SALVATION TO PEOPLE TWICE ON SUNDAY - CHURCHES CLOSE FOR UNION MEETING - THREE THOUSAND PEOPLE ASSEMBLE IN FIRST BAPTIST CHURCH, WITH TWO OVERFLOWS*
>
> A large number of prominent local citizens frankly confess that the Commander's weekend campaign at Greenville, S. C. was the event of the year.
>
> At any rate the citizens of the weekend did full justice to the people and considering the physical ills also of the Commander...
>
> A throng had gathered at the station at whose head stood the Mayor. It was a civic and popular event in one, in which many of the Office-Holders and Industrial and Religious Leaders had a part...
>
> Passing through the double wall of human bodies, the Commander entered the awaiting motor-car, where

standing by the door the Mayor made a brief and informal speech of welcome. He brought, he said, the official welcome of the city and hoped that the reports of the Commander's illness were exaggerated. The program must of necessity be changed and formal addresses (by the Commander) must be dispensed with...

Out upon a hill just within the city limits, yet standing on its own grounds which are the dimensions of a park, is what Dr. Hart describes as the best and most complete hospital of its class in the United States...

The dedication of the institution was the first task of the day. The way to the building was beset with no mean difficulties, the least of which was the long section of hub-deep mud, which must have been a damper of spirits. But at peril to themselves motor-cars by the score threaded their miry way to the foot of the hospital hill, some of them parking in the deep mud...

The first song whose notes waved through the corridors and wards was one of praise to God, and the spirit of it inspired the first prayer by the Rev. DR. C. C. Herbert...

Mr. B. E. Geer, president of Judson Cotton Mills, practical and warm-hearted friend of the Salvation Army, took the direction of the program, calling first upon Dr. H. H. Hart, connected in an important official capacity to the Russell Sage Foundation. Dr. Hart said that he had come from New York to be present at the dedication, which he affirmed possessed great significance to Greenville, to Western South Carolina, and to the South generally. The South was backward in the matter of social relief, but was rapidly awakening and moving forward, led by Virginia and South Carolina, especially the splendid Board of Charities of South Carolina backed by a progressive and liberal Governor who was responsible for much of this advance.

He had advised some years before, the appropriation of $50,000 to each of three institutions in the South, one of which was the Salvation Army's Rescue Home for Women and maternity hospital in Greenville...

He congratulated the Salvation Army, the Commander, and the city and state upon the acquisition of the property. 'The building, upon which it stands,' he continued, 'will be a model to which the States will come for ideas and suitable and efficient architecture.'

Congressman J. J. McSwain, a typical orator of the south, made an elegant eulogy of The Salvation Army generally, and the work in Greenville in particular. He paid a tribute to those "broad-minded, liberal, philanthropic gentlemen of Greenville and vicinity" whose generosity had made the building possible - the mill owners - who had contributed together as much as all the remaining contributors of the city and state together. Special mention of and credit was given to Mr. Thomas F. Parker who was the leading spirit in the entire project...

Colonel Mrs. Bovill was introduced as representative of the Commander, and in a brief talk told of the ideals of the work of the hospital.

It again fell to Colonel Holz to explain the absence of the Commander, and again the people bore the disappointment with great 'generosity.' Major Hodges and Major Malice provided music.

On Sunday, Eva Booth, the Commander addressed thousands at the Downtown Presbyterian Church.

The meeting was so crowded and overflowing with congregation that the Elks Club, who gave massive and important service to the building of the hospital was crowded out of their reserved seats. The club was given a private meeting with the Commander, who spoke glowingly of the spirit of benevolence rendered by them.

1927

The School of Nursing was established and operated by The Salvation Army in the Emma Moss Booth Hospital in Greenville. Following is a roster of the staff and the student body from the Disposition of Forces of February 1927.

WOMEN'S HOME AND HOSPITAL GREENVILE, SOUTH CAROLINA — EMMA MOSS BOOTH MEMORIAL HOSPITAL Vardry Heights (Bell phone 3080) (Adults 50, Children 40)

Nurses, training school- Adjutant Myrtle Marshall, Superintendent; Captain Kathleen Lord, S.S. Officer; Miss Gladys Ayers, R.N., Supervisor Training School;

Miss Mary Rushing, R. N. Supervisor Operating Room; Miss Kyle Marshall R. N., Supervisor Surgical Department; Miss Ora Paige R. N., Night Supervisor.

Student nurses- Eunice Neeley, Cornelia Kaminer, Orenia Ray, Helen Laurence, Mamie Davis, Lena Kirby, Martha Watson, Gladys Ray, Hattie Abererombia, Dewie Armstrong, Anna Wade, Mae Murphy, Alice Lord, Theo Kirby, Mary K. Johnston, Julia Hill, Honor Hendrix, Ina Millhouse.

Thus, in 1931-32 the Salvation Army ended its program of hospitalization in Greenville and the administration of a separate Women's Social Service Department, which had operated since 1908 in the city. The Home and Hospital program was transferred to other cities. Local Salvation Army Officers made referrals to these consolidated hospitals. All other Social Work was transferred to the local Corps Social Welfare System.

CHAPTER XV

GREENVILLE, SC BOYS AND GIRLS CLUB HISTORICAL PROGRESSION
&
SALVATION ARMY-OPERATED COMMUNITY PLAYGROUNDS AND CAMPS

"Jesus loves the little children"

Let the Little Children...

Thirty-four years after the enduring establishment of the Salvation Army in Greenville, S C, the Boys and Girls Club was added to the arsenal of weapons against poverty and need. The year was 1938.

This program was conceived and implemented by concerned citizens of the community, notably, Mr. P. D. Meadors, in partnership with the Salvation Army. It is enduring proof of the worthiness of investing in the youth of today to insure the success of tomorrow.

Following is a listing of some of the accomplishments and a partial roster of the leadership of the Greenville, SC Boys and Girls Club from inception in 1938 to the present.

1938-1948 (Ten Charter Years)

SA Officer: S/Captain Arne Lekson
Founder: P. D. Meadors
BCC: W. W. Pate
BCAC: Mrs. W. W. Pate
BCED: The first Boys Club Executive Director was newly commissioned Lt. Robert Burchett.

Founding Committee:

P. D. Meadors-Principal Originator, Joe E. Sirrine, Ellis M. Johnston, W. W. Pate, C. Douglas Wilson, Robert E. Henry, Joseph R. Bryson, Captain Arne Lekson.

IN THE BEGINNING

The Greenville, SC Salvation Army Boy's Club was formed in 1938. According to historical records, a local candy manufacturer, Mr. P. D. Meadors was being raided at night by a group of boys who were stealing candy and the promotional coins placed in the wrappers.

Not wanting to put the boys in jeopardy with the law, after they were apprehended, he approached the local Salvation Army Officer, S/Captain Arne Lekson, to seek a solution, which would remedy his problem and help the boys to become better citizens.

The result was the formation of the Red Shield Boys Club at the Salvation Army Citadel on Broad Street. An add-on building was attached to the Citadel and the Greenville, SC Boy's Club was born.

Mr. P. D. Meadors was convinced that the boys needed, instead of punishment, a place to congregate, and Christian guidance in order to help them grow into law abiding and productive adults. With the help of a group of local business leaders such as Joe E. Sirrine, Ellis M. Johnston, W. W. Pate, C. Douglas Wilson, Robert E. Henry, and Joseph R. Bryson the Red Shield Boy's Club was established.

An addition was built on the back of the Salvation Army Citadel at 26 E. Broad Street to accommodate the new program for boys.

The First Boys Club Executive Director

Retired Brigadier Robert Burchett, now deceased, provided the following information in 1995 through Mr. Sam Piper, a member of the Boy's Club Council.

Brigadier Robert Burchett was stationed in Greenville on three different occasions—1938, one year; 1941-44, three years; and 1947-56, 9 years. He was married at the Woman's College on College Street in Greenville to Molieva Ball in 1944. She is also deceased.

Captain and Mrs. Robert Burchett

I quote, excerpted and edited:

In 1938 The Salvation Army commanding Officer, Major Arne Lekson, requested an Officer be assigned to Greenville to help start and run the Boys Club. On June 6, 1938 the School for Officers Training assigned an assistant Officer to Greenville to help establish the Boys Club.

Probationary Lieutenant Robert Burchett set right to work securing volunteer help and donated equipment and supplies to staff to equip the new club.

The first recorded donation by Mr. B. Y. Jordan, a barber shop owner on broad Street, was a set of boxing gloves so the first sport engagement became boxing. They entered the golden gloves competition shortly after that.

Where he learns to "give and take"

The first SA Boys Club Activity in Greenville-1938.

Lieutenant Burchett secured the volunteer service of a gentleman from the Dry Cleaning Company up on North Main Street in front of the Old Mackey Mortuary to act as boxing coach.

They actually conducted the boxing lessons in one of the classrooms in the Citadel. At one time, they entered the golden Gloves championship at the old Textile Hall.

Also involved in the formation of the Boys club were Douglas Wilson, Marion Sanders, Wilbur Hicks, George Ross, and W. B. Cox. The mayor at that time was Fred McCullough.

Mayor C. Fred McCullough meets with Red Shield Club Mayor and Commissioners.

Mayor of Greenville Fred C. McCullough with boys
Lt. Bob Burchett at right c1938-41.

Staff members of *The Greenville News and the Piedmont*, Mr. Paul Barrett and Mr. David Tillinghast provided good publicity for the club. Mr. Meadors and Mr. Pate secured donations from their friends and concerned citizens of Greenville.

The only paid employee was a Mr. Jim Dawson. There were several volunteers at work with the boys programs.

The National Youth Administration Program provided Federal grant money and a number of workers. The Woodwork Inspector, the Physical Director and the Program Director were also provided by the NYA organization.

A Miss Laura Baugh who taught psychology and social work at the Women's College furnished several women from the college students to help with the programs of tutoring and mentoring in the Boys and Girls Club. A lady named Mrs. Kissing provided substantial donations to assure that girls were also included in the Club membership.

The program consisted of sports of all kinds, homework help and tutoring, musical instructions, and every interesting kind of contest to keep the young boys and girls busy and happy.

All this took place in a rather small 60X16-foot building added to the back of the Citadel at 26 East Broad Street. There were about 300 members in very short time.

The membership extended beyond the problem children of the city. Every boy and girl who wanted it could have membership for a quarter to a dollar a year.

he can play games with his pals away from street hazzards and temptations.

n" he has great fun playing games and learns the value of teamwork

The Salvation army Club Kids at play in the gym and game room. c1938-41.

Its All for the Kids

Some of the standout members mentioned are Thurmond Hutchens, Tom Maddus and Jimmy Maddus. These boys went on to excel in sports in high school and college. Some other boys who went to the club and now lead successful lives are Sam Pittman, Warren Taylor, Charles Posey, Henry, Harry, Billy and Bob Mansfield, Jimmy Thompson, Paul Barnell, Rick Lull, Babe Bolden, and Stokley Raines (a "Bruner," who later married a Salvation Army Officer who resigned her commission in order to marry him).

Unusual Funding Sources

Two interesting Boys Club Committee members, Mike Shelton of the Bluebird Bus Company, and Henry Theodore of the Eagle Bus Lines had great fun in arguing about who would get to pay for some of the awards banquets. They usually ended up splitting the tab. It was great fun for them and a godsend for the club.

Mr. Spivey Spears arranged for free admission to the Greenville High School football games for the boys in the club.

Another very interesting and beneficial program at the Boys Club was the Thanksgiving dinner each year. Mr. Fred Curtis and his father would provide a free movie for the club about 10:00 AM. Then the kids would go back to the gym where a sumptuous turkey feast was waiting for them prepared by the Red Shield Ladies Auxiliary members. Following the dinner the entire club attended the high school football game of the season, free of charge, of course.

Easter Extravaganza

The Boys and Girls Club also hosted an Easter egg hunt for the members and their families in Cleveland Park each year. The program was sponsored by the Civitan Club and became a huge success, often involving whole families. Attendance numbered in the hundreds.

Boys and Girls Club members hunting Easter Eggs.

Cleveland Park Easter egg hunt c1940s.
(The Reedy River flows through Cleveland Park.)

The Lions Club was instrumental in securing free eye examinations and eyeglasses for the children who could not afford the cost of the care. This was an ongoing program and the children benefited greatly in having corrected vision.

Local Future Leaders

According to Lt. Colonel Jack Waters, the basketball team of that era was made up of some locally successful citizens of this present day:

- Jimmy Maddox: Chosen as high school teacher of the year, basketball coach, State Senator.
- Tommy Maddox: Clemson graduate, High School Coach
- Jimmy Landreth: Owned his own business
- Colonel Jimmy Owens: (US Air Force)

- Lt. Colonel Jack T. Waters (Salvation Army) Lt. Colonel Jack Waters said, “In retirement, one of my passions still is to raise capital funds to build Boys and Girls Clubs and Corps Community Centers. These young people are the future of our Army and our Country.”

Note: Mrs. Judy Campbell reports also the spelling of the two brothers’ names is Mattos (Jimmy and Tommy). It is possible that all were involved in the Boys and Girls Club at one time. All three spelling styles are listed in the local current telephone book.

YOU BETTER WATCH OUT! (Better not cry...)

Each year the Red Shield Women’s Auxiliary sponsored and hosted a mammoth Christmas party for the kids in the Club. Christmas treats and gifts were given out and a pageant of Christmas programs was presented.

Donations and gifts came from the community-spirited citizens and volunteer hosts and hostesses made the children feel loved and appreciated.

A Community-Wide Project

Some other outstanding and unselfish individuals whose names were recalled by Brigadier Robert Burchett (in retirement in 1995 when this report was written) are as follows: Mrs. P. D. (Gladys) Meadors who served as the Auxiliary Chairman at one time, and Mrs. W. W. Pate who was the founding chairman of the Auxiliary in 1938.

Both Mrs. Pate and Mrs. Meadors were long-time supporters of the Club and contributed many hours of service in obtaining funds and equipment to operate both the Club city programs and the Camp programs.

The many chairpersons and members whofollowwere just as dedicated to the cause and moved the programs to ever-higher successes.

Also mentioned were Mr. John P. Ashmore County Supervisor, who provided manpower and materials for the Community camp and the City Club program to provide maintenance and improvements. As well, he spent time with the boys of the club; Mr. Bill Reynier of Rey's Jewelry Store who one year gave the entire membership each a Mickey Mouse or Minnie Mouse watch; and Mr. Russell Ashmore of Ashmore Paving Company who provided roadwork and paving at the camp as needed. Mr. Ashmore was a member of the Civitan Club.

Every Little Bit Counts

Funding was augmented during the WWII years by recycling newspapers and magazines. About forty boys participated and raised several thousand dollars to help fund the programs. The program was also seen as a good patriotic endeavor for the times.

Many persons who gave generously of time, talent and treasure must go unnamed due to unsecured records.

A huge debt of gratitude is offered in appreciation to the thousands who were instrumental in securing and operating such a large humanitarian endeavor which has touched thousands of lives and is continuing today as a force for good in the community.

The Legacy Lives On

The Salvation Army Boys and Girls Club of America in Greenville is alive and well and thriving in this year of the centennial celebration of service.

The dedication and devotion to the club of the present leaders and volunteers is equally as compassionate and effective to the task of growing good citizens to the "Glory of God and the Benefit of Humanity." —Inscription on the cornerstone of the Citadel at 26 East Broad Street.

A Formal Dedication Service

A report in *The Greenville Daily News* dated November 9, 1938 reports that the dedication was held on November 10, 1938 by Lt. Commissioner Ernest I. Pugmire.

I quote, excerpted:

> SALVATION ARMY SLATES PROGRAM FOR DEDICATION. MEETING TO BE HELD AT POINSETT HOTEL PRIOR TO DEDICATORY SERVICE.
>
> EXPECT LARGE GROUP.
>
> Lieutenant-Commissioner Ernest I. Pugmire of Atlanta, southern Territorial leader of the Salvation army will make the principal address at the dedication service of the Greenville Salvation Army Red Shield boys club tomorrow night in the gymnasium of the recently -competed building adjacent to the Salvation Army Citadel here.
>
> The dedicatory address will follow a 'Dutch' luncheon at the Poinsett hotel tomorrow afternoon at one o'clock at which time Commissioner Pugmire will be presented before a group consisting of members of the Advisory Board, The Red Shield Club Committee, and the Red Shield Club Women's Auxiliary.
>
> With Commissioner Pugmire will be his wife, who will lead the dedicatory prayer at the service tomorrow.
>
> SEEN AS A BOON
>
> The Red Shield Club is expected to fill a long want in the lives of many boys and girls of Greenville who have been denied because of circumstances a well-rounded home life and training. The club will provide these youths with opportunities to get these advantages through a regular schedule set up for both boys and girls seeking to provide training for 100.

The complete program for the dedication follows:

Opening song: Onward Christian Soldiers-Lt. Colonel A. Taylor
Prayer- Dr. Alexander R. Mitchell, President of Greenville Ministerial Association
Scripture-Boys and Girls in unison
Introduction of Chairman-Major Arne Lekson
Chairman's remarks-Joseph R. Bryson, Congressman-elect
Musical number-Charlotte Temple Band
Presentation of Mayor, C. Fred McCullough, and special guests-Joseph R. Bryson
Song-Stand up for Jesus-Lt. Colonel A. Taylor
Introduction of Lt. Commissioner Ernest I. Pugmire
Dedicatory address-Commissioner Pugmire
Dedicatory prayer-Mrs. Pugmire

BOARD MEMBERS

On the Advisory Board are the following members: J. R. Bryson-President, W. W. Pate-V-President, Thomas McAfee Sr., R.R. Bishop, G. Fred McCullough, L. W. Carter, E. L. Snipes, J. W. Chapman, P. D. Meadors, J. B. Orders, J. P. Williamson, W. J. Hicks, Douglas Wilson, J. Britt, and Herbert Mims.

Serving on the Red Shield Club Committee

W. W. Pate-Chairman, C. Fred McCullough-Vice Chairman, Dave Tillinghast-Secretary, Maj. Arne Lekson-treasurer, Joe H. Britt, P. D. Meadors, J. B. Orders, W. M. Saunders, and E. L. Snipes.

The Red Shield Women's Club Auxiliary

Mrs. W. W. Pate-President, Mrs. Roy F. Hunt-Secretary, Mrs. G. W. Race-Treasurer, Mrs. R. R. Bishop, Mrs. Joe H. Britt, Mrs. Paul Browning, Mrs. Joseph R. Bryson,

Mrs. G. P. Campbell, Mrs. Judson Chapman, Mrs. Malcomb Davenport, Mrs. L. M. Glenn, Mrs. Deckard Guess, Mrs. J. W. Hicks, Mrs. Grice Hunt, Mrs. J. M. Lesesne, Mrs. Arne Lekson, Mrs. P. D. Meadors, Mrs. Herbert Mims, Mrs. Thomas McAfee Sr., Mrs. C. Fred McCullough, Mrs. R. F. Neilson, Mrs. J. B. Orders, Mrs. Dixon Pearce, Mrs. C. O. Shell, Mrs. Elisha Snipes, Mrs. J H. Speer, Mrs. P. M. Taylor Jr., Mrs. J. P. Williamson, Mrs. C. Douglas Wilson, and Mrs. F. McKissick - honorary member.

They Number in the Thousands

The above lists are representative of the large group of volunteer local business and professional citizens who stand behind the Salvation Army in every program and service delivered to the local community. The above group served in Greenville in 1938.

In previous and subsequent years the Advisory groups added and deleted members to keep the numbers constant and allow for a one-third rotation of members to generate new ideas and involvement as the years go by.

Some members attain lifetime membership status by being elected many years in succession.

The Boy's Club has operated continuously in Greenville since 1938.

BOYS CLUB ONLY...NO GIRLS ALLOWED...NOT!

In 1938, when the Red Shield Boys Club was formed, many people who contributed did so with the understanding that girls would be served in this program also.

On January 13, 1948 the Greenville Salvation Army Red Shield Boys Club became affiliated with the Boys Club of America. At that time, it was the first and only Salvation Army Boys Club so affiliated in South Carolina.

Since May, 1969, The Salvation Army Boys and Girls Club sits upon a sprawling tract of land on Owens Street complete with outdoor playing fields and additional acreage for expansion.

The Club serves the youth of Greenville and the surrounding communities. It is open to any and all young people who sign up for membership. There is no cost associated with membership.

The Boy's Club has had a long and illustrious list of Advisors who have made possible the continuous upgrading of both facilities and programming over the years.

The Boys Club Advisory Council, while operating independently, is parented by the Salvation Army Advisory Board. Inter-membership keeps the duties of both groups solidly united in purpose and ideology of the Boys Club of America and The Salvation Army.

Purpose and Aim

The purpose and aim of the Red Shield Boys and Girls Club is to "build citizens." The Boys and Girls Club is strictly non-sectarian; however, every member is urged to attend regularly the religious persuasion of his choice. The Boys and Girls Club is a positive low cost approach to the prevention of juvenile delinquency and crime which exacts yearly a heavy financial and spiritual toll from the community.

The Red Shield Boys and Girls Club offers the following to the children of the community:

- Free-time activity under Christian leadership.
- Guidance programs dealing with issues such as behavior and attitude toward others, family and church relationships, education, employment, and government.
- Physical training, athletics, and development of physical fitness.
- Development of vocational skills and work ethic

The Red Shield Club has been affording boys and girls a better playground than the city streets and finer fellowship and wiser counsel than can be found in neighborhood gangs.

The staff of the Boys and Girls club is made up of the Executive Director, Program Directors, office manager, and volunteer program leaders.

Executive Directors

P/Lieutenant Robert Burchett was engaged as the founding Executive Director of the Boys Club. In a later Annual Meeting pamphlet Captain Bob Burchett is named as the Executive Director of the club. This would be the second assignment to Greenville for Captain Burchett.

In his letter Brigadier Robert Burchett names Jim Dawson as the only employee listed at the founding of the Boys Club in 1938. It is unclear what his function was and what part he played in the formation of the club.

It is not known when Buck Traynam, later the director, began his association with the club. There is no record available. A Mrs. K. A. Traynham is listed as a member of the Bruner Home Auxiliary in 1949. This could possibly have been a family member.

The original Executive Director was probably engaged in that position until the first non-officer Executive Director could be hired. It is unclear when that actually occurred.

In 1978, in a newspaper article, Major (now Lt. Colonel) Jack Waters alludes to the personal influence of Mr. Buck Traynam in the forties before Mr. Norman Eoute was hired. The newspaper account alludes to Mr. Traynam's being a director.

Lt. Colonel Waters adds the notation that George Worthy was the Boys Club director in the early years and Buck Traynam was later named director. Other spelling from the current phone book possible-Traynham, Traynum.

No other mention is made of either man in available Boys Club records. Boys Club historical data for the early forties is very scarce.

Oral and written reports from local citizens and some Officers attest to certain Officers, listed as Assistants, being actually employed as Boy's Club Officers. This would explain the absence of the Executive Directors position during this time. Official confirmation is not available.

Lieutenant Bob Burchett	1938
Captain Arthur Kinlaw	1944
Captain and Mrs. Jack McCune	1945
George Worthy	middle 1940s
Buck Traynam	late 1940s
Norman Eoute	July 1955 to 1990
Mike Foss	From 1990 to present.

Norman Eoute and his wife Kay came from Williamsport, PA in 1950 to attend Bob Jones University. "I had enlisted at nineteen and served three years in World War II," he explained, "and like many young men in the service I had no religion, no direction to my life until I became converted and interested in helping young people." After graduation, the couple decided to make Greenville their home and Mr. Eoute, who had been active for sometime in the Youth Crusade, went to work for the Salvation army in February 1955.

About five months later he became director of the Boys Club, often called the Red Shield Club. A year later he started directing the Civitan Club's Fresh Air Camp and continued to do this for nine years.

> "That was one of the most rewarding experiences I've ever had," he says. "You can do more with a boy in working with him for one week at camp than from just seeing him once a week for a year. Completely separated from old ties and associates, he responds to a new environment." —from Elizabeth Stiff, *The Greenville Daily News, 9/1987*

Mike Foss came to Greenville on transfer from Charlotte in 1990 to assume leadership of the Salvation Army Boys and Girls Club upon Mr. Eoute's retirement.

Prior to coming to Greenville, Mike Foss was affiliated with The Salvation Army Boys Club since he was 11 in Pinellas County, FL as a member. He showed outstanding leadership ability and was employed as part-time helper in the club's game room at age 18. In 1966 he served as a unit and programs director.

After graduation he was hired as the executive director of a Salvation Army community center and at the same time was taught special education classes.

He graduated from St. Petersburg College with a BA in Business Administration and has been a director of various clubs for almost fifty years.

The Boys and Girls club is operated as a part of the Citywide Salvation Army program under the general direction of the Corps Officer. However, the day to day oversight is vested in the Executive Director. The Boys and Girls Club Council is the guiding and supporting volunteer unit behind the club.

The Boys Club was founded to provide a place for youth of limited means and opportunity to congregate off the streets.

A Living Testimonial

A testimonial to the effectiveness of the Boys and Girls Club is found in correspondence from Reverend Robert C. McIntyre of Annandale, VA. He was an orphan in Greenville and reared by Frank and Mae McIntyre in the early and middle forties. (Mae was a "Bruner" and is a Soldier of the Greenville Corps).

Robert was sworn in as a Junior Soldier in Greenville on 2/7/1943 and a Senior Soldier on 1/31/46. He entered the Salvation Army School for Officers training in 1950 and was commissioned in 1951. He subsequently resigned his commission to attend Moody Bible Institute in Chicago and later Wheaton College where he obtained his BA and MA degrees. He went on to establish a Ministries Mission in Washington, D C. where he and his wife, Mary Frances Payne McIntyre, serve the needs of the people to this day.

I quote from an email from Reverend Robert C. McIntyre:

> I am not blood related to Mae McIntyre, but was raised by her and her husband Frank and have the McIntyre name. I was actually raised a Roman Catholic, but through a series of circumstances, including membership in the Red Shield Boys Club, I was in the Corps Sunday School on April 22, 1945 for a 'Decision Sunday,' and met the Lord in a powerful expression of His saving grace. Brigadier and Mrs. Breazeale were Corps Officers at the time and Capt. and Mrs. Jack McCune were in charge of the Boys Club. I was greatly encouraged by them in my new relationship with the Lord. I don't remember the dates, but soon thereafter Capt. and Mrs. Fred Boyette came as Corps Officers and they took a special interest in me. I became a Corps Cadet and a member of the band. I was taught how to play a baritone and was assigned to teach others what I knew. I proudly wore my uniform and was given excellent discipleship training. I was taught to teach and preach and was preaching when I was 15-16.
>
> I love the Army deeply and will be eternally grateful for the good foundation I received in its ranks. It was 'family' to this orphan. (Though I was never in the Bruner Home, Mae McIntyre actually spent several years there when she was a child.)
>
> The Army was God's instrument as the most formative influence in my life.

1949-1959

BCC: W. Marion Sanders (1959)
BCED: Norman Eoute from 1955
BCAC: Mrs. Paul E. Storey (1959)

In 1951 The Citadel on Broad Street became the Salvation Army Boys and girls Club. The Citadel moved permanently to 417 Rutherford Street Photo c1951.

In 1951, when the *Citadel program was moved to 417 Rutherford Road, the Boy's Club occupied the entire building at the Broad Street location and continued there until it was moved to its present location on Owens Street.

The Social Service conglomerate was called the Social Service Center and contained all the welfare services.

(Note: These names are interchangeable with other descriptive names of the above sections, and are not official in nature, but descriptive of the programs carried out in the centers. rwk)

The name “Citadel program” is used in connection with the Broad Street location because it was a many-faceted program that defied description. It was simply The Salvation Army. There was no other name to adequately describe it.

At a later date the official designation of the Salvation Army religious services and Character Building activities on Rutherford Street was referred to as the Corps Community Center.

The Service Center, also in the same location, contained the welfare and transient facilities. It was the official point of entry for welfare and social service work.

The designation “Corps Community Center” is slowly changing in many communities to reflect the all-inclusive nature of Salvation Army work, which eclipses simply a community center operation.

A standard, descriptive name other than “The Salvation Army” has not been identified in the entire world. “Specific-named” operations are in use throughout the world to identify the activity offered within specific buildings. No matter what it is called either formally or informally, it is The Salvation Army

The Staff in 1959 consisted of the following members:

Norman Eoute, Club Director; Jack Rodenhamel, Program Director; Jack Kirby, Athletic Director; Ray Fouet, Craft Director; and John Sanders, Canteen and Program Assistant

The Red Shield Council consisted of the following members:

W. Marion Sanders, Chairman; John P. Batson, Vice Chairman; James C. Thompson, Treasurer; and Austin Griffeth, Secretary.

Members of the Boys and Girls Club Council:

P. D. Meadors, W. W. Pate Sr., George Ross Sr., Claude Cato, C. Heyward Morgan, Thomas W. Miller, Vardy D.

Ramseur Sr., Steve Kelly, Thomas S. Hartness, Ben D. Harvey, C. A. Thrasher, M. L. Knight, M. M. Stokley, Henry Theodore, Leonard M. Todd, Charles H. Garrison, D. J. Touchberry, Henry B. McCoy, J. M. Clary, James A. Dusenberry, James White, Lythgoe Wier, William B. Price, Leonard H. Robinson, and William Norwood.

The Red Shield Ladies Auxiliary consisted of the following:

Mrs. Paul E. Storey, President; Mrs. A. N. Bozeman, 1st V. President; Mrs. C. T. Allen, 2nd V. President; Mrs. John P. Ashmore, Recording Secretary; Mrs. J. J. Massey, Corresponding Secretary; and Mrs. J. F. Welborn, Treasurer.

Members:

All are married taking the given name of the husband in keeping with the custom of the period with the exception of Miss Stella Bobo. Three other members used their own given names.

This form of addressing husband and wife was also the prevailing method in the Salvation Army during this period. Mmes. E. L. Adams, C. T. Allen, Thomas Anderson, John P. Ashmore SR, C. B. Attaway, M. D. Barton, C. W. Bell, R. P. Barry, D. A. Boyd, Joseph R. Bryerson, A. N. Bozeman, Joe L. Carter, C. F. Cato Sr., F. H. Eskew, H. D. Evatt, Frank Ferguson, E. C. Forole, C. W. Garrison, E. A. Gillfillin, Hattie Hardy, G. F. League, J. D. Lanford, C. E. Linville, A. W. Lockwood, B. G. Lollis, Mattie B. Long, F. A. Luben, F. C. Lupo, S. A. Massey, W. P. Meares, W. H. Miller Sr., T. W. Morton, S. S. Newell, M. Ousley, Arthur Pollard, R. G. Ridgewood, C. H. Roper, L. C. Shelton Sr., W. B. Simmons, J. W. Smith, E. L. Snipes, Paul E. Storey, W. King Thackston, Louis Thomas, R. M. Thomason, H. P. Watson, J. F. Welborn, Mamie G. Wilson, and W. C. Woodward.

The Annual Stewardship Report

The Annual Report to the community for 1959 (year 1958) lists the progress and production of the Boys and Girls Club for that year. It is typical of year to year operations with growth and strength shown year over year:

Receipts:

United Way of Greenville, $23,100.00: other income, $876.61

Total Receipts, $23,976.61

Disbursements:

Salaries and Wages/Retirement and Social Security, $11,428.79: Operating Expense, $5,487.39: Service Expense (Camp), $7,060.43

Total Disbursements, $23,976.61

Activities:
Athletic, Meetings 1078-Attendance 17389
Group club, Meetings 24-Attendance 539
Special Interest Groups, Meetings 195-Attendance 3320
Games Rooms, Meetings 260-Attendance 12668
Assemblies and Parties, meetings 88-Attendance 7159
Educational Trips, Meetings 9-Attendance 318
Movie Programs, Meetings 12-Attendance 1387
Note: The Camp statistics are listed in the section of this chapter covering camps and playgrounds.

1968-1978:

BCCC: Unknown
BCAC: Mrs. Jerry Gleits, 1968
Mrs. Sue Ashmore, 1972
Mrs. W. H. Miller. 1973
Mrs. Dorothy Gleits, 1975
BCED: Norman Eoute (1955-1990)

In 1969 the Boys and Girls Club operations were moved to the West Side of Greenville on Owens Street. The old Citadel and Boys Club properties were sold and subsequently demolished to make way for the Greenville News parking lot.

Following is a quote from *The Greenville News and Piedmont*, Saturday November 4, 1978:

> EX-NEWSPAPER BOY HONORED
>
> In the late 1940's a newspaper delivery boy would wile away his time downtown at the Salvation Army Boys Club, then on Broad Street behind the Greenville News-Piedmont building. He would go to the nearby club, known in past years as the Red Shield Club, to play basketball until his stack of papers was ready.
>
> Last year that delivery boy - now Major Jack Waters - was honored for his long and distinguished service in the Salvation Army. The proximity of his newspaper work and The Salvation Army Boys Club led to a successful Salvation Army career.
>
> Major Waters' current duties as Community Relations and Development Director (Secretary) for the fifteen Southern States involves a lot of traveling. He assists with Capital Campaigns, disaster work, and endowment trusts.
>
> It is ironic that the major, who initiated the Distinguished Service medallion when he was Carolinas' Youth Director, was designated a recipient of the award. He said he established the award for others and never dreamed he would get it.
>
> A native of Easley, Major Waters attended Parker High School where he played baseball and football.
>
> After a lifelong Salvation Army career, Major Waters is still boosting the Club program. "I think it is a tremendous asset to the community being a product of the Boys Club. I can give testimony to its good work. The preventive quality," he said, "is probably the greatest asset of the Boys Club, in relation to delinquency. There is no way we can measure the amount of good instilled in the boys," he said.

> Buck Traynam was the stalwart in Major Waters' youth. "He had a stabilizing influence", he said, "he was responsible for my staying close to the club," Major Waters said about the director of the Boys Club in the forties.
>
> He also lauded the Reverend Norman Eoute, the current (to 1990) director of the Club.

It is noted that Major and Mrs. Jack and Magdalene Arrowood Waters served in many Divisional and Territorial appointments and, as Divisional Commanders/Directors of Women's Ministries each with the rank of Lieutenant Colonel, in several Divisions before their retirement to North Carolina in 1997.

They are presently serving as capital campaign consultants to the Salvation Army in the Southern Territory and around the Nation.

1978-1988:

BCCC: Wally Mullinax, 1987-1989
BCAC: Mrs. Maude Cashion, 1977-1979
Mrs. Ellen Brady, 1980-1981
Mrs. Lila Ruth Godfrey, 1982-1983
BCED: Norman Eoute (1955-1990)

1988-1998:

BCCC: Wally Mullinax, 1987-1989
Jack Watson, 1990-1992
Sam Piper, 1993-1995
Al Phillips, 1996-1997
Carlisle Rogers, 1998-1999
BCAC: Mrs. Evelyn Brady, 1992
BCED: Norman Eoute to 1990, Mike Foss from 1990

In 1990 the official name was changed to the Salvation Army Boys and Girls Club of America in keeping with the

National Boys and Girls Club organization. Currently, boys and girls are served with equal consideration given to every program.

1998-2004:

BCCC: Duke McCall, Jr., 2002-Present
BCAC: Discontinued 1998.
BCED: Mike Foss

In a Greenville news interview by Sonia Chopra with Mike Foss, Executive Director of the Salvation Army Greenville Boys and Girls Club of America is found the following snapshot:

Currently the program has 1500 young people between the ages of 6 and 18 enrolled and the average number of students participating daily is 260.

The club operates on an annual budget of $648,000.00 with 15 staff members, both part time and full time. They are assisted by 340 volunteers from Furman University, Bob Jones University and the University of South Carolina and from organizations such as United Way and Hands on Greenville.

Two of those volunteers are profiled.

- Miss Kelly Fitzgerald is a graduate of Eastside High School and a student at Furman University. She says that she learned the importance of volunteering by following her parents' example. She also says, "My father always said 'We are put on earth to help others,' and my mother is a caring, compassionate person who gave herself and her time to us kids and anyone who needed help. She's always the first to help anyone in need. I want to be able to give people the same opportunities I had." Her parents are Frank and Janet Fitzgerald.
- Christian Stevenson, a volunteer coordinator with HOG and a member of the First Presbyterian Church writes in a guest column in the Greenville News, "All my life

I have searched for opportunities in my church and community to work with children. For the past six and one-half years I've lived in Greenville, I have continued to work with children . Volunteering with Hands On Greenville (HOG) has presented me with many opportunities to do this through tutoring and other programs. For the past four years, I have been the HOG coordinator for the Salvation Army Boys and Girls Club. This segment of The Salvation Army provides an after-school program for young people in neighborhoods where there is a need." She continues, "Every day of my life I realize how blessed I am to have the quality of life I do. Unfortunately, not everyone enjoys the same opportunities for success and happiness."

SMART CENTERS - TUTORING PROGRAMS

With education and problems associated with keeping at-risk children in school at an all time high, the Salvation Army Boys and Girls Club began to explore more effective means to help the kids with school work, especially homework assignments.

In an article written by staff writer Dale Perry for the Greenville News on 9/1/2000 there was an update on a very successful Boy's Club program.

SALVATION ARMY TUTORING PROGRAM GETS ANOTHER $50,000.00 DONATION

Mike Foss (Greenville Boys and Girls Club Director) started a program four years ago to help young students learn, and in it's short life, it has caught on as one of the Army's best successes.

"I'm so glad we went forward with this program," said Foss after a Thursday luncheon at The Salvation Army's headquarters on Rutherford Street, where officials announced another $50,000.00 donation from the

Sargent Foundation to help fund the tutoring program for students in the first through eighth grades.

Foss said the program called "After School Smart Centers" started four years ago with 30 students and $35,000.00 contribution from the Sargent Foundation. And next week, about 310 students are expected to enroll for weekly tutoring classes in reading, writing, math, science, history and English.

Bob Wilson, chairman of the Sargent Foundation, said that in addition to helping students make greater academic achievements, it provides spiritual guidance.

"The Salvation Army in this program is feeding body and soul and they are getting amazing results," Wilson said.

The Sargent Foundation, which also assists other Salvation Army programs, was created by Earl and Eleanor Sargent in 1954 from their own personal savings.

The Smart Centers program has grown and now encompasses several sites around the city and serves several hundreds of "at risk" children.

The Salvation Army Boys and Girls Club Advisory Council of 2001-2002 is as follows:

Officers: John Baker, Chairman, Duke k. McCall, Jr., Vice Chairman; Greg Jansen, Secretary; Jack H. Watson, Treasurer

Members: John E. Austin, Tony Barnhill, Brodie Brigman, Johnny Mack Brown, Richard L. Crain, Jim freeland, Les Hodge; Alva Phillips; Sam Piper; Amber Richards; Rita Smith; Mike Spivey; E. Roy Stone Jr.

PRESIDENTIAL RECOGNITION

Among the Salvation Army's most prized accomplishments over the years has been the favorable attention of a wide-ranging compliment of public and private corporations, individuals, and political entities.

A case in point is a visit to Greenville, SC by President George W. Bush on March 27,2002.

The following is from an article by Cindy Landrum of *The Greenville News:*

TEEN TO GREET (GEORGE W.) BUSH
GREENVILLE TEEN TO MEET PRESIDENT

Southside High School senior Gus Samuel will be among the first to shake President (George W.) Bush's hand when he lands at Greenville-Spartanburg International Airport.

The 17-year-old was chosen to meet the President because of his volunteer work at the Salvation Army's Boys and Girls Club.

He'll meet Bush under the wing of Air Force One, then ride in the presidential motorcade to the Greenville Fire Deportment, the first stop in the President's visit. "It's an honor," Samuel said.

But Samuel wasn't out for recognition when he began volunteering at the Boys and Girls Club four years ago.

It was to repay a program that helped him, starting at age 10.

"They showed me a lot of things I didn't know about, like responsibility," he said, " I went every day after school."

Greenville teen to meet president

Southside senior is active volunteer in the community

By Cindy Landrum
EDUCATION WRITER
clandrum@greenvillenews.com

When Air Force One lands at the Greenville-Spartanburg International Airport this morning, Southside High senior Gus Samuel will be among the first to shake President Bush's hand.

Samuel, 17, of Greenville, was chosen to meet the president because of his volunteer work at the Salvation Army's Boys and Girls Club.

He'll meet Bush under the wing of Air Force One, then ride in the presidential motorcade to the Greenville Fire Department, the first stop in the president's whirlwind visit.

"It's an honor," Samuel said.

But Samuel wasn't out for recognition when he began volunteering at the Boys and Girls Club four years ago.

It was to repay a program that helped him, starting at the age of 10.

"They showed me a lot of things that I didn't know about, like responsibility," he said. "I went every day after school."

Now, the honor roll student works as a junior staff member, volunteer basketball, football and soccer coach, a part-time recreation aide, field-trip leader and after-school tutor.

"He's able to speak to them on their level," said Mike Burdine, Salvation Army program director. "He's a role model. He's led by example. The kids know he's been where they are and that they have to get where he is."

OWEN RILEY JR. / Staff

To greet Bush: Southside High senior Gus Samuel has been chosen to greet President Bush when Air Force One lands this morning in Greenville.

Friends and family were stunned at the news of Samuel's visit with the president.

Samuel said his mother's reaction when the White House called Sunday was "to try to figure out why the government was calling." And when a White House advance man called Southside High on Tuesday, principal Steve Chamness said everybody thought it was a joke, reminiscent of the movie, "The American President."

Samuel said he doesn't have a predetermined question to ask the president.

"I'm sure one will pop into my mind when I see him," he said.

Outstanding Greenville Boys Club teen volunteer meets President of the United States George W. Bush c2002.

> Now, the honor roll student works as a junior staff member, volunteer basketball, football and soccer coach, a part-time recreation aide, field trip leader, and after-school tutor.
>
> "He's able to speak to them on their own level," said Mike Burdine, Salvation Army program director. "He's a role model. The kids know he's been where they are and that they have to get where he is."
>
> Samuel said his mother's (Mrs. Sonja Johnson) reaction when the White House called Sunday was to try to figure out why the government was calling. And when a White House advance man called Southside High on Tuesday, Principal Steve Chamness said everybody thought it was a joke, reminiscent of the movie, The American President.

Gus Samuel is a standout. He volunteers because he wants to make the world better, not to gain personal attention.

As a note of interest, in December 2002 Gus Samuel enlisted in the United States Marine Corps and is now serving his country in that branch of the military service.

There are many more stories such as the above in existence and many more not told of the spirit of dedicated volunteers who have both benefited by, and are benefiting from, the Salvation army's vast array of "character builders" all across the landscape of the world.

The Red Shield Boys and Girls Club (now The Salvation Army Boys and Girls Club of Greenville) is firmly ingrained into the Greenville landscape and will continue for many years as a growing force for good and decent citizenship among our young people.

The ongoing and ever-expanding programs march right on with the changing of the times and tides of fortune within the community.

In 2004 The Salvation Army Boys and Girls Club celebrates its 66th year of continuous operation in

Greenville. The Boys Clubs of America organization nationwide celebrates its 100th year in 2004.

The program is updated year-by-year. Outdated programs are discontinued and programs to meet the current needs of the young people are added.

Each year brings new challenges and begs solutions for problems encountered by the Club as new and sometimes radical changes in society evolve.

Thanks to the untiring efforts of the Advisory Board, the Boys Club Council, and the Salvation Army Administrative Officers the changes are identified and addressed on an ongoing basis.

The object is, as always, to produce better citizens and give the most underprivileged children a decent chance to grow and succeed in the battle of life.

EXPANDED BOYS AND GIRLS CLUB SERVICES SALVATION ARMY RED SHIELD CLUB-OPERATED COMMUNITY PLAYGROUNDS AND CAMPS

1942-1960s:

Salvation Army Boys Club kids at Camp Watacoo, a Salvation Army operated camp c1953.

One of the outstanding programs operated in the past by the Salvation Army Boys and Girls Club in Greenville, SC is the community camping program.

This program was conceived in 1942 and was in full operation through the 1960s with the exception of 1946-49.

Thousands of children and adults in the Salvation Army program were afforded a week or two in the outdoor setting of a summer camp and a healthy outdoor experience.

The Red Shield Club operated the camp and the Civitan Club sponsored the program with volunteers and donations of time and money. The Greenville Community Chest provided operating expenses, as did the campers themselves and the general public.

According to an Annual Report dated 1954, the Salvation Army fresh air camp was founded by interested and involved local citizens and staffed by the Salvation Army directors and counselors. It was nurtured and supported by a number of local civic clubs, corporations and individuals.

I quote from that Annual Report:

> A group of local businessmen, who were Boys Club Council members, formed a corporation known as Charities, Inc. These businessmen are E. L. Snipes, J. Wilbur Hicks, R. A. Jolley; W. W. Pate; P. D. Meadors; W. Marion Sanders; and George Ross.
>
> The Greenville Fresh Air camp is located at Blythe Shoals, S C just three miles above Cleveland, SC and twenty miles from Greenville, SC on US Highway No. 276.
>
> The Local Salvation Army staff operates the Fresh Air Camp.
>
> THANK YOU, Greenville!
>
> We are grateful to the many individuals, groups, clubs. And churches who provided a

> camping experience for the following needy and neglected families of Greenville.
>
> 334 boys and girls ages 7 through 15
> 29 mothers
> 39 kiddies under 5 years of age
> 402 campers for 1954

A note of appreciation is added to the report.

> It is to the needs of boys and girls of needy, broken homes The Red Shield Club at 26 East Broad Street serves twelve months throughout the year at no cost to the child. The Club is open daily from 2 PM to 9 PM for your inspection.
>
> The Red Shield Club is supported through the Greater Greenville Community Chest while the Greenville Fresh air camp is supported through individuals who contribute $10.00 per week for a child to spend one week in the mountains.

The Salvation Army was operator of unique community programs in conjunction with the Civitan Club and other service Clubs in the community. Two of these are the Community Fresh Air Camp and the Community playground.

Brigadier Robert Burchett gave the following excerpted report on the establishment and operation of the specialty Camp programs:

> George Ross, Joe Britt, and Maurice Jolley were the men who started the fresh air camps for the Salvation Army for the Greenville Boys Club.
>
> Ben Geer, President of Furman University, owned the camp. Local volunteer groups secured by Speedy Spears, the Greenville High School coach, staffed the camp.

The camp capacity was 125 youngsters and staff; it was filled for each of the two-week sessions each summer. A total of 500 boys and girls were given a time of fresh air and sunshine and a good old fashioned dose of Christian love by the people who operated the facility.

The program consisted of a Daily Vacation Bible School type program, sports, swimming, and a campfire program at night.

Brigadier Burchett says that swimming and eating were the favorite activities. Of course classes in good habits, hygiene, citizenship and worship were included in each camp session.

The Advisory Board and the Boys Club committee used a mail appeal and personal collections to provide operating and upkeep maintenance funds for the Community Camp. The fund raising amounted to about ten dollars per week for each camper.

The merchants of the Farmer's Market and other people who had in-kind donations to give donated the remaining substance.

A Surprise Donation

Making his rounds in the old pick-up truck, which was unstable and badly in need of repair, Captain Burchett was surprised by a donation of a new truck which the merchants had collected money to buy.

Such was the esteem of the community toward the Greenville Boys and Girls Club.

The Greenville Health Department provided physical examinations for the campers free of charge. A local barbershop provided free haircuts, if needed. This shop is unnamed but was located about three doors down the block from the Citadel at 26 East Broad Street.

Equipment was donated and solicited by members of the Boys Club Council and other citizens, such as Johnny Holmes, Director at the YMCA.

Monk Mulligan, who was the program and physical director, was also instrumental in securing donations of equipment for the camp

Woody Wilbanks, Dunean Mills Representative and coach and director of athletics, volunteered time and money to the camp and Boys Club regular program.

Norman Eoute was hired in 1955 by Captain Burchett to direct the camp program and later to direct the entire Boys Club operation in Greenville. He was employed for more than thirty-five years in that capacity.

A Well Earned Salute to a Solid Citizen

When Mr. Eoute retired, Brigadier Burchett along with Monty Dupre, radio and television announcer, and J. Roy Stone, an outstanding contributor, were the principal guests. Other participants in the retirement program were as follows:

Norvin Duncan presided over the program. Major Evans Colbert gave the invocation. Remarks were made by Lt. Governor Nick Theodore, Brigadier Robert Burchett, Shane Powell, Mickeal Burdine, Billy Hughes, Sammy Leppard, Major Clay Satcher and Major Cecil Brogden.

A special presentation was given by Wally Mullinax:, remarks were made by Norman Eoute and the benediction was given by Captain John Carter.

SUMMER CAMP PROGRAM

The following excerpts appeared in a copy of the *Greenville Piedmont* dated August 1, 1953

Free Summer Camps: A Noble Work

In this interim between the time summer begins to wane and fall and school days arrive, all Greenvillians should pay tribute to those who have operated successfully those camps, which provide camping experiences for children whose parents are unable to provide for them. These camps are those of the Elks Lodge and the Red Shield Club.

The other camp for the less fortunate, the Red Shield Fresh Air Camps, took care of 307 children between the ages of 7 and 18 years. Here the story of juvenile development is much the same; some youngsters gained on the balanced diet and others who were accustomed to an unhealthy diet consisting mainly of cheaper starchy foods and unwholesome fat gained healthy muscle.

The Red Shield Camp also offered an unusual activity, a camp period for mothers and small children. This program reached 19 mothers and 36 children under 5 and the cost was paid by a group of Women's Clubs. The almost appalling need of this group is indicated by the fact that the program included instruction in bed-making, sewing, hygiene, diet, and practices that enable a family to make the most of the little it has.

We especially commend The Elks who have done their job from their own resources. We are also indebted to the citizens who gave monetary contributions to the Red Shield Camp and to the Salvation Army which provided the leadership.

This is indeed a noble work. In many instances those actively directing it have done so at considerable sacrifice to themselves. It is our hope that proper appreciation of their efforts may make easier their job next year and in the years to come.

Excerpted from the 1952 Annual report of the Salvation Army:

> The camp was formerly known as Watacoo and is located at Blythe Shoals, S. C. on US Highway 276, 21 miles from Greenville, SC. Several members of the Red Shield Advisory Council in 1942 purchased this camp from Dr. B. E. Geer for the use of underprivileged children.
>
> These members of the Red Shield Council received a state charter in the name of Charities Incorporated. The Salvation Army has conducted a camp for underprivileged children annually since March 1942 with the exception of the years 1946-1949. A Mothers' and Kiddie Camp for children under five years of age was begun and will continue to be an annual part of the camping program. The fresh air camp operates two weeks for girls and six weeks for boys and any child in Greenville County who cannot afford to pay for his or her camping is eligible to attend.
>
> Children recommended by children's court, Department of Public Welfare, Family Services, Baptist, Presbyterian, Methodist missions along with members of the Red Shield can attend at no cost to the child.
>
> The Greenville fresh air camp is supported by contributions of interested individuals who contribute $10.00 a week for one child.
>
> The Greenville Fresh Air Camp has provided a summer vacation for over 1900 children during the years it has been under the supervision of the Salvation Army.

ACCOUNTIBILITY ALWAYS
CIRCA 1958 ANNUAL REPORT

The following information is representative of the report to the community filed annually at an Annual Report meeting given for each year. This reported information is from the year 1959, courtesy of Mr. Jack Rodenhamel of Spartanburg, South Carolina. I quote as nearly as possible to the original script.

The 1958 camping season of the Civitan fresh air camp, under the direction of The Salvation Army Red Shield Boys Club has completed its finest year.

Hundreds of boys and girls recommended by Children's Court, Department of Public Welfare, Family Services, Baptist, Presbyterians, and Methodist Missions; along with members of the Red Shield Club were able to experience one or two weeks of camp life without any cost to them as a courtesy of the United Fund of Greenville County.

The season began June 9 with 86 Sunbeams, a girl's organization of the Salvation Army ages 12 and under. They came from several other Corps in nearby towns and communities.

This camp was directed by Mrs. Sr. Captain Henry (Bernice Lyons) Gillespie, with 46 visitors and 1,239 meals being served.

The next two weeks, June 16-June 30 were for girls between the ages of 7 and 17 with 177 in attendance. The 189 visitors of this two-week period included The Women's Auxiliary, The Salvation Army, Red Shield Boys Council members, and many Civitans. There were 4,383 meals served.

Boys Camp began June 30 and continued to July 28 with 263 boys in attendance. We had 202 visitors during this four-week period and served 6,012 meals. These weeks were directed by Norman Eoute, Executive Director of the Red Shield Boys Club.

Mother-Kiddie Camp, July 28 to August 1 had 66 in attendance and 28 visitors. 1,181 meals were served. Again, Mrs. Sr. Captain Henry (Bernice) Gillespie did a fine job. The kids were five and under.

Lt. Charles Sinclair directed the *Band Camp from August 4 to 7, with 21 bandsmen and three visitors. There were 411 meals served.

August 11-14 was the Girl Guard camp for senior girls of the Salvation Army. Lt. (Charles) and Mrs. (Louell Hensley) Sinclair were in charge with 18 guards in attendance, serving 336 meals.

We had 175 Schoolboy patrols and Guards in camp for a two-day session August 19 and 20 in connection with the Greenville Police Department and the Civitan Club.

A total of 810 boys and girls used the facilities during the 1958 camping season. 13,565 meals were served, and 468 visitors were recorded.

The operating expenses of the fresh air camp are supported by the United Fund of Greenville County.

The Civitan Club of Greenville has as its major project the building of new buildings and major improvements.

This past year they built a storage room adjacent to the kitchen and a new building to house a large boiler, which was purchased to provide hot showers for the campers.

Improvements at the swimming pool included a cement patio and a four-foot fence around the pool. These projects are financed primarily with the proceeds from the Ice Vogue and Christmas fruitcake sales.

*Note: A young man, Henry Arrowood, who was a guest of his sister, Captain Magdalene Arrowood Waters in Anderson, SC won the "Mr. Salvation Army" award at that music camp. He later entered the School for Officers Training and went on to become a Salvation Army Missionary Officer.

The above schedule of camping sessions is typical and continued in Greenville from the year the camp opened until it was phased out. The camping program was continued at the Salvation Army Divisional Camp in North Carolina to effect better staffing and more adequate programming. It is still an operating program in the divisional structure.

The local Community Camping program of the Salvation Army at Camp Watacoo was phased out in the 1960s to allow for expansion of the Divisional Camp operated by the Divisional Headquarters for all of North and South Carolina. Children and adults are given the same camping program in an expanded setting at Camp Walter Johnson in North Carolina.

In 1968 the name of the camp Watacoo was changed to Camp Spearhead and is now sponsored/operated by the Greenville County Recreation District, the Greenville County and South Carolina Disabilities and Special Needs Board, the United Way of Greenville, and the Civitan Club.

The focus is now upon children and adults with disabilities and special needs.

CHAPTER XVI
SPECIFICS
"By His Own Hand, He Leadeth Me"

A specific listing of events, places, and persons who impacted the history of the Greenville Salvation Army over the past 100 years is provided here for quick reference.

LOCATIONS:

Manly Street

Manly Street is in the Historic Pettigru Section of Old Greenville. It is named for one of the original professors of the Southern Baptist Theological Seminary, Basil Manley, who was engaged in 1859 by the founder of the school, James Pettigru Boyce. The Southern Baptist Theological Seminary was established under the leadership and sponsorship of Furman University. The original property extended from East North Street to the Reedy River in 1855. It was known as the Waddy Thompson Estate.

Mr. Pettigru changed the name to the James Pettigru Boyce Estate upon purchase.

—Source, *Greenville News*/Judith Bainbridge/1/15/2003

The Salvation Army Officers' living quarters and headquarters of operation early 1904 through 1907 were located on Manly Street. The correct street number is not known, nor is it known whether this was a house or an apartment building.

Present day Manly Street numbers run from 0-121, from East Washington Street to East North Street, only two blocks, and no other street numbers are listed in that period.

In 1904 the numbers were listed as in the 200s. The location of the house used by the Officers is thought to be where the Baptist Courier is located.

The Southern Baptist Missionary Children's Home on Rutherford Street was ultimately to become the Bruner Home for Orphans, and in 1917, The Salvation Army operated Bruner Home. In 1927 the Bruner Home was deeded to the Salvation Army which became sole owner and operator.

Brown and East Washington Street

This is thought to be the first location of the tent used for services in 1904. According to J. V. Breazeale, although the exact corner is not clearly identified, it was most likely located in front of the Pates and Allen Livery Stables.

The stables were located at the east side of Brown Street and East Washington Street, at 201-207 East Washington Street. There is no further corroborating evidence on record. This location is now the headquarters for the Regions Bank.

East Court Street

This is the first identifiable location of the tent and the location of the first recorded meeting of the Salvation Army in Greenville in June 1904.

This general area was in the center of Greenville's operational activities and a hub of endeavors of all sorts in the early years. It is, today, one of the main attractions of the city of Greenville.

The tent was located behind the Carpenter Brothers Drug Store and next to the Cigar Factory. A photo of the first contingent of Salvation Army Soldiers and Officers taken in front of the Cigar Factory c1904 appears on Page 62.

South Laurens Street

The first building used by the Salvation Army in Greenville was a meeting hall above a livery stable just south of the (1960s) bus station on Laurens Street. The exact location has not been identified.

The City Directory of 1903-04 places a storage room at number 107, Gowers Hall at number 108 and W. P. Rowley Stables at 110 South Laurens Street.

There were two other livery stables and a couple of businesses, plus city hall, the jail and the police station crowded into the same block. It was a perfect place for the Army to be conducting services and making war on the devil.

West McBee Street

A tent was set up in a vacant lot behind the First National Bank and beside the Downtown Baptist Church one block from South Main Street. This is one of the locations of the tent in 1905. It again became the tent location while the Citadel was being built in 1905-1907.

Falls Street at McBee Street

The site of the old Columbia and Western Carolina Railroad station is now the location of the Central Carolina Bank complex. There was a two-story frame house on this property, which was the Army's home for a short while prior to 1905. The top story burned away, forcing a move back to the McBee Street tent.

26 East Broad Street

This was the building constructed by the Salvation Army as its permanent Citadel in 1905-1907. The home of the Salvation Army Citadel until 1951, it is said to be the first Salvation Army building constructed in the South specifically for the use of The Salvation Army.

It was also the home of the Salvation Army Boys Club from 1938 to 1969.

The building also served as the Officers living quarters until a house was located to serve the function. It is now a part of the parking lot for the Greenville News.

17 Jones Avenue

The Officers Quarters in 1939-1961was located on 17 Jones Avenue, also known as Jones Street.

125 East Earle Street

The Officer's Quarters during the sixties and seventies (1961-1974) was located at 125 East Earle Street.

6 Overton Avenue

The Officer's Quarters from the seventies (1974) to the present is located at 6 Overton Avenue, also known as Overton Drive .

617 Rutherford Street

This was the original Women's Social Service location. It housed the home for wayward and homeless ladies, and served as a home and hospital for unwed mothers.

It was called the Women's and Children's Rescue Home. 1908-17.

517 Rutherford Street

This is the address of the original "Bruner Home" before the purchase of the property at 417 Rutherford Street from the Southern Baptist Missionary Board in 1914. The transfer was made before the Salvation Army entered the picture.

Rutherford Street and Stall Street

The men's shelter lodge was located here in the early 1900s.

417 Rutherford Street

This location served as the Bruner Home for orphan children from 1906 to 1949. The Salvation Army operated the home from 1917 to 1949. Salvation Army took ownership of the property in 1927.

This in now the location of the Salvation Army Citadel and Social Service Complex. It has served in that capacity since 1951.

There is a granite marker here attesting to the operation of the Southern Baptist Association's Home for children of the missionaries serving in foreign lands prior to 1914, c1904-1914. The Bruner Home for Orphans purchased the property at a later date for operation of that program. The Salvation Army assumed operational responsibility in 1917 and ownership in 1927.

318 West Stone Avenue, 221-B Croft Street, 419 Rutherford Street, and 1608 Pinecroft Drive, Taylors, SC

These addresses were used as Assistant Officer's quarters over the years. None are presently listed.

East McBee Street, number unknown

This was the location of the homeless shelter program prior to WWII.

300-310 Pinckney Street

This was the location of the women's and men's shelters after the war years.

120 Buist Street

This was the location of the Women's Transient lodge in the 1950s.

Stratham Street

The Playground Program operated by the Salvation Army and sponsored by the Civitan Club was facing this street in the 1950s.

Camp Watacoo on State Route 276 (Now Camp Spearhead)

This is the location of the Community Camp operated by the Salvation Army and sponsored by the Civitan Club about 1940s through 1960s.

St Francis Drive in Vardry Heights

This is the location of the Salvation Army's Emma Moss Booth Memorial Hospital. It opened in 1921 and continued as the Salvation Army Home and Hospital for unwed mothers and mill workers until 1932. It also operated a complete and certified nursing school in the later years.

At that time it was the most modern and complete hospital building in the Upstate.

It was sold to the St Francis Little Sisters of the Poor and they operated it as the St. Francis Hospital until 1971 when it was demolished to make way for the new hospital complex. The original site is right beside the present emergency entrance. It is a part of the parking lot.

Springwood Cemetery

Captain William Orr Hannah is buried here. He was the second Commanding Officer and the builder of the Citadel at 26 East Broad Street. He died three weeks after the dedication of the new Citadel in 1907. His grave is located in section C of the cemetery.

Section U of the same cemetery is the burial place of indigents who were buried by the Salvation Army in the early 1900s.

Conestee Cemetery in Conestee, SC

This is the burial place of the first Corps Sergeant Major of the Salvation Army Corps in Greenville, CSM Roland Smith (1935) and his wife, Fannie Sizemore Smith (1961)

Cleveland Park/Reedy River

The Salvation Army Ladies Auxiliary (The Red Shield Auxiliary) sponsored a citywide Easter egg hunt for neighborhood children of the Boys Club for a number of years in this park.

LOCAL CITIZENS WHO IMPACTED THE SALVATION ARMY IN GREENVILLE

Roland and Frances Smith

One of the early converts, Roland Smith served as the beloved Corps Sergeant Major from 1904 to 1935. His family descendants are serving as Southern Territorial Officers and Soldiers in Greenville today. His wife served right along beside him.

J. Rivers Lebby

Lebby was the first Cadet sent from Greenville to the Training School for Officers in New York City in 1905. He attended the Southern Theology Seminary in Atlanta before it became the Salvation Army School for Officers Training School.

He was assigned as an assistant officer in Greenville in 1906 following his training session. In 1927-28 he was appointed as Divisional Commander of the Georgia division.

John V. and Emma Kirby Breazeale

He was converted in the tent on Court Street in 1904. Her conversion is not recorded, but is evident.

He assisted Captain R. E. Holz with the setting the cornerstone at the first citadel on Broad Street in 1905. Both went to Salvation Army School for Officers Training and served two terms as Corps Officers in Greenville. Major Eugene Breazeale, their son, served as a Salvation Army Officer in the Southern Territory until August 2004, when he was promoted to Glory at age 84. His wife, Major Martha Kellner Breazeale was promoted to Glory in 2003.

Moiedna Fletcher

She was born in 1871 and is the first member of the Fletcher family in Greenville to join The Salvation Army in 1930. Her descendents are still active in the local Salvation Army.

C. E. Graham

Founder/owner of the Camperdown and Huguenot Mills

He contributed the lot for the building on Broad Street and $1000.00 to build the new Citadel Building on Broad Street. It is said that he did so because one of his "ornery" workers was saved in the tent and spared him a lot of grief at the mill. He became a staunch supporter of the Salvation Army in its formative years.

Pablo D. Meadors

Mr. Meadors, a local businessman and candy manufacturer, was the founder/originator of the Salvation Army Boys and Girls Club in 1938.

Waldo Norman Leslie

A civic and business leader of Greenville, Mr. Leslie was a lifetime member and served on the Salvation Army Advisory Board from 1945 to 1994, at the time of his death.

He was born in 1907, the year of the completion and dedication of the Citadel on 26 East Broad Street.

He made many significant contributions, along with his wife, Angeline Dempsey Leslie, to the successful operation of the Salvation Army during his lifetime.

Mr. and Mrs. Leslie's daughter, Jane Shaw, a present day member of the Advisory Board relates the following information via E-mail:

My parents were Waldo and Angeline Leslie. The Social Services Center was named in memory of my father who served on the Advisory Board in Greenville for over 49 years. His life reminded me much of the Salvation Army. If he saw a need, he did what he could to meet that need without calling attention to himself.

When Daddy died Norman Eoute (the former Executive Director of the Boys and Girls Club here) came to see Mother. They were laughing about the times Mother and Daddy drove their Cadillacs to the Club and loaded them up with children to drive them to wherever they needed to go. I think he said they bought the first bus for the club. I know they were very interested in every area of the Salvation Army ministry.

The present social Services Building on Rutherford Street, the Waldo Leslie Service Center bears his name.

William Marshall

Mayor of the city of Greenville in 1909

He was a strong supporter of the Salvation Army and encouraged it to take innovative steps to serve the community. Under his administration, a Salvation Army Officer, Captain William Purdue, was appointed to the office of Youth Parole Officer for the city.

Thomas F. Parker

The principal innovator and motivator of the establishment and construction of the Emma Moss Booth Memorial Hospital, he received special recognition as such in the dedication service of the hospital in 1921.

Excerpted from the dedication of the Hospital in 1921:

> Mr. B. E. Geer, president of Judson cotton Mills, practical and warm-hearted friend of the Salvation Army took the direction of the program, calling first upon Dr. H. H. Hart, connected in an important official capacity to the Russell Sage Foundation. Dr. Hart said that he had come from New York to be present at the dedication, which, he affirmed possessed great significance to Greenville, to Western South Carolina, and to the South generally. The South was backward in the matter of social relief, but was rapidly awakening and moving forward, led by Virginia and South Carolina, especially. The splendid Board of Charities of South Carolina, backed by a progressive and liberal Governor, was responsible for much of this advance.

Dr. Thomas Wylie Sloan c1904.

Dr. Thomas W. Sloan

Pastor of the First Presbyterian Church 1902-1931, Dr. Sloan was friendly to the work, allowing meetings to be held in his church and giving encouragement to the Officers who pioneered the work in Greenville.

In 1921, at the time of dedication of the Emma Moss Booth Hospital in Vardry Heights, the 1st Presbyterian Church invited Commander (Eva) Booth, National Commander of the Salvation Army since 1904, and other high officials of the Army to speak in behalf of The Salvation Army.

Jack T. Waters

A local newsboy in the forties who joined the Boys and Girls Club, he went to The Salvation Army School for Officers Training in 1949. He married Magdalene Arrowood, a Salvation army Officer, and they advanced to the rank of Lt. Colonels with commanding assignments in several Divisional districts as Divisional Commanders.

Willard and Marie Fitton Evans

Willard and Marie Fitton Evans were Soldiers of the Greenville Corps in 1947-49. At that time they were students in college. They were active soldiers and Willard was the corps Bandmaster. He also taught music in the Bruner Home program. They entered into The Salvation Army School for Officers Training from Greenville and advanced to the rank of Commissioners with responsibility for the Salvation Army's work at the Territorial level as Territorial Commanders.

United Way of Greenville, South Carolina

This report would not be complete without acknowledging the partnership of The Salvation Army and The United Way of Greenville. From the inception of the first United Way efforts, the Salvation army has been linked with the organization in purpose and unity of ideals. That union has been a large factor in the success of both organizations. It is as strong today as it has ever been.

The numbers of local citizens and organizations who have made an indelible impact upon the colorful history of the Salvation Army in Greenville actually soar into the thousands. The above list is representative of that great roll call of heroic volunteers who placed their hands to the plow, some pulling and some guiding

...And never once looked back.

IN THE RANKS OF THE DEAR OLD ARMY...
(From an old Salvation Army battle chorus)

Ranking of Officers

Generally, the Salvation Army at the outset of the work in 1878 (When the Christian Mission was renamed The Salvation Army) used almost every conceivable rank in the military jargon to identify and categorize officers and members.

This has been pared down to a handful of ranks for convenience and clarity in later years.

Below is a partial list of yesteryear ranks:

Cadet, Probationary Lieutenant, 1st Lt., 2nd Lt., Lieutenant, Ensign, Probationary Captain, Captain, Senior Caption, Staff Captain, Adjutant, Commodore, Major, Senior Major, Brigadier, Lt. Colonel, Colonel, Lt. Commissioner, Commissioner, and one General.

The ranks of non-commissioned officers was that of Envoy, Supply, Sergeant, and Warrant officers.

Members were Soldiers, Junior and Senior, Local Officers, and Adherents.

The present day rankings are shortened to Cadet, Captain, Major, Lt. Colonel, Colonel, Commissioner, and one General.

The Soldiers rankings remain much the same as the in the past.

The rank of Lieutenant is used to denote Non-Commissioned Officers of rank. It applies to limited term Officership on an employee basis. It can lead to appointment to full Officership under certain conditions.

The rank of Lieutenant replaces the non-commissioned ranks of Sergeant, Envoy, Auxiliary Captain, and other locally generated designations.

There is also a non-commissioned employee designation of Corps Administrator where there is no Officer stationed. This is sometimes intermixed with the rank of Sergeant.

No matter what the rank or designation all Salvation Army Officers are committed to the ideals and mandate of the founder, to save and to serve.

EPILOGUE - ONWARD TO THE FUTURE
"What a Work the Lord has Done"

This account of the beginning and progression of The Salvation Army work in Greenville, South Carolina covers the entire history from 1888 (with parenthesis) to 2004. The story is still unfolding and will continue do so as long as there is a need for the services of The Salvation Army in Greenville.

Most of the material is substantiated by at least one and often two or more independent sources and constitutes a true record of the main happenings and events associated with the establishment and growth of the Salvation Army work within the city.

However, the compilation of 116 years of history in Greenville South Carolina, especially when precise record-keeping was not the priority of the participants, is bound to have gaps and omissions which are pertinent to the story.

Perhaps a historian in future years will have access to more and better information and can construct a more accurate history line.

The International Salvation Army evolved from a street tent meeting mission and was founded by William Booth and his wife Catherine Mumford Booth in 1865 in the East End of London. The name 'Salvation Army' was adopted in 1878. Today it is a multifaceted operation touching almost every segment of society, by the Grace of God.

It is very evident that there is more and greater work for the Salvation Army to do in the future, for as long as the world stands in its present form.

Jesus Christ said, "The poor you have with you always." Where the poor are found you will find The Salvation Army. It will be attacking the root cause of poverty—sin. At the same time the Army will be inviting the "sinners" to come away and sit at the feet of Jesus, who is the only true remedy for sin and poverty of spirit, mind and body, and learn of him.

Figuratively, one can hear the multitudes of Salvation Army Officers, Lay Leaders, Volunteers, Donors and Workers saying almost with one worldwide voice, “Come in and rest awhile. May I wash the dust from your feet? Here’s a cup of cold water in the name of Jesus.”

“Are you Saved?”

“Christ is the answer, to my every need, Christ is the answer, He is my friend indeed. Problems of life, my spirit may assail, with Christ my savior, I shall never fail, for Christ is the answer, to my need.”

“He can be yours, too!”

Into the future! Whither?

General Albert Orsborn (General 1946-1954) a prolific songwriter hit upon the gist of the power and purpose of The Salvation Army in one of his songs written as a song of personal request for Holy help. It could be well applied to the corporate underpinning of the Army of today.

Song number 641 SASB (Salvation Army Song Book)

Unto Thee will I cry, Shepherd hear my prayer!
Poor and needy am I, Shepherd hear my prayer!
Deep is calling unto deep,
Rugged are the heights and steep:
Guide my steps and keep:
Hear O hear my prayer! Hear O hear my prayer!

Where the tempest is loud, Shepherd hear my prayer!
‘Mid the darkness and cloud, Shepherd hear my prayer!
Let me hear thy voice afar,
Coming with the morning star;
True thy mercies are!
Hear O hear my prayer! Hear O hear my prayer!

Let the foe not prevail, Shepherd hear my prayer!
My resources would fail, Shepherd hear my prayer!
Order all my steps aright,
Carry me from height to height;
Yonder shines the light.
Shepherd lead me there! Lead me safely there.

Into the Future! Yonder!

General William Booth, the founder and first General of the Salvation Army until 1912, in the latter years of his active leadership of the Army, at the age of 83 on May 9, 1912 uttered the near-perfect charge to all the Salvation Army of past, present, and future years. In his last speech in Royal Albert Hall he said,

> *"While women weep as they do now, I'll fight. While little children go hungry as they do now, I'll fight. While men go to prison in and out, in and out as they do now, I'll fight.*
>
> *While there is a drunkard left, I'll fight. While there is one poor lost girl in the streets, while there remains one dark soul without the light of God, I'll fight.*
>
> *I'll fight to the very end."*

On August 20, 1912 the founder and first General of the Salvation Army was "promoted to Glory" to receive his heavenly reward for a lifetime of crusading for the lost sinners and downtrodden creatures of the world. His salvation was procured and secured by the blood of his beloved Savior, Jesus Christ.

His Salvation Army is still running the race with patience to the light of God's high calling in Christ Jesus. The light is still shining yonder. The Salvation Army will, no doubt, go there.

As General William Booth would say. *"That and better will do".*

—END—

APPENDIX

THE CENTENNIAL CELEBRATION

In 2002 Major Stanley Melton commissioned retired Major Raymond Kitchen to study the feasibility of a centennial celebration in Greenville, SC. His report follows:

METHODOLOGY

This Centennial report has been prepared by Major Raymond Kitchen, (retired.) for Commanding Officers Major and Mrs. Stanley and Carlene Melton,

The report required approximately four months, from February 3 to May 30, 2002, to compile and complete.

The dates and events have been researched through readily available materials and records, mainly the Greenville news, The Salvation Army War Cry, local citizen and soldier interviews, previous officer reports and interviews, National Headquarters records of Officer Assignments, and information found in the Corps files. No extraordinary efforts were made to obtain or verify the contents.

The material is not guaranteed to be accurate and includes some non-verified information. However, the main items are accurate for planning the "Century of Service" program and can be relied upon to portray a fairly accurate history from 1904 through 2002.

Periods covered are 1888-1903 and 1904-2004.

Events covered are significant openings and events of the founding and the subsequent reestablishment of The Salvation Army in Greenville, S. C.

CENTENNIAL DEFINITIONS

The Salvation Army began work in Greenville, South Carolina in January 1888 and was officially recognized as a functioning Corps operation until May of the same year.

It was removed from the Disposition of Forces in May 1888 and did not reappear until January 1904. No other information can be found in the usual, available sources about the 1888-1903 Salvation Army history.

Therefore, the official Centennial date for the establishment of the first Salvation Army operation in Greenville, S. C. would have been January 1988.

The next date available for a reasonable initial Corps opening celebration date is 125 years in the year 2013, or 150 years in 2038.

Note: the Salvation Army Southern Territory policy on Centennial, and future celebrations is to use the date of the original Corps opening as the base point. Other celebrations can be staged as "Years of Continuous service" in the case of broken service years.

I quote from an email sent to me by Mr. Michael Nagy of the Salvation Army Southern Historical Center,

"Our Policy on Corps Anniversaries is that a Corps can celebrate a centennial anniversary of the Corps opening, or a centennial of service to the Community.

In the case of Greenville, 1988 would have been the centennial of the first Corps Opening. 2004 will be a Century of Service to Greenville, and 100 years of continuous service".

It is possible to recognize the centennial date of significant openings of other units of Salvation Army operations as the one-hundredth birthday is reached. In Greenville we have several units that would possibly merit a centennial celebration date. These are as follows:

1. The completion of the first Temple Corps Building on Broad Street in 1907-2007. This building was turned over to the Boys Club in 1951 and operated as such until 1969. It was sold and demolished in 1971.

2. The commencement of the Women's Social Service Program in 1908-2008. This program was discontinued in 1931 and the services are now disbursed through the Corps Social Service operation.

3. The commencement of the Salvation Army's operation of the Bruner Home for orphaned and abandoned Children in 1917-2017. This program was discontinued in 1949 and the site of the Bruner Home is now the Corps/Social program.

4. The establishment of the Boys and Girls Club in 1938-2038. This program was operated in an "add-on building" to the old Citadel until the Corps was moved to the Rutherford Street address in 1951. The Club then took over the entire Citadel building. Later in 1969, it was moved to Owens Street in a building built especially for the Boys and Girls Club.

5. The construction of the Women's Social Service Department's Hospital in 1921-2021. The Salvation Army operated this program until 1931. It was sold to the Catholic Little Sisters of the Poor and became Saint Francis hospital that year. It was used for their operation until it was demolished in 1971 to make way for the new Saint Francis Hospital system.

6. The completion of the present day Citadel and Social Service complex on Rutherford Street in 1951-2051. This program has been upgraded and enlarged to accommodate the entire Salvation Army range of services and is in use today as the Salvation Army Corps/Social Service complex.

7. The completion of the Salvation Army Boys and Girls club building on Owens Street in 1969-2069. This program is presently in use and is an ongoing program of The Salvation Army. Many additions and improvements have been made since its completion.

8. All of these events could be incorporated into one huge citywide gala and celebrated as "a century of service to the City of Greenville" in the year 2004, or they could be fragmented and celebrated throughout the year as individual components of the total celebration.

HISTORICAL PROGRESSION OF THE SALVATION ARMY IN GREENVILLE, SC FROM JUNE 5, 1904 UP TO THE PRESENT DAY, JUNE 30, 2002

In 1904 Ensign and Mrs. J. W. McSheehan and Cadet Pearl Hewitt reestablished the Salvation Army in Greenville, South Carolina. The Salvation Army in Greenville has operated continuously since that date.

According to a letter from Brigadier J. V. Breazeale (R), now deceased, to Captain Robert Burchett, now deceased, dated January 29, 1954, the McSheehans came from Atlanta, Georgia in January 1904 after helping with the Christmas work in that city.

Note: Brigadier Breazeale was a native of Greenville and was converted in the tent in 1904. He and Mrs. Brigadier Breazeale later came back as the Commanding Officers of the Greenville Salvation Army in 1930-31 and March 3, 1942.

Since the window for a centennial of Corps founding passed in 1988, the next course of action could be to celebrate a 'Century of service to the community' or some other appropriately named event in the year 2004. There are several other dates and locations mentioned as the first meeting of the Salvation Army in Greenville. These are unsubstantiated by other creditable evidence, or unclear in content, so they have been eliminated as viable historical celebration events. There is enough validity and creditability for them to be considered, however. They are as follows:

1. An Apartment building at 317 N. Manley Street where the Officers lived and held "open air" meetings. The date is uncertain and the location is not in existence at the present date.

2. The Corner of E. Washington and Brown Street where a tent was used for meetings. The date is uncertain. The correct corner of the intersection is not identified.

3. There is also an account that mentions the Officer being in Greenville in 1903 but no further corroboration is available. It is apparent from the size and scope of the operation on June 5, 1904 at the dedication service that the officers had been here for some time prior to the opening. There is also a statement that they were here in January 1904.

4. There is a report by a Salvation Army Officer stationed in Greenville in 1964-1966 that states that the work began in a tent on October 10, 1904 at 317 N. Manley Street and at the corner of E. Washington and Brown Streets. According to the official record the October 10, 1904 date is the official date of commencement in Greenville.

5. There is another location mentioned. This is the corner of Falls and McBee Streets in a two-story frame house where the C and W C railroad station was later located. The report states that the top floor of the house was burned away and the railroad station was built to replace the house.

The Army moved to a tent on McBee Street behind the First National Bank Building until the Citadel was completed. This was in 1905-1907 and Captain and Mrs. Orr Hanna had replaced the McSheehans as commanding officers.

The Central Carolina Bank building complex occupies the McBee and Falls Street's corner site today.

On June 6, 1904 The GREENVILLE DAILY NEWS reports that the official opening campaign of The Salvation Army was conducted in a tent erected on E. Court Street next to a cigar factory behind the Carpenter Brothers Drug Store in the open air.

The Divisional Commander, Captain Berriman and an assisting officer, Ensign Widgery, also presumably from the Divisional Headquarters in Atlanta, GA. conducted the services. Soldier recruits were enrolled.

The beginning date of the two day campaign was June 5, 1904. The official Salvation Army Corps re-opening date is recorded as October 10, 1904. The newspaper account would be a more reliable source.

Thus, it is my opinion that the E. Court Street location and the date of June 5-6, 1904 would be the unofficial Corps re-opening weekend and location for Greenville, SC.

The Divisional Officer was also a guest speaker at the local Presbyterian Church on Sunday morning June 6, 1904.

Today East Court Street is one block long and runs from Main to Falls Street. There are two lanes running east and west from Main Street with a public parking lot in the center. In the early 1900s this area was referred to as "the slums of Court Street" and was more than a few blocks long. Surrounding are local businesses and offices.

Both the Cigar Factory and the Carpenter Brothers' Drug store are still there. The Cigar Factory has been restored and the Carpenter Brothers' Store is slated for restoration and conversion to a sandwich shop. The building will retain basically the same appearance.

Note: The Cigar Factory built/completed in 1902-1903 was used and occupied by SEIDENBERG AND COMPANY. This is according to a photo of the building from the Greenville News special, "Guide to Greenville/2002", published in May 2002.

There is a small landscaped island there, which would make a good location for the site of a standing historical statement plaque. The little plot could be named the McSheehan/Hewitt Historical garden, or something of that nature, in honor of the first Corps officers. Perhaps, William Booth Garden, or something else would be appropriate.

The actual site of the tent, which was located adjacent to the Cigar Factory, and behind the Carpenter Brothers' Store is a fenced part of the renovated Kent Court Building. (The Cigar Factory).

This also would be the prime spot for a marker. Perhaps a "tintype" of the first contingent of Soldiers and Officers, if the original picture could be found, could be mounted on the wall at the exact spot where the photo was taken. I have a picture of the photo. The original site is still intact.

SUGGESTIONS AND CONCLUSION

There are a number of enticing, possible avenues of celebration of the century of service.

Below is a possible, workable plan. It is neither complete nor exhaustive but can serve as a generator of thoughts and ideas.

Suggestion

1. Obtain from the Greenville Historical Society and the City Council permission to erect a historical plaque or a marker on a pole on the site of the tent. Place a sidewalk marker or a standing plaque at the site of the "open air" meetings in front of the Mansion House

(present day Poinsett Hotel) and/or at the corner of Main Street and W. Washington Streets.

2. Conduct a rededication service on the spot of the tent and perhaps an open-air meeting in front of the Poinsett Hotel on the corner of Court and Main Streets. Perhaps a tent could be set up at that location for the service.

3. A march of witness around the downtown locations of the early Salvation Army would be appropriate for the occasion.

4. The route could trace the Army's first steps through the downtown section during the years 1904-1907. From E. Court Street (Founding location) west to Main Street. ("Open air" service in front of the old Mansion House). This is now the second edition of the Poinsett Hotel.

- Right on Main Street to Washington Street (favorite 'Open air' location),
- Left on Washington Street to Laurens Street (Meeting Hall above an old livery stable), this location is not pinpointed but it was on Laurens Street near the old Bus Station.
- Left on Laurens street to McBee Street (tent location behind the First national Bank Building while waiting for the Citadel to be completed),
- Left on McBee street to Main Street,
- Right on main Street to Broad Street (first Citadel dedicated in 1907 at 26 East Broad Street) It is presently a parking lot for the Greenville News.
- Left on Broad Street to Falls Street
- Left on Falls Street to East Court Street
- Left on East Court Street to the original location of the tent.

In a copy of a photograph of the first contingent of Officers and Soldiers in front of the Cigar Factory in 1904 there is depicted the first band instrumentation.

- a bass drum (Bub Breazeale, wearing a suit with a SA cap)
- a snare drum (Tommy Turner, young man regular dress)

- a large tambourine (Miss Know, teen girl regular dress),
- a small tambourine (Bessie Breazeale, pre-teen girl regular dress)
- a guitar (Bula Davis, young woman, regular dress)
- a 2nd guitar (Cadet Pearl Hewitt, young woman, in uniform)
- a cornet (Mrs. Captain McSheehan in uniform)
- Captain McSheehan in uniform (no instrument apparent)
- Mr. Honeycutt in uniform (no instrument apparent)
- a zither, or some other object, (Mr. Norris, young man in regular dress)
- A Salvation Army Flag (Major J. C. Morgan in uniform) This is a Soldier who was enrolled in 1904 and could have been the Corps Sergeant major of that time. The caption of the photo refers to him as Major Morgan.
- A United States Flag (Mr. Turner in uniform)
- All together there are thirty people in the photograph, including several small children and a baby. There is no mention of the occasion of the photograph. Joseph L. Arnold of Danville, VA who appears in the photo on the front row donated the photo to The Salvation Army, or to whomever published the picture.
- This little band (or the entire contingent of members) could be replicated in period costume and placed at the head of the marching unit with a Divisional, regional or Corps band behind perhaps followed by a local school band or the Greenville Community Band, or the like.

Note: I have left the Manly Street, Brown and Washington Street tent, Hospital, present Corps location, Boys and Girls Club, and Falls Street locations out of the parade route in order to facilitate a smooth progression of the parade.

5. A walking (or riding) tour could be planned for the entire route including the omitted locations with a narrative of the times and events, as a part of the

celebration year. This would be good for Advisory Board, Corps Council, United Way, interested friends, etc. The ideal plan would be to place a marker at each of the primary sites of The Salvation Army historical events. A map and a running commentary could be developed to guide visitors and interested people to the spots for years to come.

6. As an alternate plan, the celebration could cover several important dates and be divided into a celebration each quarter (or, in the month of each occurrence) of a significant opening. Some suggested events are the completion of the Citadel, the beginning of the Women's Social Work, the opening of the Hospital in Vardry Heights, the initial Bruner Home acquisition and operation, the beginning of the Boys and Girls Club program. There is also the Community Camping program, the opening of the present Corps Complex, and the completion of the new Boys and Girls Club facility.

7. Distribute mementos in the form of Salvation Army memorabilia items to as many people as possible. The theme, "a century of service to the Glory of God and the welfare of mankind" in Greenville 1904-2004, or something appropriate. In keeping with the inscription on the cornerstone laid in 1905 of the Citadel Building first erected at 26 E. Broad Street in 1907, perhaps a small facsimile of a cornerstone could be offered. The completion of the Citadel building could be an occasion of a celebration. There was a celebration and dedication in 1907. The cornerstone mentioned by several people was not recovered when the old Citadel was demolished.

8. Tie the 2004 regular Corps sponsored homecoming and/or the Advisory Board Annual meeting to the century of service program and do massive publicity in the print and broadcast news and the *War Cry*, *Southern Spirit* before and after the occasion.

9. Invite Salvation Army officers and the citizens of Greenville who have been in touch with, and are founding partners of, the Army in Greenville through the years to come and help celebrate. Many still prominent past Officers and citizens are involved.

10. Feature the Women's Auxiliary as a very important generator of support and service to the Army. The auxiliary is no longer functioning but the people who were members are still here. Many of them were very involved and moved the army along in its early days.

11. One other avenue of celebration could be to replicate the order of dedication in 1904. The visiting Divisional Officer was invited to speak at the First Presbyterian Church on the Sunday Morning of the dedication weekend. Meetings were held in the tent and in the open air throughout the day. This could be a good focal point for the Army in the community.

ABOUT THE AUTHOR

Major Raymond W. Kitchen is a life-long Salvation Army member. He was born into a Salvation Army family of ten siblings in Logan, West Virginia in 1929 and became a recipient of services, a soldier, a lay leader, and a commissioned officer/ordained minister and appointed administrator.

In the 1960s-1970s, the Kitchen family claimed the largest contingent of sibling Salvation Army Officers in the world with eight of its members serving as Officers at the same time.

He married Hope Bernice Casarez in Huntington, West Virginia in 1948. They have three children; two are deceased.

During the Korean War he was drafted by the US Army but opted for the US Navy as an enlistee in 1951. After four years in which he attained the rank of first class Non-Commissioned officer he was honorably discharged and took a position as estimator and project manager with a mechanical/electrical contracting firm in Norfolk, Virginia administering US government contracts for five years. He attended the college of William and Mary Technical School in the 1950's.

In 1961 Raymond and Hope Kitchen applied for Officership in the Salvation Army and were graduated/commissioned/ordained in 1963. Together, Ray and Hope Kitchen have served in numerous Corps appointments, both miniscule and large. Duties included planning and directing Corps Community center expansions, feasibility studies, fund drives, construction of new facilities, and administrators and acting as pastors to the local Christian community of the Salvation Army members, as well as divisional and local responsibilities related to the appointments.

As social services directors and community relations directors of Louisville, Kentucky, they planned and executed that city's centennial celebration. Major Raymond Kitchen served as the divisional music director as an added responsibility.

They served briefly as the City Commanders of the Charlotte, NC Salvation Army operation.

Retired after 30 plus years of service as officers, the Kitchens moved to Greenville, SC in 1993 and have served as volunteer workers and Salvation Army members filling many positions in the local corps operation, from volunteer workers to musicians, and are church members.

Both serve on the local Corps Council and Major Raymond Kitchen serves on the advisory board as a public relations and long range planning committee member. Together, they teach the Soldiership classes for new and aspiring corps members in Greenville.

Major Kitchen has published several dozens of articles in Salvation Army magazines including short stories, series articles, poems, feature articles, and reports. In the 1970s he was unofficially dubbed the poet laureate of the Virginia and Southern West Virginia division by the then divisional commander (the late commissioner John Needham), for his penchant for poetry and other writing.